Tribute and Trade

China and the West in the Modern World

William Christie, Series Editor

China and the West in the Modern World publishes original, peer-reviewed research on cultural, diplomatic, and trade relations between China and the West from the accession of the Manchu Qing dynasty in 1644 to the present. The series aims to map and interpret historical and cultural interactions during the gradual opening up of China to an enterprising and expansive West, as a sequence of Chinese governments developed policies of accommodation and exclusion in reaction to pressure from Western commerce, culture, and religion. The series brings into play different national and disciplinary perspectives to achieve a more thorough and cross-culturally nuanced understanding of the political, economic, and cultural background to the negotiations and realignments currently underway between China and Western nations.

The Poison of Polygamy
Wong Shee Ping, translated by Ely Finch

Tribute and Trade: China and Global Modernity, 1784–1935
Ed. William Christie, Angela Dunstan and Q.S. Tong

Tribute and Trade

China and Global Modernity, 1784–1935

Edited by William Christie,
Angela Dunstan and Q. S. Tong

SYDNEY UNIVERSITY PRESS

First published by Sydney University Press
© Individual contributors 2020
© Sydney University Press 2020

Reproduction and communication for other purposes
Except as permitted under the Act, no part of this edition may be reproduced, stored in a retrieval system, or communicated in any form or by any means without prior written permission. All requests for reproduction or communication should be made to Sydney University Press at the address below:

Sydney University Press
Fisher Library F03
University of Sydney NSW 2006
Australia
sup.info@sydney.edu.au
sydneyuniversitypress.com.au

 A catalogue record for this book is available from the National Library of Australia.

ISBN 9781743326008 paperback
ISBN 9781743325995 epub
ISBN 9781743326916 mobi
ISBN 9781743327050 pdf

Cover image: The waterfront at Canton with the American, British and Danish factories and the Protestant church, Studio Tingqua, c. 1847–56. Caroline Simpson Collection, Sydney Living Museums.

Cover design by Nathan Grice.

Contents

Figures   vii

Introduction: China and the West in the Long Eighteenth Century   1
William Christie

1   'That full complement of riches': China and the Problems of   23
    Political Economy in Adam Smith's *The Wealth of Nations*
    Robert Markley

2   Cultural Cross-Dressing in the House of Pankeequa   53
    William Christie

3   The *Lady Hughes* Affair, Extraterritoriality, and the Limits   79
    of Liberalism
    Q. S. Tong

4   Once Upon a Time in 1784: American Mercantile   109
    Biographies and the Romance of Free Trade Imperialism
    Kendall A. Johnson

5   'What stories I shall have to tell!': Mediating China in the   145
    Writings of Charles Lamb and Thomas Manning
    James Watt

6	Global Contacts of Canton in the Qing Dynasty: A Discussion of Export Painting *Yinghe Jiang*	165
7	'A desperate traffic': John Francis Davis, China, the Opium Trade and First Opium War *Peter Kitson*	183
8	Walter Scott's Writing, Collecting and Reading China *Kang-yen Chiu*	205
9	'Sheer Memory': The Victorian Idea of Confucian Education *Dongqing Wang*	225
10	The Life and Death and Life of Augustus Raymond Margary *Elizabeth Hope Chang*	243
11	Linguistic Nationalism and Its Discontents: Chinese Latinisation and Its Practice of Equality *Lorraine Wong*	273

About the Contributors   303

Index   307

Figures

Figure 4.1 Frontispiece to Samuel Shaw and Josiah Quincy, *The Journals of Major Samuel Shaw, The First American Consul at Canton: With a Life of the Author* (Boston: Wm. Crosby and H.P. Nichols, 1847). Courtesy of the Rare Book and Manuscript Library, Van Pelt-Dietrich Library Center, University of Pennsylvania. 111

Figure 4.2 Portrait of Columbus, Joseph Delaplaine's *Repository of the Lives and Portraits of Distinguished Americans* (Philadelphia: William Brown, 1815), 2 volumes; vol. 1, no page. 121

Figure 4.3 Cover page of Freeman Hunt's *The Merchant's Magazine and Commercial Review* (August 1839). 129

Figure 4.4 Frontispiece of Thomas G. Cary, *Memoir of Thomas Handasyd Perkins: Containing Extracts from His Diaries and Letters. With an Appendix* (Boston: Little, Brown and Company, 1856). 133

Figure 6.1 Chinese artist, *Portrait of Mrs and Miss Revell in a Chinese Interior*, about 1780. Reverse painting on glass, 46.673 x 40.958 cm. Purchased with funds donated anonymously, 2000. AE85763. Courtesy of Peabody Essex Museum. Photo by Mark Sexton and Jeffrey Dykes. 170

Figure 6.2 *View of Canton* (detail), 1780s, aquatint, 920 x 74 cm, 075041, The King's Topographical Collection of the British Library, United Kingdom. Courtesy of the British Library. 174

Figure 6.3 Anonymous Painter of Canton, Painting of the Foreign Factories, c.1825, Gouache on paper, 50 x 76 cm, Courtesy of Guang Dong Provincial Museum, Guangzhou, China. Photo by Liu Guzi. 175

Figure 6.4 Painting of the Foreign Factories by You Qua or his Studio, Oil on canvas, c.1855, 65 x 111 cm, Courtesy of Guangdong Provincial Museum, Guangzhou, China. Photo by Liu Guzi. 176

Figure 6.5 Lamqua, *La Grande Odalisque*, after 1826. Oil on canvas, 28.734 x 45.403 cm. Purchased in part with funds donated by the Asian Export Art Committee and The Meserve Fund, 2010. 2010.28.1. Courtesy of Peabody Essex Museum. Photograph by Bob Packert. 180

Figure 7.1 'Mandarin with opium pipe'. 191

Introduction: China and the West in the Long Eighteenth Century

William Christie

Not surprisingly, given the rise of China in the global economy and the rapid extension of its political and cultural interest, the last ten to twenty years have seen a comparably rapid growth in the number of studies of Sino-European cultural exchange over the course of the eighteenth, nineteenth, and early twentieth centuries. The essays in this volume developed out of a research network of scholars from both Western and Eastern universities which was established six years ago with the broad aim of mapping and interpreting events and cultural interactions during the gradual opening up of Qing China to an enterprising and expansive West, as respective Chinese emperors developed different policies of accommodation and exclusion in reaction to different and accumulating pressures from Western trade and religion. The focus of the network – and the focus of these essays – is on the way different events, as well as the different ideas, beliefs, and cultural practices of China and the West, were understood and evaluated – and misunderstood and misevaluated – by each other. Art, architecture, literature, music, science, politics, gender and family relationships, cooking, dress – how did China and the West see each other, and how did they interpret what they saw? What artistic and cultural (including scientific) influences resulted from contact and trade, with what long-term benefits or legacies? What passed for knowledge in the different regions, and how were these different knowledges and knowledge economies modified by their contact? The aim of this volume is to extend and deepen scholarly inquiry into this vital period, bringing into play different national and disciplinary perspectives to achieve a more thorough and cross-culturally nuanced understanding of the political, economic, and cultural background to current negotiations and realignments taking place between China and other nations of the world.

The Idea of China in the West

As an idea or ideal of political, social, and (later) economic organisation and as a remote source of exotic objects, China was a constant presence in the European imagination from the seventeenth century onwards, thanks to two influential media. The first was print, starting with the reports and histories of the Jesuit missionaries, who from the arrival of Fr Matteo Ricci in Beijing in 1601 had a monopoly on China-knowledge until around the early to middle eighteenth century, and the publication of the French Jesuit Jean-Baptiste du Halde's four-volume *Description géographique, historique, critique, chronologique, politique, et physique de L'empire de la Chine et de Tartarie chinoise*, first published in 1735. Du Halde's *Description* was an 'authoritative ethnography', in the words of Chi-ming Yang, undergoing 'a craze of rival translations into English in book form and popular magazine installments between 1738–42'.[1] Du Halde, as it happens, was not a missionary at all. His *Description* is an encyclopaedic anthology of China, a compilation of translated and abridged accounts by fellow

---

1   Chi-ming Yang, 'Virtue's Vogue: Eastern Authenticity and the Commodification of Chinese-ness on the 18th-Century Stage', *Comparative Literature Studies* 39:4 (2002), 326–46 (326). (Du Halde's compilation had been quickly translated into English, first, as *The General History of China* the following year, in 1736, then as *Description of the Empire of China*, which came out between 1738 and 1741.) 'The volumes of du Halde served generations of European naturalists as a storehouse of information about Chinese flora and fauna', writes Fa-Ti Fan, *British Naturalists in Qing China: Science, Empire, and Cultural Encounter* (Cambridge, MA: Harvard University Press, 2004), 95.

Jesuits over the previous century, including information and material from the cumulative *Lettres édifiantes et curieuses écrites des missions étrangères par quelques missionnaires de la Compagnie de Jésus* (1702–), as well as an assortment of relevant statistics, summaries of the Confucian texts, and Fr Joseph Henri de Premare's translation of the Chinese play *The Orphan in the House of Chao*: 'Fictional sources were thus set alongside historical and state documents to produce a compendious impression of the territory represented'.[2]

Though the representation of China to be found in the Jesuit writings was largely positive, in the seventeenth and early eighteenth century the Jesuits could not be said to have had it all their own way. The maritime world, for example, had for some time been passing on negative knowledge from sailors with access only to coastal ports and to Chinese emigré settlements elsewhere in Asia – stories of Chinese mendacity, cunning, greed, gambling and cruelty.[3] Insofar as this, too, had entered conventional wisdom, the eighteenth- and nineteenth-century Europeans inherited a bi-polar image of the Chinese nation and its people, which allowed them to move between extremes in their own responses, according to historical and ideological exigencies. What appeared to one European commentator as an enviable stability and order imposed by a benign autocracy, acting on the advice of an educated literati and reproducing itself through the conservative ethico-political philosophy of Confucius – as it did to Leibnitz, Voltaire, and Quesnay, for example – appeared to another (to the conflicted antiquarian, Rev. Thomas Percy, for example) as 'servile submission, and dread of novelty, which enslaves the minds of the Chinese, and while it promotes the peace and quiet of their empire, dulls their spirit and cramps their imagination'.[4] As David Porter has shown, Percy's own, sometimes bizarre oscillations and characteristic ambivalence towards the Chinese can be read as an index to Britain's

---

2   Ros Ballaster, *Fabulous Orients: Fictions of the East in England 1662–1785* (Oxford: Oxford University Press, 2005), 46.
3   Donald F. Lach and Edwin J. Van Kelly, *Asia in the Making of Europe*, Volume 3, *A Century of Advance*, Book Four: *East Asia* (Chicago and London: University of Chicago Press, 1993), 1563–1753 (1568–69). Cp. Eric Hayot, *The Hypothetical Mandarin: Sympathy, Modernity, and Chinese Pain* (Oxford and New York: Oxford University Press, 2009), 14–16.

developing national self-consciousness and cultural assertiveness.⁵ However we choose to interpret the phenomenon, '[t]hrough the course of the eighteenth century', as Ros Ballaster observes, 'writings on China became increasingly critical, especially of its apparent political and moral stagnation. What looked like security and ancient lineage to the Jesuits began to look like xenophobia, paranoia, and stultification to Protestant trading powers'.⁶

From the middle of the eighteenth century, moreover, the Jesuit reports were overtaken by the miscellaneous memoirs of (besides sailors) traders, tourists, official visitors, and later Protestant missionaries, as more and more Europeans took the limited opportunities offered to them by the Qing government to visit Canton. Certain prominent features of Chinese culture isolated and praised by the Jesuits – its rational Confucianism and meritocratic examination system, for example, its complex writing practice and its sheer antiquity – became 'objects of impassioned speculation and controversy in polemics on language reform, natural religion, the philosophy of taste, economic policy and the like', to quote Peter Kitson.⁷ (The essays in this volume will be seen to take up this speculation and controversy from where it has never left off.)

Familiarity with China for the bulk of the European population, however, came less from social and intellectual history and geography, translated from Latin into the vernacular, than from the second influential medium of exchange: an extensive range of exotic 'Chinese and Chinese-styled goods' – pre-eminently tea for ritual consumption and porcelain for domestic display. Indeed, given the severe limitations

---

4   Thomas Percy (ed.), *Hau Kiou Choaan or The Pleasing History, A Translation from the Chinese Language*, trans. James Wilkinson (and Thomas Percy), in vols (London: R. and J. Dodsley, 1761), 1:xii–xiii (Web access: 12 July 2012).
5   David Porter, *The Chinese Taste in Eighteenth-Century England* (Cambridge: Cambridge University Press, 2010), 154–83. Just how characteristic Percy was can be gleaned from the essays in Adrian Hsia (ed.), *The Vision of China in the English Literature of the Seventeenth and Eighteenth Centuries* (Hong Kong: Chinese University Press, 1998).
6   Ballaster, *Fabulous Orients*, 208.
7   Peter Kitson, *Forging Romantic China: Sino-British Cultural Exchange 1760–1840* (Cambridge: Cambridge University Press, 2014), 21.

on access to China imposed by the Qing government in the eighteenth century, 'Sino-European encounters in this period', as Kristel Smentek has written, 'were mediated more by things than by people'.[8] These imported luxury objects, according to David Porter, embodied an 'alien aesthetic sensibility' that both informed and challenged European ways of seeing and understanding.[9] A number of scholars interested in cultural relations between China and the West over the course of the long eighteenth century, and particularly in relations between China and Britain, have written on the ubiquity and implications – variously social, aesthetic, sexual, and ideological – of the Western taste for Chinese *things*: the economic and cultural commodities that, along with the 'intelligence' of China that came through print, mediated European–Chinese encounters.[10]

China and the West in the Modern Era

The first recorded European visit to China in the modern era had been in 1514 by the Portuguese, who forty-three years later, in 1557, established the first European settlement at Macao on the south-east coast. Western access to China proper did not come until Ricci arrived in 1582 and nineteen years later established a missionary residence in Beijing.[11] Contact between Britain and China throughout most of the sixteenth and seventeenth century, however, was only occasional and peripheral, at least until the lifting of the maritime trade ban in 1676

---

8   Kristel Smentek, 'Global Circulations, Local Transformations: Objects and Cultural Encounter in the Eighteenth Century', in *Qing Encounters: Artistic Exchanges between China and the West*, ed. Petra Ten-Doesschate Chu and Ning Ding (Los Angeles: Getty Research Institute, 2015), 43–57 (43).
9   Porter, *The Chinese Taste in Eighteenth-Century England*, 4.
10 David Porter's *The Chinese Taste in Eighteenth-Century England* speculates insightfully in this productive area of research. See also Elizabeth Hope Chang, *Britain's Chinese Eye: Literature, Empire and Aesthetics in Nineteenth-Century Britain* (Stanford, CA: Stanford University Press, 2010) and Eugenia Zuroski Jenkins, *A Taste for China: English Subjectivity and the Prehistory of Orientalism* (New York: Oxford University Press, 2013).
11 Liam Matthew Brockey, *Journey to the East: The Jesuit Mission to China, 1579–1724* (Cambridge, MA: Harvard University Press, 2007), 32–49.

when commercial relations between the two nations got underway. The establishment by the British East India Company of a factory at Canton at the turn of the eighteenth century gave those relations more formal recognition and continuity, but the rationale remained trade and that trade was circumscribed – as indeed were the British themselves, who along with other Europeans were confined to Canton. Of the Europeans, only the Jesuits were tolerated anywhere near the central government, though from the advent of the Qing dynasty in 1644 relations with the Jesuits were themselves often strained. While certain priests enjoyed respect and even power within the Chinese government, and their mathematical and astronomical expertise meant they were in demand for institutions like the observatory and for surveying, only some factions within the Chinese administrative government were supportive, while others deplored the Jesuits' presence and influence. Christianity itself, moreover, in spite of the Kangxi Emperor's Edict of Toleration in 1692, had always been under suspicion, until it was declared heterodox by the Yongzheng Emperor in 1724 and a decade of clearing the Christian missionaries out of China had begun.[12]

Even with regard to trade, China became wary of foreign influence, and with the Yongzheng (1723–35) and Qianlong (1735–95) Emperors came 'more security-conscious policies toward European trade'.[13] China would only cautiously meet Britain's apparently insatiable appetite for porcelain, silk, and, of course, tea. Still, the supply of tea from China to Britain rose from 2lb 2oz in 1664 to nearly 6 million pounds in 1783, and thence to 30 million pounds in the 1830s.[14] Because the Chinese neither needed nor wanted to encourage and

---

12 See John W. Witek, S.J., 'Catholic Missions and the Expansion of Christianity, 1644–1800', in *China and Maritime Europe 1500–1800: Trade, Settlement, Diplomacy, and Missions*, ed. John E. Wills, Jr. (Cambridge: Cambridge University Press, 2011), 135–82.

13 John L. Cranmer-Byng and John E. Wills, Jr., 'Trade and Diplomacy with Maritime Europe, 1644–c. 1800', in *China and Maritime Europe 1500–1800*, ed. Wills, 183–254 (200).

14 Ulrike Hillemann, *Asian Empire and British Knowledge: China and the Networks of British Imperial Expansion* (Basingstoke and New York: Palgrave Macmillan, 2009), 25.

Introduction: China and the West in the Long Eighteenth Century

expand trade with the Europeans, trade relations began as comparatively modest and decidedly one-sided, with the balance of payments favouring China. The disproportionate demand for Chinese goods – by way of return, until late in the eighteenth century, Britain as China's major European trading nation had only cotton and wool to offer, brought in from India by the British East India Company – created a trade imbalance that, while it satisfied a Chinese mercantilist policy of accumulating silver, remained a matter of comparative indifference to them.[15] In the mid-1750s, the 'Canton System' was imposed on all traders, who were obliged to deal exclusively with a merchant guild or 'cohong', a limited co-operative of Chinese merchants established and overseen by a single Chinese government official, the 'Hoppo'.[16] 'Foreign merchants or officials could not approach the Chinese local or provincial authorities directly', in the words of David Steeds and Ian Nish, 'but communicate with them only through the hong merchants, and only in the form of a petition, symbolizing inequality'.[17]

Having said that, however, with the expansion of the European community and the growing assertiveness of the British in particular, the same 'local or provincial authorities' faced varying degrees of complaint, defiance, and intimidation. 'The Portuguese, French, and Dutch also complained about the Canton System and China's restrictions on foreign trade', writes Li Chen, 'but the British were particularly bellicose from the mid-eighteenth century onward as they became increasingly confident in their cultural and material superiority'.[18] This was especially the case with issues or incidents

---

15   David Steeds and Ian Nish, *China, Japan and 19th Century Britain* (Dublin: Irish Academic Press, 1977), 22.
16   Cranmer-Byng and Wills, 'Trade and Diplomacy with Maritime Europe, 1644-c. 1800', 193. For more detail, see two works by Paul A. Van Dyke, *The Canton Trade: Life and Enterprise on the China Coast, 1700–1845* (Hong Kong: Hong Kong University Press, 2005), passim, and *Merchants of Canton and Macao: Politics and Strategies in Eighteenth-Century Chinese Trade* (Hong Kong: Hong Kong University Press, 2011), 1–30.
17   Steeds and Nish, *China, Japan and 19th Century Britain*, 21. See my chapter below.
18   Li Chen, *Chinese Law in Imperial Eyes: Sovereignty, Justice, and Transcultural Politics* (New York: Columbia University Press, 2016), 49.

involving cross-national crime and punishment – like the notorious *Lady Hughes* case of 1784, when a gun fired by a British country ship severely damaged a Chinese boat and took the life of one of its Chinese crewmen, Wu Yake. This and other incidents invariably led to the foreign community's demand that their countrymen be tried and judged according to their own laws, rather than by those of China (known as 'extraterritoriality'), which when formally instituted after the Treaty of Nanjing in 1842 would become a major source of Chinese humiliation.[19]

The Macartney Mission

Historically and imaginatively crucial to the narrative of cultural relations between China and the West, and therefore to this volume of essays, is the (in)famous Macartney embassy of 1792–94, which represents a more or less fortunate fall in the complex history of Britain's historical engagement with China. One of the main aims of the mission was to put formal trade relations between Britain and China on a more equal basis. Britain hoped to address various grievances caused by slow processing at Canton and to negotiate the opening up to trade of new ports in north and central China. At the same time, Britain also – and more ambitiously – aspired to establishing a trading factory and permanent envoy in the capital, Beijing, from which, along with all the other European nations and unlike Russia, they were excluded.[20] Like other major voyages and diplomatic missions of the eighteenth century, however, the embassy had a number of motives. James Hevia, for example, identifying 'a ceremonial and a business phase', argues convincingly for the national vanity and sense of exceptionalism driving the British mission.[21] It was also a voyage of exploration: 'at

---

19 Li Chen, *Chinese Law in Imperial Eyes*, 25–68.
20 Cranmer-Byng and Wills, 'Trade and Diplomacy with Maritime Europe, 1644-c. 1800', 243.
21 James L. Hevia, *Cherishing Men from Afar: Qing Guest Ritual and the Macartney Embassy of 1793* (Durham and London: Duke University Press, 1995), 58.

the public expense in pursuit of knowledge and for the discovery and observation of distant countries and manners', according to the instructions Macartney received from His Majesty's Government.²² After all, although China was the oldest developed civilisation in the world and there was an abundance of information, misinformation, and conjecture circulating in the European world, the country was forbidden to the kind of unmediated gaze of the empirically trained eighteenth-century investigator and to that extent remained as much *terra incognita* to the European inquirer as some of the more remote parts of the Antarctic, Africa, and Australia.

The Macartney embassy, then, was an important one and the British government planned it with care.²³ Foreign embassies, however, were considered by the Chinese government as tribute-bearing missions and 'all representatives sent to China by the Western powers were expected to follow the rules laid down for tributary missions': '(i) the point of entry and departure in China and the route to be followed by the tributary envoy to Peking were specifically determined, (ii) upon his arrival at Peking and at his audience with the emperor the envoy was expected to perform a full kowtow of three kneelings and nine knockings of the head, and (iii) the Chinese authorities provided an escort who accompanied the tributary envoy on his journey to and from the capital'.²⁴ Insofar as performing the kowtow before the emperor implied submission on the part of the ambassador's sovereign to the Chinese emperor, the British objected to it as a humiliating ritual, one which Macartney had been instructed to negotiate and avoid.²⁵

---

22 P. J. Marshall, 'Britain and China in the Late Eighteenth Century', in *Ritual and Diplomacy: The Macartney Mission to China, 1792–1794: Papers Presented at the 1992 Conference of the British Association for Chinese Studies Marking the Bicentenary of the Macartney Mission to China*, ed. Robert A. Bickers (London: Wellsweep, 1993), 11–29 (14).
23 Earl H. Pritchard, 'The Kotow in the Macartney Embassy to China in 1793', *The Far Eastern Quarterly*, 2:2 (Feb. 1943), 163–203 (163).
24 Steeds and Nish, *China, Japan and 19th Century Britain*, 24. Here again, Hevia offers a corrective to more paranoid interpretations of Chinese policy by looking at the tribute system and comparing Chinese relations with its immediate neighbours, *Cherishing Men from Afar*, 9–15, 29–56.
25 Pritchard, 'The Kotow in the Macartney Embassy to China in 1793', 163–64.

Opinion was (and would remain) divided. In choosing to make an issue of it and refusing to kowtow, Macartney set a precedent of national pride that 'exceeded the calculated political and economic objectives of the British', according to Lydia Liu, 'and led to costly and fanatical destruction of human lives and property in military campaigns'.[26] However we interpret the various diplomatic incidents in the lead-up to Macartney's audience in the summer palace, his challenge to the supremacy and prerogative of the emperor sank the mission. What the British might have gained by conforming to the ritual, however, remains uncertain. For good and ill (corruption was rife and the eighty-nine-year-old Qianlong Emperor was in thrall to the self-aggrandising eunuch Heshen), the Chinese were predisposed to resist British ministrations. 'The reluctance of the emperor to end restrictions on international trade', as Arthur Cotterell reminds us, 'tallied with a tradition going back to Ming times', and news of revolution in Europe had only made the Chinese court more suspicious of European insubordination.[27]

If the Macartney mission was a diplomatic and commercial failure, as a scientific expedition and a media event it was a great success, generating what Elizabeth Hope Chang calls 'a complex constellation of texts'.[28] Even before Lord Macartney's valet, Aeneas Anderson, brought out his *Narrative of the British Embassy to China in the years 1792, 1793, and 1794; Containing the Various Circumstances of the Embassy, with Accounts of the Customs and Manners of the Chinese, and a Description of the Country, Towns, Cities, &c. &c* in 1795, with the characteristic swiftness of sensational journalism, 'discussion of the embassy had already featured in several publications as soon as initial reports of the embassy began to arrive back in England in July and August 1794', as Logan Collins points out.[29] Once Anderson's *Narrative* was issued, however, China and its people became an established topic in the

---

26 Lydia Liu, *The Clash of Empires: The Invention of China in Modern World Making* (Cambridge, MA: Harvard University Press, 2004), 217.
27 Arthur Cotterell, *China: A History* (London: Pimlico, 1988), 229–30.
28 Elizabeth Hope Chang (ed.), *British Travel Writing From China, 1793–1901*, in 5 vols (London: Pickering & Chatto, 2009), 1:3.
29 Logan P. Collins, 'British Periodical Representations of China: 1793–1830' (unpublished MA dissertation, University of Houston, May 2014), 39.

periodical press, as china plate and tea had become established commodities in British households. Other accounts of the embassy were soon to follow:

> Sir George Staunton, *An Authentic Account of an Embassy from the King of Great Britain to the Emperor of China* (1797).
> Samuel Holmes, *The Journal of Mr. Samuel Holmes, Serjeant-Major of the XIth Light Dragoons, during his Attendance, as one of the Guard on Lord Macartney's Embassy to China and Tartary, 1792–3* (1798).
> John Barrow, *Travels in China, Containing Descriptions, Observations, and Comparisons, made and collected in the course of a Short Residence at the Imperial Palace of Yuen-Min-Yuen, and on a subsequent Journey through the Country from Pekin to Canton, in which it is attempted to appreciate the Rank that this extraordinary Empire may be considered to hold in the Scale of Civilized Nations* (1804).
> William Alexander, *The Costume of China*, in 2 vols (1805).
> John Barrow, *A Voyage to Cochinchina, in the Years 1792 and 1793: containing a General View of the Valuable Productions and the Political Importance of this flourishing Kingdom; and also of such European Settlements as were visited on the Voyage: with Sketches of the Manners, Character, and Condition of their several Inhabitants* (London: Cadell & Davies, 1806).
> John Barrow, *Some Account of the Public Life, and a Selection from the Unpublished Writings of the Earl of Macartney* (1807).[30]

Prior to the Macartney mission, discussion of China in British print culture had been occasional, eccentric, and largely prelinguistic: neither Thomas Percy nor the Orientalist Sir William Jones had been fluent in the language they helped to translate. Percy had edited and (after Canton businessman James Wilkinson) partly rendered into English the late seventeenth-century Chinese 'scholar-beauty romance' *Haoqiu zhuan* (1683?), as *Hau Kiou Choann; or, The Pleasing History* (1761), which he had published with extensive footnotes, and which proved a controversial introduction to the Chinese empire and its culture.

---

30 See William Christie, 'China in Early Romantic Periodicals', *European Romantic Review*, 27(1), 1–13, and Shunhong Zhang, *British Views on China at the Dawn of the 19th Century* (Reading: [China Social Sciences Press and] Paths International, 2013), chapter 2, 'Views on China of the Retinues of the Macartney and Amherst Embassies', 22–56.

('Percy is at once thoroughly captivated and deeply disturbed by his sinological discoveries', writes David Porter: 'His ambivalence is dizzying'.[31]) The more positive William Jones had hoped, but failed, to publish what would have been the first direct translation into English of a Confucian text (the *Lunyu*) – this would have to wait until Joshua Marshman issued his Serampore translation of 1809 – and had been unable to obtain translations of the approved Chinese law tracts with which he had planned to furnish Europe with China's ideas and values – this had to wait until 1810 when George Thomas Staunton published his *Ta Tsing Leu Lee*, a translation of the Qing legal code.

Neither Percy nor Jones, moreover, had ever been to Canton. Like all British knowledge, Percy's derives largely from the Jesuits, as did that of members of the Macartney mission – pre-eminently, though not exclusively, from du Halde. On the eve of the departure of the Macartney mission, no one in Britain could be found competent to negotiate or interpret in Mandarin. The mission's secretary, Sir George Leonard Staunton, was obliged to go to Paris in search of linguistic competence, finally settling on two non-English-speaking Chinese interpreters from a Neapolitan seminary. The result was that all communication at the Chinese court had to be channelled through Italian or Latin. The only halfway competent Mandarin speaker among the British themselves by the time they arrived in China was Staunton's twelve-year-old son, George Thomas, who, with Robert Morrison, Thomas Manning and John Francis Davis, would become part of a collective of accomplished Chinese speakers later interpreting and translating in China.

After Macartney

The Macartney embassy instigated and generated an outpouring of cultural commentary in books and periodicals that formed the core of new knowledge and fresh (mis)interpretation. The next generation of sinologists would claim intimacy with China and the Chinese language in a way that eighteenth-century commentators could never have,

---

31   Porter, *The Chinese Taste in Eighteenth-Century England*, 154.

though it was an intimacy mediated by Baptist and London Missionary Society activity and British East India Company trade at Canton. In spite of any bias given to their inquiries by religious or commercial interests, however, what Peter Kitson calls the Canton School of Romantic sinology, formed by George Thomas Staunton and John Francis Davis, was free of the classicising, theological imperatives that had driven Jesuit and Protestant sinology alike, free of their agonising over the precise spiritual nature and value of Chinese orthodoxy and willing 'to explore the more popular and practical aspects of Chinese life and culture and to translate works about Chinese law and diplomacy, as well as popular works of fiction and drama for both a specialist and a general audience'.[32] Staunton translated tracts on vaccination and, crucially, the Qing code of fundamental laws that Sir William Jones had been unable to manage, in which he challenged such cherished European 'truths' about China as its tolerance of infanticide and the prevalence of corporal punishment, denying the ubiquity of both while at the same time sketching in a vital social context.

Despite Staunton's efforts, however, the cultural abominations identified by Percy in his footnotes to *Hau Kiou Choann; or, The Pleasing History* – infanticide, exquisite punishments, mistreatment of women (including foot binding), concubinage, homosexuality, cultural arrogance, global and economic exclusivity, and (not least) having no word for 'sin' itself – became part of a conflicted British sinology extending well into the nineteenth century and beyond. In Percy, most of the themes and all of the tensions and contradictions of Britain and the West's reception of (and attitude towards) China had come together. John Barrow's popular *Travels in China* (1804), along with numerous periodical review articles, would keep this conflicted, largely negative image of China before the minds of the British public in the lead-up to the Opium Wars and the progressive humiliation of China over the course of the nineteenth century.

---

32   Kitson, *Forging Romantic China*, 98.

The Opium Wars and Beyond

The trafficking in illegal opium that began under the eye of the British East India Company later in the eighteenth century had by the early nineteenth century dramatically reversed the balance of trade through Canton, where the Chinese demand for opium proved as insatiable as the British demand for tea. Relations between Britain and China changed correspondingly, at a national and often a personal level. It was the Chinese attempt to block the opium trade that precipitated the Opium Wars, in which the Chinese proved fatally vulnerable to a vastly more sophisticated British military technology. Britain's overpowering of the depleted and under-resourced Chinese army and navy forced the opening up of China to a quasi-imperial (and evangelical) West.

However disinclined we might be to use the First Opium War and the Treaty of Nanjing of 1842 as a dividing line between ancient and modern Chinese history,[33] they remain pivotal events in any history of China's cultural relations with Britain and the West, whose 'complex power dynamics', to quote from Li Chen, 'created some of the still influential ideas of Sino-Western difference, identities, and modernities at a time when these ideas remained seriously underdeveloped, contradictory, or contested'.[34] And it is entirely characteristic that both Staunton's and Davis's views of China should have changed during and after the Opium Wars – Staunton when consulted by the British government during the war and Davis when he later rewrote his sympathetic history of 1836, *The Chinese: A General Description of the Empire of China and Its Inhabitants*, to bring it in line with British imperial ambitions and cultural rationalisations. No amount of historical and economic revisionism is likely to gainsay the sense of national humiliation induced by the enforced opening up of China (along with Britain's demand for extraterritoriality) over the next hundred years. What we witness after 1842 is 'the untidy, unplanned scramble for China', to quote Robert Bickers:

---

33 See William T. Rowe, *China's Last Empire: The Great Qing* (Cambridge, MA: Harvard University Press, 2009), 2–3.
34 Li Chen, *Chinese Law in Imperial Eyes*, 3.

Introduction: China and the West in the Long Eighteenth Century

The chase was joined by missionaries, merchants and mercenaries, by Britons, Americans, Russians, Parsees, and Malacca-born Chinese, by all comers from all corners. The Qing Empire which ruled China had not been closed to foreign intercourse before 1832, but it regulated it tightly, and restricted it to one point on its coastal periphery. After 1842 those controls were sharply degraded, and communities of foreigners and their Chinese allies and partners developed in major coastal cities, eventually as far north as Tianjin, the coastal gateway to the imperial capital at Peking.[35]

The Essays

While the outline of an expansive and aggressive Britain, exceptionalist and Orientalist, is clearly in evidence in most of the essays in this volume – how else does one read the willingness with which, both in print and in arms, Britain prepared itself to go to war with China in the opening decades of the nineteenth century? – none of these studies interprets the impasse that precipitated the Opium Wars of 1839–42 as an inevitable 'clash of civilisations' in the Huntingtonian sense, concerned as many of the essays are no less with how things might have developed, than with how they did develop. As James Watt suggests in concluding his chapter on Charles Lamb and Thomas Manning, 'there were "stories … to tell" about China other than those that were premised on antagonism and the expectation of future conflict'.

Robert Markley reads Adam Smith's *Wealth of Nations* in the light of Domingo Fernandez Navarette's *Account of the Empire of China* (trans. 1704), Jean-Baptiste du Halde's *General History of China* (1736), and Walter and Robins' *Voyage Round the World … By George Anson* (1748), looking at the way Smith struggled to accommodate the second-hand knowledge of China he gained from these popular sources within the developmental narratives of stadial history and economic growth.

---

35 Robert Bickers, *The Scramble for China: Foreign Devils in the Qing Empire, 1832–1914* (London: Penguin, 2012), 11.

Markley shows how Smith's dependence on textual evidence problematises his economic theories and influences his choice of examples and vignettes from his primary sources. Smith's *Wealth of Nations*, as Markley points out, 'raises some fundamental questions about how first-hand accounts are used as "evidence" by eighteenth-century philosophers and economic theorists, intent on shoehorning China into overarching systems of thought'. He also discovers a powerful counternarrative to the bigoted and influential account of the Chinese people in George Anson's *Voyages* in the little known and unpublished 'A Little Secret History of Affairs at Canton in the Year 1743' (dated 1765) of Edward Page, an East India Company supercargo resident in Canton throughout the episode described in Anson's *Voyages* and obliged to mediate between Anson and the Hong merchants.

The clearly sympathetic and mutually respectful relationship between Edward Page and the Hong merchant Suqua manifest in Markley's transcriptions from Page's 'History' make the two men an excellent example of the kind of cross-cultural friendship identified and explored in my own chapter on 'Cultural Cross-Dressing in the House of Pankeequa', which acknowledges the challenge posed to mutual understanding by everyday objects like eating utensils and dress. Starting with the visit to Canton of William Hickey in 1769 and a sumptuous banquet offered by the Hong merchant Pankeequa to his European business acquaintances and friends, my survey of cultural interaction and emulation looks at accounts of similar festive occasions in the travel memoirs of a string of British and American visitors. What interests me is the alternative history of Britain's relations with China, the fact that the Chinese and the British were never so far apart that occasional acts of mutual understanding and even friendship – what Leela Gandhi calls 'minor narratives of crosscultural collaboration'[36] – were impossible.

Through the lens of the 1784 *Lady Hughes* affair mentioned earlier, Q. S. Tong's chapter examines the significance of this extraordinary battle for judicial authority, which raised complex questions about the

---

36 Leela Gandhi, *Affective Communities: Anticolonial Thought, Fin-de-Siècle Radicalism, and the Politics of Friendship* (Durham and London: Duke University Press, 2006), 6.

Introduction: China and the West in the Long Eighteenth Century

way in which conflict between the Qing and British legal systems could be mediated and the chasm between the Qing and British ethical and jurisprudential matters navigated. Considered in the context of laws developed in the spirit of modern liberalism, writes Tong, extraterritorial privileges are a contradiction in terms: 'What would extraterritoriality be, if not an imposition on the other whose legal sovereignty must be denied, rejected, and violated?' Tong's chapter examines the limits of liberalism in the context of an undeniable cultural impasse, and productively complicates the role of laws in the Qing Dynasty by emphasising their performative and politico-diplomatic dimensions. Tong argues that the *Lady Hughes* affair escalated the mutual distrust between China and Britain and suggests that the ethical and legal dilemmas raised by the affair continue to haunt us today.

Kendall Johnson's chapter also takes 1784 as pivotal, only in his case it is the arrival in China from the newly formed United States of America of Major Samuel Shaw as the first American supercargo and 'first American consul' that makes it a year of 'global historical significance with implications for China's relationship to global modernity'. Examining a series of American mercantile biographies, Johnson complicates the term 'free trade' as it was understood after the Revolutionary War. American traders provided an interesting counterpoint to the British for, as Johnson argues, '[u]ncorrupted by imperial monopolies or the project of colonial land acquisitions in China or India, they had showcased new potential for American free trade in the global co-ordination of speculative enterprise through their private companies'. The 'American merchant' emerges from Johnson's accounts of nineteenth-century mercantile biographies as an identifiable 'type' and Carlylean hero who operated with relative neutrality between the Opium Wars. Johnson shows how celebratory accounts of American commerce attempt to downplay involvement in the opium trade, revealing the merchant biography as a vehicle for American nationalism which offers an alternative representation of the relationship between China, America, and Britain during the Opium Wars.

Through an examination of the writings of Charles Lamb and his friend, the elusive but accomplished sinologist Thomas Manning, James Watt reflects on the period before the First Opium War as a key moment during which China could be represented by Westerners without antagonism – indeed, with a great deal of frivolity and affection, if occasionally (as with Lamb) that frivolity betrayed something of the reflex contempt fast becoming characteristic of the British response to China and the Chinese. Through a sensitive analysis of Manning's writings, which drew on his first-hand experiences travelling in Asia and working in the East India Company factory at Canton, and comparing his and Lamb's writings with their correspondence, Watt shows how Manning 'challenged Lamb's sense of the strangeness of China in the letters that he wrote from Canton, [and] emphatically rejected any idea of an essential Chinese inscrutability of the kind that is evident in De Quincey's opium nightmares'.

Yinghe Jiang's essay considers Qing export paintings, or trade paintings, as artefacts of Canton's 'hybrid culture shaped by Chinese and Western interaction' and also as individual works of art in a complex global marketplace during the Qing Dynasty. Produced for European and American markets, few traces of export paintings remain in China but, as Jiang shows through a series of intriguing examples, the paintings and their histories 'profoundly influenced the globalisation of Canton Port' and were a pivotal and evocative means of representing heavily mediated portrayals of China to the Western world. While the low social status of the painters and the 'factory line' production of set images make it easy to subsume export or trade paintings under global commodity trading (as their title suggests), along with tea, silk, and porcelain, Jiang argues that they also represented precocious examples of Chinese artists assimilating Western styles and subject matter (the example she gives is of export painter Lamqua's reverse imitation of Ingres' *La Grande Odalisque*) and have a place in the global history of art, no less than in the global history of trade.

Opium, as Peter Kitson reminds us, is the 'most ambiguous of commodities, both medicine and poison'. Ambiguity, not to say hypocrisy, also characterises the historical representation of Kitson's subject, sinologist and diplomat Sir John Francis Davis, in a close and extended analysis of Davis' involvement with the British opium trade to China over the course of a long public career, first as a clerk with the East India Company, then as president of the Company's select committee and its chief superintendent after the lapse of its monopoly

(1834), and later as the governor of Hong Kong and a servant of the British crown. Kitson's study of Davis's personal and political relationship with China, using as a commentary the changes Davis introduced over the decades to his popular study *The Chinese: A General Description of the Empire of China and Its Inhabitants*, untangles the many contradictions inherent in his writings and career and reveals how Davis, 'who opposed the abolition of the Company monopoly on the China trade and characterized the opium trade as desperate and destructive', eventually came to support the war and oversee the legalisation of opium in Hong Kong. Through this fascinating case study of an influential sinologist's lifelong relationship with China, Kitson traces the complex web of influences which shape an individual's interactions with a foreign culture, including the personal, institutional, political, and geographical.

In his essay on Walter Scott's relationship with China, Kang-yen Chiu contributes to an increasing body of scholarly work on the imaginative and occasionally direct connections between the canonical Romantic writers and the Far East. Analysing references to China in Scott's novels, journals, and private letters, Chiu builds a case for Scott's long-held interest in China, which later materialised in his collection of Chinese artefacts at Abbotsford and in his library of books on China. Among the Chinese items in the eclectic Abbotsford that could be associated unequivocally with Scott as its first owner, Chiu focuses on the Chinese wallpaper, a gift of the novelist's cousin, Hugh, which clearly intrigued and delighted him. Extending his survey of Chinese objects in Scott's possession to include discussion of nine books on or about China in Abbotsford's library, Chiu argues for Scott's 'nuanced appreciation of the nation and culture these objects represented'.

Dongqing Wang's chapter explains how and why '[t]he Opium Wars marked a key moment when the admiration of Confucian meritocracy began to be questioned and the limits of classical Chinese learning came into discussion among the Westerners'. Examining a range of British writings on Confucian education during the period that focus, in the first instance, on the Chinese pedagogical practice of rote learning, then on what the commentators stigmatise as the narrow, 'unscientific' curriculum of an imperial examination system privileging 'words' over 'things', Wang carefully traces shifts in conceptions of what

Confucian education entailed and how it related to 'the rise of liberal education as a product of cross-cultural social debates on industry, culture, and democracy in the context of global modernity'. Wang's essay concludes by outlining the complex role of Orientalism in furthering not only revolutionary criticism, but also cultural conservatism in China.

In her essay on the textual lives of the young British vice-consul Augustus Raymond Margary, Elizabeth Hope Chang examines the 'brief but intense crisis in Sino-British relations' that followed his murder in 1875 while seeking to establish a trade route from China through Burma to British India. Chang's account traces the nature and impact of Margary's posthumous representation in Victorian travel narratives and their importance in the struggle for power between Britain and China and in shaping British conceptions of China. Taking up the narrative and theoretical discussion of sovereignty and extraterritoriality in Q. S. Tong's essay, Chang complicates it by considering a sensational event that took place in the undemarcated borderlands of *both* the Chinese *and* the British imperium. 'The paradoxical impulse to attach a name and sentimental history to a broader phenomenon of extra-national mobility allows us to trace the evolution of this boundary space across the span of many different journeys to the west.' Chang points us beyond the narratives of the 'life, death and afterlife' of Margary to argue that such personal stories give 'a false but instructive individual biographical outline to the in fact trans-personal function of place-making in the Victorian understanding of China', at the same time demonstrating the significance of rhetorical constructs in travel writing and establishing Margary as a case study with important implications for our understanding of mobility, extraterritoriality, sovereignty, and the relations between place and person.

Building on longstanding projects and critiques of linguistic nationalism in the West, Lorraine Wong considers 'the simultaneous rise of linguistic nationalism and communism in the non-Western world, as is found in China', where 'linguistic nationalism was complicated by the struggle for social equality and the communist revolution against capitalism'. The cultural phenomenon that Wong analyses is the Chinese Latinisation movement of the 1930s and 1940s, focusing on the poet and creator of the New Writing, Qu Qiubai, and his dream of using the Latin alphabet to overcome the ingrained inequalities of Chinese characters and thus of 'reconfiguring the existing discursive order'. Alert to the difficulties and contradictions inherent in an egalitarian enterprise at once national (creating a level playing field for the different classes and different language communities of China) and international (uniting the workers of the world), Wong examines Qu's struggle to make meaning semantically and grammatically out of incompatible media, and uses the Latinised translation of Lu Xun's *Diary of a Madman* – *Igo fungz di rhgi* (1936) – to isolate some of the interpretative challenges involved. In the process, she provides insights into hierarchies of power at local, national, and global levels, while considering, not just the limitations of the enterprise, but also the way in which Latin script could enable 'the democratic participation of people in linguistic activities (such as reading and writing) that affect their material lives' and 'facilitate national awakening and social equality simultaneously'.

1
'That full complement of riches': China and the Problems of Political Economy in Adam Smith's *The Wealth of Nations*

Robert Markley

Although Adam Smith devotes only a few pages to discussing the Middle Kingdom in *The Wealth of Nations*, China nonetheless plays a significant role in his treatise as the world's primary example of a nation that has, he says, 'acquired that full complement of riches which the nature of its laws and institutions permits it to acquire'.[1] As a country that has reached the limits of its growth, China exemplifies a fundamental tension in Smith's thought between the limits that 'nature' puts on agricultural productivity, and therefore on a nation's wealth, and his belief that international trade and laissez-faire economics can help extend national prosperity (at least in theory) indefinitely. Yet Smith never travelled to China and had little access to economic data on the Qing Dynasty. Consequently, his comments, like those of his contemporaries, represent an effort to reconcile competing textual traditions: the dozens of eyewitness accounts by Catholic missionaries and Western emissaries that praised the socioeconomic stability, orderly government, and techno-cultural sophistication of China with the 'modern' conceptual frameworks – political, economic and cultural – promoted by writers during the Scots Enlightenment that

---

1 Adam Smith, *An Inquiry into the Nature and Causes of the Wealth of Nations*, ed. R. H. Campbell and A. S. Skinner (Oxford: Oxford University Press, 1979), 1: 89.

championed Western European, especially British, exceptionalism. In this regard, exploring Smith's treatment of China requires examining some of the ways these complex textual traditions influenced late eighteenth-century thinkers and raises some fundamental questions about how first-hand accounts are used as 'evidence' by eighteenth-century philosophers and economic theorists, intent on shoehorning China into overarching systems of thought.[2]

In trying to fit China into his analysis of economic principles, Smith confronts the significant challenges that the Middle Kingdom posed to European exceptionalism: it was an advanced non-Christian civilisation that had thrived for centuries; it rejected international commerce as a primary driver of national prosperity; it lacked Western commitments to scientific knowledge and technological innovation; and its laws, to many Europeans, seemed inimical to the rights and liberties of property owners.[3] For many writers in the second half of the eighteenth century, China remained where many Jesuits had placed it – at the apex of civilisation. The Aberdeen philosopher James Dunbar wrote, 'if the honors of nations were, in reality, to be estimated by riches, by

---

[2] On the dominance of China in the global economy before 1800, see Frank Pomeranz's *The Great Divergence: China, Europe, and the Making of the Modern World Economy* (Princeton: Princeton University Press, 2000), and his response to his critics, 'Ten Years After: Responses and Reconsiderations', *Historically Speaking* 12.4 (2011), 20–25.

[3] A wealth of recent studies emphasise, in a variety of ways, the complex role that China played in shaping Western conceptions of literary and cultural modernity. See David Porter, *Ideographia: The Chinese Cipher in Early Modern Europe* (Stanford, CA: Stanford University Press, 2001), and Porter, *The Chinese Taste in Eighteenth-Century England* (Cambridge: Cambridge University Press, 2010); Robert Markley, *The Far East and the English Imagination, 1600–1730* (Cambridge: Cambridge University Press, 2006); Eugenia Zuroski Jenkins, *A Taste for China: English Subjectivity and the Prehistory of Orientalism* (New York: Oxford University Press, 2013); Chi-ming Yang, *Performing China: Virtue, Commerce, and Orientalism in Eighteenth-Century England, 1660–1760* (Baltimore: Johns Hopkins University Press, 2011); Ashley Eva Millar, *A Singular Case: Debating China's Political Economy in the European Enlightenment* (Montreal and Kingston: McGill-Queen's University Press, 2017); and Eun Kyung Min, *China and the Writing of English Literary Modernity, 1690–1770* (Cambridge: Cambridge University Press, 2018).

1 China and the Problems of Political Economy in *The Wealth of Nations*

population, by the antiquity of arts, or by the stability and duration of civil government, it is not any of the European nations, it is the Chinese, and the Indians, who must be placed at the head of the species'.[4] Dunbar identifies four criteria that are central to his assessment of civilisation; and, as we will see, Smith acknowledges China's status in precisely these terms of population, wealth, antiquity and stability. Moreover, China's sociopolitical stability and wealth over centuries suggested, to some, that it remained 'a singular case', seemingly removed from stadial theories of socioeconomic history so essential to the Scots Enlightenment: the progress of humankind from stateless bands of nomadic hunters and gatherers; to herding societies centred on the domestication of livestock; to agricultural states that developed urban centres of calculation and distribution; and ultimately to the advent of commercial society – and with it the arts, culture and refinements of civilised nations.[5] In the context of changing perceptions of China in the later eighteenth century, the Qing Dynasty's seeming lack of interest in Western notions of progress produces both the rage and bafflement that characterise George Anson's version of events in Canton and the complicated strategies that Smith employs to explain the paradoxes of the nation's wealth and the low wages of its labouring classes.

In what follows, I situate Smith's comments on China in relation to two of the important texts on China in his library and, as importantly, to emerging debates about the East India Company's trade to China, prominently on display in the official account of George Anson's voyage, published in 1748 as *A Voyage Round the World, in the Years MDCCXL, I, II, III, IV*, written by Richard Walter and Benjamin Robins.[6] Smith's

---

4   James Dunbar, *Essays on the History of Mankind in Rude and Cultivated Ages* (Dublin: B. Smith for William Colles and William Gilbert, 1782), 121–22.
5   See Jeng-guo S. Chen, 'The British View of Chinese Civilization and the Emergence of Class Consciousness', *The Eighteenth Century: Theory and Interpretation* 45 (2004), 193–205.
6   Walter [and Robins], *A Voyage Round the World, in the Years MDCCXL, I, II, III, IV. By George Anson* (London, 1748). The authorship of the text is vexed; the title page attributes the text to the ship's chaplain Walter, but he left the *Centurion* in 1742 when it first docked in Canton and sailed to England on a merchant ship; he was not present during the events in 1743. Glyndwr Williams suggests that much of the text was ghost-written by Robins but

library contained the English translation of *Tratados históricos, políticos, éticos y religiosos de la monarquia de China* (Madrid 1676) by the Dominican missionary Domingo Fernandez Navarette, who spent years in China in the late seventeenth century, and the compilation of Jesuit sources published by Jean-Baptiste du Halde in 1735 and translated the next year under the title *The General History of China*.[7] In his treatment of China, Smith does not comb assiduously through sources so much as he gathers anecdotes and examples that he uses to illustrate the larger operations of political economy. He cherry-picks some of Navarette's observations and ignores others, radically alters the tone and substance of passages he finds in du Halde, and ultimately elevates to sweeping generalisations the kinds of derogatory comments about China that are legion in Walter and Robins' *Voyage Round the World*. What is at stake in Smith's reshaping of these competing views of China are not only particular views of that country but also the nature of political economy itself as a series of particular emphases, rewritings, suppressions and displacements. To illuminate the implications and consequences of some of these displacements, I turn in the final pages of this essay to examine one of the most significant first-hand accounts of doing business in eighteenth-century China, the unpublished manuscript by the East India Company merchant Edward Page, who was the supercargo, the head of that year's trading mission, in Canton in 1743 when Anson was embroiled with Chinese officials in a dispute about custom duties and the disposition of the Spanish prisoners he had captured at sea.[8] Page's 'A Little Secret History' contests Anson's account

---

ventriloquises Anson's views. See *The Prize of All the Oceans: The Dramatic True Story of Commodore Anson's Voyage Round the World and How He Seized the Spanish Treasure Galleon* (New York: Viking, 1999), 237–41. Although there is no evidence that Smith owned a copy of this text, its popularity and influence makes it likely that he was familiar with its attack on the Chinese.

7   Jean-Baptiste du Halde, *The General History of China*, 4 vols (London, 1736).
8   Markley, 'Anson at Canton, 1743: Obligation, Exchange, and Ritual in Edward Page's "Secret History"' in *The Culture of the Gift in Eighteenth-Century England*, ed. Linda Ziokowski and Cynthia Klekar (New York: Palgrave, 2009), 215–33; Glyndwr Williams, 'Anson at Canton, 1743: "A little secret history"', in Cecil H. Clough and P. E. Hair, eds., *The European Outthrust and Encounter. The First Phase c. 1400 to c. 1700* (Liverpool: Liverpool University Press, 1994), 271–90.

1 China and the Problems of Political Economy in *The Wealth of Nations*

at every turn and underscores the limitations of armchair theorising about China's role in the late eighteenth-century world.[9] As a text that lies seemingly outside the system that Smith describes, Page's secret history acts as a heuristic means to put Smith's comments on China into a less Eurocentric context.

Domingo Navarette in China

The translation of Navarette's text, *An Account of the Empire of China, Historical, Political, Moral, and Religious,* is by far the longest account in the Churchills' collection of previously unpublished voyages and among the most influential, both for its attack on the Jesuit mission and its account of life in seventeenth-century China during the early years of the Qing Dynasty.[10] Navarette devotes much of his account of China to chronicling his travels, defending his mission and detailing its conflicts with Jesuit missionaries over the course of two decades, discussing at length controversies that arose over Jesuit accommodationism (the effort to make Christian piety and practices conform to Chinese culture), and offering his readers comments on law, government, agriculture, gender relations, and everyday life in the Qing empire. To a greater extent than some of his fellow missionaries, Navarette provides sketches of life for the labouring classes. Farmers in China, he writes,

> work without ceasing, and if they had the Feeding and Wine those of *La Mancha* in *Castile* have, no men in the World would outdo them at their Business. They are continually about their Land ... The Land in *China* never lies Fallow; generally the same Ground produces three Crops a Year; first Rice; and before it is reap'd, they

---

9   Edward Page, 'A Little Secret History of Affairs at Canton in the Year 1743 when the Centurion, Commodore Anson was Lying in the River', Ms. 2894, Oregon Historical Society, 1765. All quotations are from this manuscript. The manuscript is dated 18 November 1765.
10 See David E. Mungello, *Curious Land: Jesuit Accommodation and the Origins of Sinology* (Honolulu: University of Hawai'i Press, 1985).

sow Fitches; and when they are in, Wheat, Beans, or some other Grain: Thus it continually goes round.[11]

By comparing the parts of eastern China that he knew to the wine and wheat-growing region of La Mancha, Navarette emphasises both the productivity of the land and the tireless labour required to harvest three different crops a year. Although multi-cropping was practised widely in the Ming and Qing eras, his comments seem less an exact description of agricultural practices than a fleshing out of his overall impression of the countryside: contiguous fields bearing a variety of crops (but no wine), with no land lying neglected or fallow.

In this regard, Navarette's description of the countryside conforms to the accounts of other Europeans who travelled in the interior of China in the seventeenth century. Whatever qualifications Smith and other critics of Jesuit accounts of China might offer, it remained difficult in the eighteenth century to discount reports of agricultural abundance and the virtues of the local, regional and national governments that were responsible for maintaining this depiction of socioeconomic stability. Navarette claims that:

> [There is] not a foot of waste Land in all *China*; and if it were not all till'd, the Product would not suffice to maintain such Multitudes. The Husbandmen are generally poor People, and have but a small parcel of Land they farm from others: The general Rule is, that the Landlord pays Taxes and has half the Crop, the Husbandman tills the Ground and has the other half for his pains. There is not a Horn, Bone, or Feather, but what they burn to make Ashes to manure their Ground. *Horace* and *Cicero* wrote much in praise of Husbandry. (58)

---

11   'An Account of the Empire of China, Historical, Political, Moral, and Religious' in Awnsham and John Churchill, compilers, *A Collection of Voyages and Travels, Some Now First Printed from Original Manuscripts*, 4 vols (London, 1704), 1: 1–424 (57). All references are to this edition. 'Fitches' refers to nigella sativa, a plant whose seeds are used as a spice, variously called black caraway, black cumin, fennel flower, nigella and Roman coriander.

1 China and the Problems of Political Economy in *The Wealth of Nations*

Navarette's seeming non sequitur, invoking Horace and Cicero in praise of farming, places the Chinese 'Husbandmen' within a universal system of moral and social virtues. Their industriousness promotes a socioeconomic system able to feed the 'Multitudes' of their countrymen and women, and their work ethic, as they labour tirelessly to support themselves and pay their landlords, becomes a cornerstone for what Navarette describes as the entrepreneurial character of the people. Not only do they turn all the byproducts of their farming (horns, bones and feathers) to use but also their enterprises have beneficial consequences for commerce and the living conditions in towns and cities, thanks to a thriving trade in human and animal dung as fertiliser. 'There is', Navarette maintains, 'no Dung but what is put to this use. Human Dung is sold, and the Countrymen go about the Streets, crying, Who will exchange this Commodity for Wood, Oil, or Herbs?' (57). The value of fertiliser helps ensure that the unsanitary conditions familiar to European readers are minimised. The Chinese collect dung in 'small Tubs very close cover'd', and Navarette emphasises the cleanliness of streets in cities as a by-product of the peasants' industriousness: 'the Houses are cleans'd every day, and [they] get something' – that is, they profit from selling excrement as fertiliser. The entrepreneurial spirit of Chinese dung-collectors does not stop there, according to Navarette, because 'a great many go about the Streets with Baskets, and little Iron Shovels, picking up all the Filth there is, whether it be Dogs, Swine or other Creatures Dung, so that all places are constantly kept clean' (57). The specificity of his observations – the sellers' cries, the closed collection tubs, the small shovels – place the reader imaginatively on the streets of a Chinese city that apparently is not plagued by the 'Filth' and stench that, Navarette implies, are familiar to readers living in European cities. This scene, in brief, offers an experiential sense of the virtues of a profitable recycling of human and animal waste. Chinese farmers and dung-sellers not only help to ensure the smooth functioning of the agricultural system but encode those values of thrift, labour and ingenuity associated with familiar ideas of moral virtue.

The same entrepreneurial spirit defines both Chinese merchants and workmen in urban areas. Impressed by the 'number of Traders and Merchants in *China*', Navarette writes that 'whatsoever Town or City a Man comes into, there seem to be more Sellers than Buyers'; and yet, in contrast to the hard-bargaining Japanese, Chinese merchants 'are all very obliging and civil; if they can get any thing [that is, make a profit] they don't slip the opportunity' (60). The Chinese are motivated by the same desire for gain as European merchants but apparently are willing to accept lower profit margins ('any thing'). Despite the rampant competition in a buyer's market, they retain their 'obliging' manners, and their civility, for Navarette, brings them within a transcultural system of civilising values.

The goods for sale in Chinese cities match or exceed in quality and price what the upper classes can buy in Europe. Navarette describes Canton as a city of superb workmen, who produce both exotic items and knockoffs of European imports 'counterfeited ... so exactly, that they sell them in the Inland [of China] for Goods brought from *Europe*' (58). In seizing this market opportunity, the Chinese demonstrate the business acumen that Smith in the 1770s associates with the 'advanced' economies of Western Europe. Even as they undercut the market for European imports, the Chinese more than hold their own against Europeans as manufacturers of luxury merchandise:

> The Curiosities they make and sell in the Shops amaze all *Europeans*. If four large Galeons were sent to the City *Nan King*, to that of *Cu Cheu*, to *Hang Cheu*, or any other like them, they might be loaden with a thousand varieties of Curiosities and Toys, such as all the World would admire, and a great Profit be made of them, tho sold at reasonable Rates. All things necessary to furnish a Princely House, may be had ready made in several parts of any of the aforesaid Citys, without any further trouble than the buying, and all at poor Rates in comparison of what is sold among us. (58)

Navarette is unambiguous: the Chinese are excellent workmen and seemingly better businessmen than their counterparts in the West. They can match or better the quality of desirable European goods at cheaper prices and manufacture those items, 'Curiosities and Toys', unavailable in Europe. The trade in luxury goods – the very markers of wealth – is widespread across cities in China and 'amaze[s]' those missionaries who historically were the only Europeans to travel widely across the country. In turn, these items 'ready made' for upper-class

1 China and the Problems of Political Economy in *The Wealth of Nations*

houses and the 'great Profit[s]' that accrue to merchants, who sell them at 'reasonable Rates', suggest that China, rather than England or Navarette's native Spain, is operating more like a model Smithian economy, a point that Kenneth Pomeranz suggests in his analysis of economic data.[12] Because 'in the Manner and Order of Governing' the Qing Dynasty 'may vie with the best [monarchies] in *Europe*' (19), China exemplifies the very virtues of historical continuity, patriarchal authority, and good governance that underwrote many of the justifications of the socioeconomic, moral and political systems of Western nations.[13]

Adam Smith on China

Smith's discussion of China in *Wealth of Nations* occurs at a significant point in his treatise when he gives voice to a theory of socioeconomic change that seeks to account for the causes and effects of economically thriving, already wealthy, wealthy but stagnating, and decaying nations. He begins by asserting that rising wages and therefore rising standards of living do not depend on 'the actual greatness of national wealth, but [on] its continual increase', so that labourers benefit most in 'thriving' countries that 'are growing rich the fastest'. Consequently, although England 'is certainly, in the present times, a much richer country than any part of North America', wages nonetheless 'are much higher in North America than in any part of England' and the 'price of provisions ... much lower' (1: 87). The demand for labour and the self-sufficiency of colonial workers, in turn, helps to fuel its rapidly growing population, and, as Smith reminds his readers, the 'most decisive mark of the prosperity of any country is the increase of the number of its inhabitants' (1: 87). In explaining the difference between North

---

12 Pomeranz, *Great Divergence*, 107.
13 See Porter, *Ideographia: The Chinese Cipher in Early Modern Europe*; David E. Mungello, *The Great Encounter of China and the West, 1500–1800*, second ed. (Lanham, MD: Rowman and Littlefield, 2005); Jonathan D. Spence, *The Cham's Great Continent: China in Western Minds* (New York: Norton, 1998); and Rachel Ramsey, 'China and the Ideal of Order in John Webb's *An Historical Essay*', *Journal of the History of Ideas* 62 (2001), 483–503.

America and England, Smith discloses some of the assumptions and values that he has inherited – from the French physiocrats, among others – and that he promotes.[14] Rapid economic growth and population increases go hand in hand, and the availability of agricultural land that fuels economic expansion means that the inhabitants of North America and other 'thriving' nations do not need to rely on the practices of intensification that lead to environmental stress and declining standards of living.[15] Smith's argument about standards and costs of living in England and North America is cast in the relational calculus of demographic expansion, agricultural production, and trade: rapidly accumulating national wealth, as in the American colonies, can produce enough food, goods, and surplus for trade to forestall the economic and environmental dead end that Thomas Malthus envisioned a generation later.

Smith's comparison between England and North America allows him then to turn to the Qing empire in order to explain the paradox of a wealthy nation that restricts international trade and (from an eighteenth-century free trader's perspective) economic freedom. Smith begins by echoing the kind of assertions that Navarette and other writers make about China: it 'has been long one of the richest, that

---

14 See Christian Marouby, 'Looking for (Economic) Growth in the Eighteenth Century', in Richard Barney and Warren Montag, eds., *Systems of Life: Biopolitics, Economics, and Literature on the Cusp of Modernity* (New York: Fordham University Press, 2019), 36–55. See also Robert L. Heilbroner, 'The Paradox of Progress: Decline and Decay in *The Wealth of Nations*', in *Essays on Adam Smith*, ed. Andrew S. Skinner and Thomas Wilson (Oxford: Clarendon Press, 1975), 524–39; Joseph J. Spengler, 'Adam Smith on Population Growth and Economic Development', *Population and Development Review* 2, 2 (1976), 167–80; Vivienne Brown, *Adam Smith's Discourse: Canonicity, Commerce and Conscience* (London: Routledge, 1994); Christian Marouby, 'Adam Smith and the Anthropology of the Enlightenment: The "Ethnographic" Sources of Economic Progress', in *The Anthropology of the Enlightenment*, ed. Larry Wolff and Marco Cipolloni (Stanford, CA: Stanford University Press, 2007), 85–102; and Ted Benton, 'Adam Smith and the Limits to Growth', in *Adam Smith's Wealth of Nations: New Interdisciplinary Essays*, ed. Stephen Copley and Kathryn Sutherland (Manchester: Manchester University Press, 1995), 144–70.
15 On intensification, see Marvin Harris, *Cannibals and Kings: The Origins of Cultures* (New York: Random House, 1977).

is, one of the most fertile, best cultivated, most industrious, and most populous countries in the world' (1: 88). Its natural fertility apparently is matched by the industriousness of its people. His next sentence, however, suggests that China marks both the logical culmination and ultimate limits of the 'thriving' that has enriched Britain and is enriching North America: the empire, Smith writes, 'seems, however, to have been long stationary. Marco Polo, who visited it more than five hundred years ago, describes its cultivation, industry, and populousness, almost in the same terms in which they are described by travellers in the present times' (1: 88). As evidence for the 'stationary' nature of the Chinese economy, Smith relies on what he sees as a static descriptive vocabulary: 'the same terms' that have persisted in travellers' accounts for 500 years indicate that conditions in the country have not changed. This transhistorical consensus about China's long-lived prosperity allows him to cast it as a nation that seemingly has 'acquired that full complement of riches which the nature of its laws and institutions permits it to acquire' (1: 88). As Christian Marouby observes, the phrase 'full complement of riches' marks the limits of a nation's agricultural productivity; yet Smith's subsequent qualification – economic growth depends on individual nations' 'laws and institutions' – gestures towards the possibility that free trade and benign governments might extend this prosperity indefinitely by forestalling the problems of diminishing returns on overexploited resources.[16] China's prosperity, in brief, is constrained by the limits of the natural world, its reproductive success, and the nature of its supposedly restrictive 'laws and institutions'.

In one respect, Smith's China exists in a paradoxical space that has its spectral origins in a long tradition of writers grappling with contradictory images of the natural world. For many writers in the sixteenth and seventeenth centuries, nature is, on the one hand, the fallen, postlapsarian realm of scarcity and labour; yet, on the other, it remains the creation of a beneficent God that, with knowledge, skill and labour, can yield the unending profits and national prosperity.[17] This paradox finds its way into the complex role that the individual's needs

---

16 Marouby, 'Looking for (Economic) Growth in the Eighteenth Century', 48–49.

and desires play in *The Wealth of Nations*. In calling attention to the ironies that underlie Smith's treatment of the relationship between the subject and the economic system in which he (or she) exists, Catharine Packham suggests that 'nature in [his] political economy is at once expressed and corrupted, ideal and fallen' and consequently 'plural and variable rather than monolithic and determining'.[18] In Packham's astute analysis, the 'vital principle' animating human bodies becomes for Smith and other late eighteenth-century thinkers a way to imagine the self-coherent operations of an economic system. In writing about China, Smith assumes that the nation but not its labourers and farmers operate according to this vitalist logic. He denaturalises Chinese farmers and workers, cordoning them off from the very success that characterises one of the 'best cultivated, most industrious, and most populous countries in the world'. But to do this he has to recast what he finds in his sources, like Navarette's praise of the Chinese, by treating China as a 'singular case' – the exception that remains outside of his economic theorising and yet paradoxically that serves as the 'other' against which the 'thriving' subjects of North America and Britain are defined.

Smith's treatment of the Chinese peasants, workers and merchants praised by Navarette removes them from what Jan de Vries has called 'the industrious revolution', the development of craft skills, attitudes towards work, innovation across a wide range of fields, and economic values systems that prepared the ground for the Industrial Revolution.[19] Smith turns Navarette's hard-working and enterprising peasants into passive cogs in a system, held down by low wages and seemingly unmotivated by what he describes as the ostensibly universal desire for self-betterment: 'The accounts of all travellers', he observes,

---

17 I discuss this paradoxical view of the natural world in '"Land enough in the World": Locke's Golden Age and the Infinite Extensions of "Use"', *South Atlantic Quarterly* 98 (1999), 817–37.

18 Catherine Packham, 'System and Subject in Adam Smith's Political Economy: Nature, Vitalism, and Bioeconomic Life', in Barney and Montage, eds, *Systems of Life*, 93–112; quotation on 108. See also Packham, 'The Physiology of Political Economy: Vitalism in Adam Smith's *Wealth of Nations*', *Journal of the History of Ideas* 63 (2002), 465–81.

19 Jan de Vries, 'The Industrial Revolution and the Industrious Revolution', *Journal of Economic History* 54 (1994), 249–70.

1 China and the Problems of Political Economy in *The Wealth of Nations*

'inconsistent in many other respects, agree in the low wages of labour, and in the difficulty which a labourer finds in bringing up a family in China. If by digging the ground a whole day he can get what will purchase a small quantity of rice in the evening, he is contented' (1: 88). There is an inferential logic at work in Smith's comments: the low prices that delight Navarette must mean that the peasant – removed as an exemplar from the social contexts of village life and extended family – labours without any hope or intention of improving his lot. He and his family merely subsist rather than strive for self-betterment. In this respect, he lacks the interior life, the drives, the motivation that animates farmers in North America or Britain. The Chinese peasant's hard work does not lead either to prosperity or, as significantly, the *desire* for prosperity: he lives, in Packham's terms, a 'fallen' existence in an ideally fertile and populous nation.

Chinese 'artificers', in Smith's view, fare even worse, and again the striking contrast with Navarette's account is illuminating. According to Smith, 'the condition of artificers is, if possible, still worse' than the subsistence existence of peasants. 'Instead of waiting indolently in their workhouses, for the calls of their customers, as in Europe, they are continually running about the streets with the tools of their respective trades, offering their service, and as it were begging employment' (1: 89). What Navarette praises as, in effect, the virtues of a free market – the artisans' initiative, self-promotion, mobility, and their concern for customer satisfaction – Smith takes as evidence that 'the poverty of the lower ranks of people in China far surpasses that of the most beggarly nations of Europe' (1: 89). His underlying logic (successful artisans become indolent) calls attention to the problems inherent in a wealthy nation like England: a consumer culture, based on customers' desires to go from shop to shop in search of what they want (or what happens to strike their fancy), threatens to erode the entrepreneurial virtues that underlie a market economy predicated on self-betterment. Yet Chinese workers running after business in the streets, seeking to underbid each other, embody the worst tendencies of an ideology of self-betterment; they do not violate Smith's view of economic principles but mark their limits by embodying an *excess* of the enterprising spirit that makes the market function. In contrast to Navarette's characterisation of artisans as 'obliging' and 'civil', Smith's workers 'begging employment' are so insistent that they violate the protocols of polite, class-appropriate behaviour that characterise their Western counterparts. Their example threatens to demystify the ideology that ensures the functioning of the economic system: the delusions and hollow promises that personal striving is the equivalent of happiness.

In this respect, Smith's Chinese peasants and artisans become lightning rods to redirect, in opposite directions, the worst excesses of political economy: unmotivated peasants, whose lack of interest in self-betterment threatens the functioning of the system as a whole, and aggressive artisans who threaten to strip the marketplace of its character as a 'natural system' and expose it instead as an inherently unstable and chaotic wilderness of desire and self-aggrandisement. Smith's Chinese peasants and workers, then, are neither truly economic subjects in their own right nor the types or classes of individuals that Navarette describes, but instead function as systemic abstractions that paradoxically exemplify and exist outside of the logic operating elsewhere in *The Wealth of Nations*. National prosperity – Smith's 'wealth' – is a by-product, Packham argues, of the 'easily deluded imagination of the worker' that Smith describes in *Theory of Moral Sentiments*. The vital principle of compulsive self-betterment serves as the engine of a depersonalising economic system that ironically sacrifices the individual to the overall benefit of national wealth. In his example of the poor man's son who strives his entire life to become rich, Smith concludes that the end is not worth the effort: he will find his life 'in no respect preferable to that humble security and contentment which he had abandoned'.[20] Having become rich after a lifetime of work, he realises only 'in the last dregs of life, his body wasted with toil and diseases, his mind galled and ruffed by the memory of a thousand injuries and disappointments' that 'wealth and greatness are mere trinkets of frivolous utility, no more adapted for procuring ease of body or tranquility of mind than the tweezer-cases of the lover of toys'.[21] The seeming contentment of Chinese peasants and the 'begging' of Chinese artisans deny them the delusive imagination that underlies

---

20 Adam Smith, *The Theory of Moral Sentiments*, ed. D. D. Raphael and A. L. MacFie (Oxford: Oxford University Press, 1976), 181.
21 Smith, *Theory of Moral Sentiments*, 181.

1 China and the Problems of Political Economy in *The Wealth of Nations*

self-betterment: because they desire so little, they escape the psychological torment of being 'galled and ruffed by the memory of a thousand injuries and disappointments'. They are neither individuals experiencing the frustrations of labouring for little gain nor parts of collectives developing a consciousness of their own situations, but rhetorical buoys that bob with the tides of market forces.[22] Their passivity implies that they tolerate, with comparative equanimity, the inequalities of wealth and grandeur that characterise Smith's vision of China and India.

Despite this assessment of Chinese farmers and workers, Smith is well aware that the prosperity of China needs to be explained because 'though [the nation] may perhaps stand still, [it] does not seem to go backwards'. Unlike the horrific conditions in West Bengal, China remains a non-Western nation that continues to thrive, even though Smith's descriptive rhetoric seems, at best, grudging:

> [China's] towns are nowhere deserted by their inhabitants. The lands which had once been cultivated are nowhere neglected. The same or very nearly the same annual labour must therefore continue to be performed, and the funds destined for maintaining it must not, consequently, be sensibly diminished. The lowest class of labourers, therefore, notwithstanding their scanty subsistence, must some way or another make shift to continue their race so far as to keep up their usual numbers. (1: 90)

This passage is constructed rhetorically around a series of implied double negatives: 'nowhere deserted', 'nowhere neglected', 'not ... sensibly diminished', 'notwithstanding their scanty subsistence'. Smith's language de-idealises the kind of rhetoric that Navarette employs but, at a crucial juncture, defers any attempt to explain the paradox of China's prosperity: peasants and workers survive 'some way or another' to keep the nation in its 'stationary' state of agricultural prosperity to support a population that pays the taxes to support its own existence and the opulence of the upper classes. In a later passage,

---

22 See Mike Hill, 'The Crowded Text: E. P. Thompson, Adam Smith, and the Object of Eighteenth-Century Writing', *ELH* 69 (2002), 749–73.

Smith offers a quasi-ecological explanation for both China's wealth and its social stratification:

> In rice countries, which generally yield two, sometimes three crops in the year each of them more plentiful than any crop of corn, the abundance of food must be much greater than in any corn country of equal extent. Such countries are accordingly much more populous. In them, too, the rich, having a greater superabundance of food to dispose of beyond what they themselves can consume, have the means of purchasing a much greater quantity of the labour of other people. The retinue of a grandee in China or Indostan accordingly is, by all accounts, much more numerous and splendid than that of the richest subjects in Europe. (I: xx)

Two growing seasons and monsoon rains produce the conditions under which a nation or region can thrive, at least until it has tilled all its arable land and reaches the condition of China: sufficient population to keep wages low and permit the wealth of the nation to be accumulated by a handful of 'grandees'. Social stratification and restricted class mobility become both cause and effect of the nation's prosperity.

Smith's discussion of China is followed immediately by his description of the conditions in the agriculturally depressed regions of West Bengal under the administrative control of the East India Company (EIC). In triangulating his accounts of North America, China and India, Smith relies implicitly on the criteria Dunbar invokes to judge the progress of civilisation: increasing population, wealth, antiquity and stability. For Smith, India's depopulation marks it as an inverted image of North American prosperity, 'a country where the funds destined for the maintenance of labour [are] sensibly decaying'. Whatever Orientalist biases one might find in Smith's description of Canton, his comments on South Asia have the effect of throwing into relief the wealth and stability of Qing China. Caught in a deflationary spiral where demands for labour decrease and wages drop below subsistence level, 'servants and labourers' in 'Indostan' 'either starve, or [are] driven to seek a subsistence either by begging, or by the perpetration perhaps of the greatest enormities'. India, not China, has

1 China and the Problems of Political Economy in *The Wealth of Nations*

fallen victim to 'want, famine, mortality', and despite its fertility, its population declines because 'the funds destined for the maintenance of the labouring poor are fast decaying'. Although Smith's description of 'Indostan' begins with an implicit contrast to China, by the conclusion of his discussion West Bengal serves as the grounds for a different comparison to explain why 'three or four hundred thousand people die of hunger in one year': 'The difference between the genius of the British constitution which protects and governs North America, and that of the mercantile company which oppresses and domineers in the East Indies, cannot perhaps be better illustrated than by the different state of those countries' (1: 92–93). In contrasting two forms of colonial control, Smith returns to the question of 'laws and institution' by condemning the monopolistic practices of the EIC, even as he fails to explain why analogous restrictions on 'free trade' in China (at least in his eyes) produce prosperity rather than decay.

Smith's critique of the Company's catastrophic policies serves as a general analysis of ecological, social, economic and demographic decline. The EIC discouraged traditional – and highly effective – irrigation techniques in Bengal in favour of cash cropping; they accumulated vast grain reserves in the form of crushing taxes on farmers; and they closed communal storehouses in the villages and provinces they controlled in the interests of furthering the EIC's monopolistic price-gouging during bad harvests. For Smith, these policies become indications of both the evils of the Company's monopoly and of the downswings implicit in his cyclical model of socioeconomic growth, national wealth, and decline: India is the opposite of North America: too many unemployed or underemployed people, too few financial resources, too few opportunities to earn a living wage. Significantly, however, China has dropped out of the comparison. Whatever the excesses of its 'grandees' and its restraints on trade, China paradoxically seems a quintessential modern economy because it is confronting, on a daily basis, the logical end of national prosperity: a society poised on the knife-edge of wealth and the social and environmental decline exemplified by West Bengal. If North America exists in a state of seemingly limitless expansion, China exemplifies the complexities of political economy: a balancing act between maintaining living standards and dealing with the spectre of diminishing returns, slower growth, and stagnation. Smith's response is to displace onto Chinese peasants and workers the inexorable consequences that, in theory, should be overtaking the nation as a whole.

Anson in Canton, Smith Imagines Canton

Smith's most devastating and, in some ways, revealing passage on life in China occurs immediately after his discussions of 'artificers' running through the streets 'begging employment'. His description of Canton, the only Chinese port to which foreigners had access, conjures up a nightmare image of subsistence living and eating:

> In the neighbourhood of Canton many hundred, it is commonly said, many thousand families have no habitation on the land, but live constantly in little fishing boats upon the rivers and canals. The subsistence which they find there is so scanty that they are eager to fish up the nastiest garbage thrown overboard from any European ship. Any carrion, the carcase of a dead dog or cat, for example, though half putrid and stinking, is as welcome to them as the most wholesome food to the people of other countries. (1: 90)

For a Scots gentleman, the lack of a freehold, tenancy, cottage or workshop dooms these 'many thousand families' to an abject existence because they neither own nor work the land. The populousness that elsewhere Smith, like Dunbar, considers an indicator of prosperity in this passage is recast as endemic overcrowding that has forced 'many thousand families' onto waterways and struggling for 'subsistence'. Although Canton, like the rest of China, is exempt from the fate of Bengal, it suffers its own affective horrors: 'half putrid and stinking' carcasses become a 'wholesome' dietary staple. As Lucinda Cole argues, carrion-eating marks the limits or breakdown of food systems and more generally civilised order in depictions of Asia; Smith casts the Cantonese beyond the pale of socioeconomic progress and wealth.[23] Yet his

---

23 Lucinda Cole, 'Gut Ecology: Meat Science, Modernity, and Carrion Aversion in Gandhi's India', *Configurations* 25 (2017), 215–35.

rhetorical construction, 'it is commonly said', unmoors Smith's comments from specific sources or eyewitness accounts.[24] It elevates anecdotes to the level of evidence and qualifies affectively as much as intellectually his earlier acknowledgement that China maintains its ability to feed its massive population and maintain social and economic order.

In this respect, it is worth considering Smith's characterisation of Canton in light of descriptions in two of the works in his library: Jean-Baptiste du Halde's *General History of China*, a compilation in four volumes of dozens of Jesuit accounts, and Walter and Robins' *Voyage Round the World*. Both texts were extremely influential in the later eighteenth century. Both the tone and subsistence of du Halde's account of Canton differ markedly from Smith's. According to du Halde:

> The River [the narrow strait leading to the port] is cover'd with a Multitude of small Barks, which contain an infinite Number of Persons, and appear like a floating Town: These Barks are placed in Ranks, and form Streets; each Bark contains a Family, and is divided into different Apartments like Houses; the common People, who inhabit them, go a Fishing early in the Morning, or to the Rice Harvest, of which they have two Crops a Year.[25]

The social arrangements that govern the 'infinite Number of Persons' living on the water mimic the ordered society of the Chinese mainland. Boats are formed into orderly 'Ranks' that are organised into the 'Streets' of a 'floating Town'; families are intact as social and presumably affective units and have 'Apartments' on the 'Barks' that are 'like Houses'. As significantly, the 'common People' who live on the water participate in both riverine and agricultural economies: they are fishing for food and profit in the morning and then earning some form of income by working in rice paddies, presumably both to supplement their diet and enter into a complex marketplace where barter and

---

24 See Mike Hill and Warren Montag, *The Other Adam Smith* (Stanford, CA: Stanford University Press, 2015), 292–96.
25 Jean-Baptiste du Halde, *The General History of China*, 4 vols (London: 1736), 1: 241.

exchange coexist. No one, at least according to du Halde, is fishing for the 'nastiest garbage' thrown from European ships or eating carrion.

Walter and Robins' *Voyage Round the World*, in contrast, offers potentially greater insight into the ways that Smith characterises Canton. In promoting a vision of British economic, political and techno-military superiority, *Voyage* becomes a foundational text for Orientalist appropriations by later writers who insist, particularly in the wake of the failed Macartney and Amherst embassies, that China is a decaying, 'beggarly' empire.[26] I have analysed elsewhere Anson's stand-off with Chinese officials in 1743 and the ways that his and his collaborators' (or ghostwriters') account rides roughshod over the complexities of the diplomatic, social, ethnic and economic tensions that marked his stay in Canton.[27] In the rest of this essay, though, I want to concentrate on a particular set of accusations in Anson's *Voyage* that, I suggest, inform Smith's insistence – 'it is commonly said' – that the Chinese routinely eat carrion.

Walter and Robins justify Anson's attacks on the Chinese by invoking the ultimate success of his voyage in dealing a telling blow to Spanish shipping in the Pacific – a success salvaged only by the capture of the treasure ship, the Manila Galleon, in 1743.[28] *A Voyage*'s characterisation

---

26 See James Hevia, *Cherishing Men from Afar: Qing Guest Ritual and the Macartney Embassy of 1793* (Durham, NC: Duke University Press, 1995). On the Amherst embassy, see Gao Hao, 'The Amherst Embassy and British Discoveries in China', *History* 99 (2014), 568–87; Eun Kyung Min, 'Narrating the Far East: Commerce, Civility, and Ceremony in the Amherst Embassy to China (1816–1817)', *Studies in Voltaire and the Eighteenth Century* (2004), 160–80; Peter J. Kitson, *Forging Romantic China: Sino-British Cultural Encounters, 1760–1840* (Cambridge: Cambridge University Press, 2013); and the essays in Peter Kitson and Robert Markley, eds., *Writing China: Essays on the Amherst Embassy (1816) and Sino-British Cultural Relations* (London: Boydell & Brewer, 2016).

27 Markley, 'Anson at Canton, 1743: Obligation, Exchange, and Ritual in Edward Page's "Secret History"', in *The Culture of the Gift in Eighteenth-Century England*, eds. Linda Ziokowski and Cynthia Klekar (New York: Palgrave, 2009), 215–33.

28 The publishing history of *A Voyage Round the World* is complicated. The *Eighteenth-Century Catalogue Online* lists twenty-two separate editions by 1796, although title pages are inaccurate: there were, for example, two 'ninth' editions published in Dublin in 1773 and 1790.

1 China and the Problems of Political Economy in *The Wealth of Nations*

of the Chinese – a people ostensibly given to 'artifice, falshood, and an attachment to all kinds of lucre' (517) – displace onto them a range of negative behaviours that resonate with Smith's understanding in *A Theory of Moral Sentiments* of the consequences of the unending drive for wealth. The narrative details various kinds of mercantile 'double dealing': ducks and chickens force-fed gravel before being sold to the English in order to increase their weight, and hog carcasses injected with water to inflate their price. These actions are offered as evidence of the inherent corruption of the Chinese in order to refute, once and for all, the praise of the Chinese 'in the legendary accounts of the *Roman* Missionaries' (519). In particular, one passage illuminates in striking fashion Smith's description of carrion-eating in Canton:

> When the Commodore first put to sea from *Macao* [in 1742 in pursuit of the Manila Galleon], they practised an artifice ... for as the *Chinese* never object to the eating of any food that dies of itself, they took care, by some secret practices, that great part of his live sea-store should die in a short time after it was put on board, hoping to make a second profit of the dead carcasses which they expected would be thrown overboard; and two thirds of the hogs dying before the *Centurion* was out of sight of the land, many of the *Chinese* boats followed her, only to pick up the carrion. These instances may serve as a specimen of the manners of this celebrated Nation, which is often recommended to the rest of the world as a pattern of all kinds of laudable qualities. (525)

The sarcasm of the final sentence papers over the sleight of hand that inflates a 'specimen' of mercantile 'double dealing' – or, from the merchants' perspective, ingenuity – into a wholesale condemnation of the 'manners' of the nation. The corrupt business practices of the Chinese exploit the readers' disgust with the prospect of eating carrion, and this affective reaction marks an extreme of what Catherine Gallagher terms 'somaeconomics' – a desire for gain and self-betterment internalised as a vital force within the human subject.[29]

---

29 See Catherine Gallagher, *The Body Economic: Life, Death and Sensation in Political Economy and the Victorian Novel* (Princeton: Princeton University

43

If reselling dead hogs indicates a market for carrion because the 'Chinese never object to the eating of any food that dies of itself', Smith's version of indiscriminate carcass-eating in Canton harbour removes the Chinese from the crass economic system that Walter and Robins describe. A *Voyage*'s condemnation of mercantile corruption becomes, in *The Wealth of Nations*, a marker of Chinese abjection.

Significantly, neither Walter and Robins nor Smith have anything to say about the well-known, highly regulated trading system in Canton on which all foreign commerce, including the EIC's, depended.[30] *A Voyage* sneeringly dismisses the efforts of Chinese officials to assess duties on the *Centurion*'s cargo as examples of the 'indefensible absurdities' (512) of the trading system in the port. The text is equally harsh in condemning Page, the EIC supercargo, as a dupe of '*Chinese* Merchants' who 'had so far prepossessed the supercargoes of our ships with chimerical fears, that they (the supercargoes) were extremely apprehensive of being embroiled with the Government, and of suffering in their interest' (530). As these passages suggest, Anson's refusal to pay customs becomes, in Walter and Robins' text, a form of heroic resistance to an intransigent regime; and Anson's example is cited repeatedly in later eighteenth-century attacks on the Qing Dynasty's refusal to open other ports to international trade.[31] Given the tendency among later writers to credit more generally aspects of Anson's description of Canton, Page's unpublished manuscript, 'A Little Secret

---

Press, 2006), 3–8. Packham argues that, for Smith, 'the human is defined in terms of the desire for self-betterment: One's very constitution as a subject therefore leads inexorably to work. The economy's vital force then is not simply an analogy but a literal force located by somaeconomics within the human subject' ('System and Subject in Adam Smith's Political Economy', 105).

30 The standard account of European trade in Canton during the period is Paul A. Van Dyke, *The Canton Trade: Life and Enterprise on the China Coast, 1700–1845* (Hong Kong: Hong Kong University Press, 2005). See also Weng Eang Cheong, *The Hong Merchants of Canton* (Copenhagen: NIAS-Curzon Press, 1997); and Hosea B. Morse, *The Chronicles of the East India Company Trading to China 1635–1834*, 5 vols (Oxford: Clarendon, 1926–1929).

31 In addition to Zuroski Jenkins, *A Taste for China*, and Millar, *A Singular Case*, see Markley, 'China and the English Enlightenment: Literature, Aesthetics, and Commerce', *Literature Compass* 11 (2014), 517–27. doi: 10.1111/lic3.12164.

1 China and the Problems of Political Economy in *The Wealth of Nations*

History', becomes vitally important in understanding how Anson, and Smith after him, recast Chinese attitudes towards international commerce in Eurocentric terms.

As supercargo for the two EIC ships then in the harbour, Page was the closest thing to an official British representative in Canton; since no permanent foreign trading factories were allowed in China (with the exception of the Portuguese tributary port of Macao), the supercargo, as lead negotiator for that year's trade, was treated as a guest of the emperor. Page's account describes the pressures under which he laboured in striving to negotiate among competing interests: orders from the EIC to maximise profits; concerns voiced by other English merchants; demands from the impolitic commodore, insisting on the privileges he believes are his due as a representative of the English nation; and responses from his Chinese hosts, who are portrayed as both trading partners and embodiments of the transcultural values of civility. His account provides an economic analysis of both the ways in which the Canton System works and the values of transcultural understanding that he takes as integral to successful commerce. He repeatedly contrasts Anson's boorish and ignorant behaviour to the civility and acumen of the Chinese whose concern with the smooth operations of business mirrors his own.

In 1743 when Anson returned to Canton, with the captured Spanish galleon, its vast treasure, and 500 prisoners, he refused to pay the customs duties on the rich cargo that his ship carried, claiming that because the *Centurion* was a man of war, 'he was prohibited from trading, and had nothing to do with customs or duties of any kind' (511).[32] To Page, Anson's intransigence was both wrong-headed and potentially dangerous to the carefully maintained trading relations maintained by the English in Canton. No provisions existed for foreign ships in Canton that were not there to trade, and in Page's view, the assessments, fees and percentages paid to local and imperial officials were simply the cost of doing business. The protracted negotiations

---

32   Williams, *Prize of all the Oceans*, 167. Loaded with silver and gold from Spanish colonies in the Americas, the Manila Galleon was one of the richest prizes taken by the English during the eighteenth century: 1,313,843 pieces of eight and 35,682 pieces of silver and plate.

about resupplying the *Centurion* dragged on for months. Anson had no way to transport or feed his prisoners on the voyage to Europe but wanted to turn them over to the Chinese on his terms, vindicating the honour of his naval victory, rather than surrender them as a symbolic pledge of fealty to the Qing emperor. Page quickly recognised that surrendering the prisoners as tribute could finesse the problem of Anson's refusal to pay customs and contain the threat that Anson's intransigence (represented in both *A Voyage* and Page's history) posed to the EIC's substantial investment in that year's trade.

Page's history contests this interpretation of events at almost every turn. He begins his history by describing the tense stand-off between the commodore and Qing officials. Anson's refusal 'to pay [customs], as all other Ships did, of every European Nation', according to the supercargo, 'was a Case Extraordinary, and could not but Create some Disgust & aversion in the Chinese Government, who fancy themselves Superior to every Nation' (1–2). Significantly, Page describes himself siding implicitly or explicitly with the Chinese against Anson's actions. Anson had no authority to be in Canton, and Page more than once describes him as 'a private man, in his apartment in our Factory and at [the] Mercy' (16) of the Chinese while he is ashore, pressuring Page and low-level officials to secure him a formal audience with the viceroy. The Cantonese officials and Hong merchants are granted a civilised interiority that *A Voyage* denies them: their motives, business acumen, cross-cultural understanding, and enlightened self-interest are a mature alternative to the demands, insults and imagined sleights that characterise the commodore's behaviour. In trying to mediate between Anson and the 'Chinese Government', Page turned to Suqua (spelled Seuqua in his history), the oldest and most experienced of the Hong merchants who traded with the EIC.[33]

Page's introduction of Anson to Suqua invokes transcultural standards of upper-class civility by investing the commodore, the son of a minor country gentleman, with a social status that he did not possess.[34] The supercargo appeals to Chinese self-perceptions of their superiority, asking that they uphold the ideals of 'Politeness' on which

---

33 See Cheong, *The Hong Merchants of Canton*, 200–05; on Suqua's career, see 134–44.

1 China and the Problems of Political Economy in *The Wealth of Nations*

the mutual obligations of economic intercourse and social privilege depend. Page's description of the subsequent conversation between Suqua and Anson makes the Chinese merchant a crucial figure in the 'Secret History' by allowing him to articulate what Page endorses as an accurate assessment of the complex situation that the *Centurion*'s return had created.

Suqua's remarkable response to Anson's hot-headed intransigence is worth quoting at length because it gives voice, within an English merchant's narrative, to Chinese perceptions of commerce:

> When Seuqua had heard all the Com[m]dore had to say (and he understood and spoke English very well) he stroked his Beard & said 'Com[m]dore, If I was to tell the Choncoon (which was then the Vice Roy's Title) all you have been telling me, truly he would look upon you as a little man, and greatly his Inferiour. ... You give Mr. Page a great deal of trouble, who had Business enough upon his hands to dispatch his Ships in time, and He tiezes the merchants upon a foolish Business. That He (Seuqua) had sometimes attended at the Mandareens himself with the merchants upon this affair, But that they found it very difficult to obtain what he so much desired. That the Merchants for This, neglected their *real* Business at their Hongs, when all the European Factorys wanted to pack their Teas and Silks with them. Truly (says he) I think it is a very Foolish Business to set your Heart so much upon. You want to see a little of the China Customs. To You it is all one as to see a play, But to others it gives much Trouble and Vexation, and perhaps after all, when you have your Visit, you will not be pleased ... and Resent it; and then much Trouble will be brought upon the Factory, and the Merchants must have their Share.' (4–5)

In ventriloquising Suqua's response to Anson, Page allows the Hong merchant to emerge as a spokesperson for 'modern' economic values.

---

34 On the significance of notions of transcultural civility in European perceptions of and contacts with Ming and Qing China, see Markley, *Far East and the English Imagination*, 104–42.

He is portrayed as a rational businessman who, in good English, quickly puts the Commodore in his place as a 'little man' trying to bluster his way into an audience with the viceroy. Precisely because the customs charges (roughly seven per cent) are comparatively small, Suqua can tell Anson to his face that the Englishman's assertion of principle is merely 'a very Foolish Business' that threatens to disrupt the EIC's '*real* Business'. Suqua empties this yet-to-be-realised audience of any idealised significance by calling attention to the performative nature of Anson's posturing: 'To You', says the Hong merchant, 'it is all one as to see a play'. In effect, Suqua casts Anson as an outsider in the complex diplomatic and commercial systems of Canton, lecturing the English commodore on the semiotics of the interlocking economies of exchange and deference that govern international trade:

> The Com[m]dore said, Why so, & Why should he not see me, and the same over again, But Seuqua repeated his Sentiments, said he had got his Ship full of Money, He was now supplied with every thing he wanted, and he thought he might be easy without giving himself and others so much trouble about such Trifles. (5)

Suqua's advice proved prophetic because Anson ultimately was not pleased with the treatment he received either from the Chinese or from the English merchants. The commodore's demands strike the Hong merchant as 'Trifles' precisely because there is no possibility that Qing officials will take seriously his self-presentation as a representative of British diplomatic and maritime power. As Page reminds his readers, Anson 'had no Credentials to the Port at all, nor was his name so much as mentioned in [Page's] Instructions' from the EIC. In mediating between Anson and the Chinese, Page 'ran a risqué of [his] Employers displeasure by encreasing the Expences of the Factory, by [Anson's], and his Officers and people, coming up' (6) to Canton from their anchorage. From the supercargo's point of view, Anson is a troublesome guest; from the commodore's perspective, the English merchants are cowards and hirelings of a private company who must defer to his authority as a representative of the crown. When Page reminds Anson that the EIC ships 'were wholly in the power of the Chineese' and that 'the Loss of the China Trade' that year would cost the crown almost 'two

1 China and the Problems of Political Economy in *The Wealth of Nations*

hundred Thousand pounds', the commodore replies 'he did not mind That, the Nation might make that up some other way' (12–13). Anson's blindness to the economic consequences of disrupting the lucrative China trade 'frightened [the English merchants] out of their Wits', who feared that his behaviour 'might be the Loss of all our priviledges, and the cause of much Trouble to [the Hong merchants who] were Security for the Good Behaviour of our Ships' (14). The merchants' fear, derided in *A Voyage*, stems from their recognition that Anson's defiance of Chinese authorities can sever the complex bonds of financial and personal trust that the English maintain with Hong merchants, landing their Chinese counterparts in 'much Trouble', and jeopardising trade for the future.

In a telling rhetorical move, Page pursues the implications of this argument by asking his readers to imagine sympathetically the dilemma that Anson's behaviour presents to the Chinese:

> And I ask, whether the Officers of *Our* Customhouse would not watch the Boats of Foreign Ships (although they might be a Man of War) or, if they would examine their Baggage if they were ordered to do so? And whether our Government would not protect *their* Officers in their Duty, & punish the Foreigners, if their Resistance to our Laws & Regulations should bring on any mischiefs. It would have given the Foreign Factorys great Joy to have seen the English involved in Broils with the Chineese Government &, lose their Trade ... For what was *our* Loss would have been their advantage. (19–20)

Page invites his readers (however secret they may be) to imagine the situation reversed, with a foreign war ship refusing to comply with English laws by rejecting England's authority to assess merchandise and levy customs. By granting the Chinese the same legitimacy and national authority that the English claim, he brings the 'Laws & Regulations' of both nations within a system of reciprocal benefit and obligation that presumably would delight even a free trader like Smith. Rather than the self-interested caricatures depicted in *A Voyage*, the Chinese act consistently, rationally and legally in their own territory. Anson's blustering renders him an external threat to international trade and to England's national interest by endangering the Company's share of the lucrative trade in Chinese silks and tea to European rivals: the French, Danish and Swedish ships that were in the harbour at the time. For Page, the future Lord Admiral of the English navy is not the embodiment of England's national strength but a loutish country cousin who jeopardises the nation's standing as a commercial power.

Economy and Abstraction

Near the conclusion of his 'Secret History', Page overtly satirises the chapters on China in *A Voyage Round the World*, mocking the smug superiority and pretensions to authority that characterise Walter and Robins' heroicising of Anson. Much of the satire is set in quotation marks both to indicate an imagined Chinese text about England and to mark his sardonic ventriloquising of Anson's account:

> Suppose that [a] Chineese that was to come to our countrey, should make Remarks upon the English Nation, at his return, and write a Book complaining 'That he met with Liars, Deceivers, Trickers, & Sharpers of every profession. That we take advantage of every Distress, and the Better sort starve the Poor to fill their own pockets. That either our Laws are defective, our Government weak, our Magistrate corrupt or Negligent, or our people Unruly or Disobedient'. (55)

Throughout this long passage, Page satirically inverts the kinds of judgements that Anson makes and that become prevalent in late eighteenth-century accounts of China, including *The Wealth of Nations*. His judgements, particularly about economics and morality, are pointed, often elevating the Chinese over the British. Anson and other critics 'accuse the Chineese of loving Money, but no people Love it more, or would do Baser things to get it than the English and the man of merit finds little Respect with them but may be buried in obscurity' (58). The conduct of his own employer, the EIC, is singled out for critique. Among these 'Baser things', according to Page, is the behaviour of the British in India where 'the good order & Government

1 China and the Problems of Political Economy in *The Wealth of Nations*

of whole Provinces are disturbed by the avarice, Wantonness, & cruelty of these Christian people, whose desire after wealth is never satisfied' (57). Although the English 'setled at first indeed under the pretence of Trade, ... now they Domineer & are likely to pretend to be Lords & Masters'; therefore, he argues that 'the Regulations in the Chineese Dominions are very wise, to watch [Europeans], and keep them at a distance' (57). For Page, China's 'Regulations' are not, as free traders claim, a hindrance to trade but a rational response to the insistent efforts of Europeans to secure greater and greater trading privilege in Canton and to open other ports in China to international commerce.

Page's satire of *A Voyage* zeroes in on its combination of outrage, indignation and bafflement, Anson's inability to process the consequences of a complex economic and diplomatic situation. In this respect, Anson's repeated questions to Suqua about his delayed audience, 'Why so, & Why should he not see me, and the same over again', points to his limited understanding of the commercial values that Page and the Hong merchant articulate. By refusing to pay customs duties, by dismissing Page's fears, Anson tries to remove himself from the protocols of international trade and, more pointedly, from a sophisticated economic system. In this respect, Walter and Robin's insistence that *A Voyage* demystifies positive views of China rides roughshod over what Page and Navarette, in different ways, offer, a kind of 'reciprocal anthropology'.[35] 'Suppose', asks Page, 'a Chineese sho^d write such an account as this of *Our* Countrey, which he had picked up in generals, by reading Newspapers and Books upon different Subjects, and from something he had seen & observ'd himself? His countreymen might be pleased with the Narration, and Yet all might not be true' (60–61). Anson's account, Page suggests, is a mishmash of 'generals', widely available sources stitched together, and limited first-hand observations that contribute to the ideology that allows Smith to deploy the telling, passive voice construction to describing life in Canton: 'it is commonly said'. Veracity is sacrificed to a pleasing 'Narration' – that is, one that uses received prejudices to shore up, for Anson, British

---

35 Bruno Latour, *We Have Never Been Modern* (Cambridge, MA: Harvard University Press, 1993).

exceptionalism and to promote, for Smith, a contrast between 'thriving' nations and an empire that has reached its 'full complement of riches'.

The problem that envelops Smith's characterisation of China is that he must rely on textual evidence – Navarette's account and du Halde's compilation – that creates problems for his larger theories of national wealth; consequently, he has to be selective in choosing anecdotes from Anson's *Voyage*, common reports, gossip and presuppositions. If China becomes in *The Wealth of Nations* a projection of the negative consequences of a political economy defined by the subjection of individual labourers to national wealth, Page suggests that the Middle Kingdom embodies the ideals of international commerce as a civilising, transcultural system that can be mutually beneficial. If both writers agree on the brutal and lethal consequences of unbridled imperialism in India, Smith's system of international or comparative economy is still tethered by anecdotes to hearsay, ideology, and an emerging Orientalist perspective overdetermined to believe the worst about Chinese peasants, artisans and merchants. The disconnect between the wealth, stability and longevity of China and the condition of its subjects becomes, in one respect, Smith's effort to wrestle with the perplexities of economic theory in general. It abstracts into a systemic analysis of 'thriving', stasis and decay the incompatible evidence of Anson's prejudices and Navarette's idealisations.

2
Cultural Cross-Dressing in the House of Pankeequa

William Christie

> [T]here is much to support the view that it is clothes that wear us and not we them; we may make them take the mould of arm or breast, but they mould our hearts, our brains, our tongues to their liking.
> —Virginia Woolf, *Orlando*[1]

What stand out in the official history of cultural relations between China and the West over the course of the long eighteenth century are the seemingly irreconcilable differences that would eventually see Britain and China at war: misunderstanding and distrust of foreigners on the part of an isolationist Chinese government and a regressive denigration of China and the Chinese people in Western opinion, as 'writings on China', to quote Ros Ballaster, 'became increasingly critical':

> What begins as a search for analogy and correspondence often serves only to generate visions of alterity and difference. Enlightened pursuit of a universal humanity gives way to a sense of relativity in the late eighteenth century. Paradoxically,

---

1   Virginia Woolf, *Orlando: A Biography*, ed. Rachel Bowlby (Oxford: Oxford University Press, 1992), 180.

knowing more about the East only tends to create rather than dispel alterity.[2]

The Western attitude to China shifts from an early idealisation – the Scottish reviewer Francis Jeffrey compared the exalted image of Chinese civilisation disseminated by the seventeenth-century Jesuit missionaries with Swift's Houyhnhnms[3] – to what, in the wake of the Macartney mission of 1792–94, were often extreme forms of demonisation. Indeed, 'Mutual mud-slinging', to quote Qian Zhongshu, 'soon became the order of the day'.[4] The inference from all this has been one of cultural incomprehension and imminent disaster, 'the incommensurability and thus inevitable clash of Sino-Western civilizations, which supposedly then led to the First Opium War and foreign extraterritoriality in China'.[5]

But British attitudes towards China, both before and after the Macartney mission, were a good deal more various, conflicted and uneven than this unitary narrative of 'a staggering reversal of fortune from admiration to degradation' suggests.[6] (At the same time, attitudes in Britain towards the British imperial project generally, as it was fast becoming apparent, betray a similar disagreement and ambivalence.)

---

2   Ros Ballaster, *Fabulous Orients: Fictions of the East in England 1662–1785* (Oxford: Oxford University Press, 2005), 364.
3   Francis Jeffrey, review of *Ta Tsing Leu Lee*, *Edinburgh Review* 16:32 (August 1810), 476–99 (476).
4   Qian Zhongshu, 'China in the English Literature of the Eighteenth Century', in Hsia, Adrian (ed.), *The Vision of China in the English Literature of the Seventeenth and Eighteenth Centuries* (Hong Kong: The Chinese University Press, 1998), 117–213 (198). 'A sublime irony lay at the heart of their long struggle', writes Piers Brendon: 'each empire thought the other utterly barbarous', *The Decline and Fall of the British Empire 1781–1997* (New York: Alfred Knopf, 2008), 102.
5   Li Chen, *Chinese Law in Imperial Eyes: Sovereignty, Justice, and Transcultural Politics* (New York: Columbia University Press, 2016), 26. See, e.g., Arthur Cotterell: 'It was an inevitable collision of two governments whose views were totally different: two diametrically opposed social and economic systems met head-on', in *China: A History* (London: Pimlico, 1988), 230.
6   Peter Kitson, *Forging Romantic China: Sino-British Cultural Exchange 1760–1840* (Cambridge: Cambridge University Press, 2013), 13.

2 Cultural Cross-Dressing in the House of Pankeequa

Just as there was no one China – 'cultural homogeneity', as John Fairbank has remarked, 'was one of China's great social myths'[7] – so there was no single attitude towards China. Critical homogeneity is one of intellectual history's great myths. Throughout the 200-year history of trade relations between China and Britain in the lead-up to the Opium Wars of 1839–42, we can always find voices of openness and sympathy, and these gestures of understanding and friendship do not end with the Macartney era.

What I offer in this essay, then, is a brief chapter in the alternative history of Britain's relations with China, as of Romantic globalisation generally. In *Romantic Globalism*, Evan Gottlieb considers British 'Romanticism's relationship with globalization' in a way that refuses to equate it with imperialism as 'a malevolent, unstoppable force that can only be cravenly justified or vainly resisted'.[8] Instead, Gottlieb finds evidence of what he calls a 'global hospitality', a development of Enlightenment tolerance and cosmopolitanism: 'a formal acceptance of otherness that holds out the possibility of greater accord between individuals as well as nations, without eliding their differences'.[9] It may well have been that, as Wang Gungwu argues, 'on the most serious matters pertaining to their deeply felt values, both the British and the Chinese people remained far apart',[10] but not so far apart that occasional acts of mutual understanding and even friendship, however fleeting, were not possible. With this in mind, I want simply to record a selection of what Leela Gandhi calls 'minor narratives of crosscultural collaboration'.[11] Taking my epigraph on clothes from Virginia Woolf, I want to address the question of how China and the West saw each other

---

7   John K. Fairbank, 'Introduction: the old order', in his edition, *The Cambridge History of China*, vol. 10, part one, Late Ch'ing 1800–1911 (Cambridge: Cambridge University Press, 1978), 1–32 (9).
8   Evan Gottlieb, *Romantic Globalism: British Literature and Modern World Order, 1750–1830* (Columbus: Ohio State University Press, 2014), 7.
9   Gottlieb, *Romantic Globalism*, 14.
10 Wang Gungwu, *Anglo-Chinese Encounters since 1800: War, Trade, Science and Governance* (Cambridge: Cambridge University Press, 2003), 4.
11 Leela Gandhi, *Affective Communities: Anticolonial Thought, Fin-de-Siècle Radicalism, and the Politics of Friendship* (Durham and London: Duke University Press, 2006), 6.

throughout the long eighteenth century, and how they interpreted what they saw, by reflecting on the phenomenon of cultural cross-dressing as a literal and metaphorical act of cultural sympathy.

William Hickey

To do this, let me start with a tale of two dinner entertainments from the journal record of the Englishman William Hickey, just twenty years old when he travelled to Canton in 1769:

> After spending three very merry days at Whampoa, we returned to Canton, where McClintock gave me a card of invitation to two very different entertainments on following days, at the country house of one of the Hong merchants named Pankeequa. These fêtes were given on the 1st and 2nd of October, the first of them being a dinner, dressed and served *à la mode Anglaise*, the Chinamen on that occasion using, and awkwardly enough, knives and forks, and in every respect conforming to the European fashion. The best wines of all sorts were amply supplied. In the evening a play was performed, the subject warlike, where most capital fighting was exhibited, with better dancing and music than I could have expected. In one of the scenes an English naval officer, in full uniform with a fierce cocked hat, was introduced, who strutted across the stage, saying 'Maskee can do! God damn!' whereon a loud and universal laugh ensued, the Chinese quite in an ectacy, crying out 'Truly much havee like Englishman.'

The two things I want to highlight in this entertainment are dress and 'taste' in the most physical sense – what things actually taste like – always bearing in mind the centrality of the more metaphorical Taste (with a capital 'T') to the aesthetic ideology of the eighteenth-century European: good taste or refined taste as a personal and social end in itself. In the Hong merchant Pankeequa's entertainment,[12] dressing up as

---

12 I have used Hickey's transliteration 'Pankeequa' as the merchant's trading or public name, though every Anglophone source has a different transliteration

2 Cultural Cross-Dressing in the House of Pankeequa

an Englishman is an act of impersonation and parody at the same time: in*habit*ing another culture through its clothes and gestures and idiom.

'The second day, on the contrary, every thing was Chinese', when the presentation and consumption of food became central and fireworks were the main source of entertainment:

> all the European guests eating, or endeavouring to eat, with chop sticks, no knives or forks being at table. The entertainment was splendid, the victuals extremely good, the Chinese loving high dishes and keeping the best of cooks. At night brilliant fire works (in which they also excel) were let off in a garden magnificently lighted by coloured lamps, which we viewed from a temporary building erected for the occasion and wherein there was exhibited slight of hand tricks, tight and slack rope dancing, followed by one of the cleverest pantomimes I ever saw. This continued until a late hour, when we returned in company with several of the supercargoes to our factory, much gratified with the liberality and taste displayed by our Chinese host.[13]

Pankeequa's choice of pantomime is telling. Though selected as representatively Chinese, pantomime aspires to a set of shared human grimaces and gestures that transcend or circumvent language – indeed, any entertainment in an unfamiliar language necessarily becomes a form of pantomime in which meaning is reconstructed from facial expression and bodily gesture. Hickey would have been familiar with English pantomime and obviously felt qualified to judge this Chinese instance of an ancient, popular art form. It is no coincidence that the artistic genre in which Britain's understanding of and contact with China was most commonly represented was in popular theatre.

---

and sometimes it is necessary to approach the English name imaginatively in order to identify the referent. In other sources, he appears as Pan-ke-qua, Poankeequa, Poankeyqua, Puankhequa, Pankeiqua, Punhyqua, Pon-qua-qua (*pinyin*: Pan Qiguan).

13   *Memoirs of William Hickey (1749–1775)*, ed. Alfred Spencer (London: Hurst & Blackett, 1913), 223–24.

Only twenty years old when the events described in his *Memoirs* took place, William Hickey was in his sixties and living in the 'very limited society' of a southern English village (in Hickey's own words) when he finally wrote them down in 1808 on his return from Calcutta, where he had settled and built a successful legal practice.[14] Hickey is an endearing character, capable of laughing at himself in ways that relate directly to our theme of mutual cultural understanding and tolerance and the way that understanding and tolerance are often obliged to negotiate ordinary things – like dress and food. Everyday objects and practices can become, disproportionately, part of the problem of cross-cultural relations, but with the right will and insight they can also become part of the solution:

> Mr. Phipps one day at dinner offered to help me from a dish that stood before him, which he described as a delicious fricassee. I accepted and found it as he had said, exquisitely good. The following day I was eating the same dish, when the gentleman next me asked if I knew what it was. I answered 'No,' but thought it chicken. 'Chicken,' replied he, 'not it indeed, it is frogs.' Strange and absurd as it may appear, upon hearing this I instantly turned so dreadfully sick I was obliged to leave the table. Such was the force of prejudice. Upon enquiry I found that frogs had long been one of the dishes at the supercargo's table; it consisted of only the hind quarters of the frog. No person was more ready to admit the absurdity of the prejudice than myself, yet had my life been at stake I do not think I could have swallowed a mouthful of the excellent fricassee after I knew of what it was made.[15]

Just as there is a long, reflective tradition on the management of chopsticks in European travel literature, so there is a long and more variously inflected tradition on the consumption of frogs, one that takes in not just the eating habits of a remote Far East, but also of Britain's immediate neighbour.

---

14   *Memoirs of William Hickey*, ix.
15   *Memoirs of William Hickey*, 224–25.

2 Cultural Cross-Dressing in the House of Pankeequa

The Canton System

However, before we get too carried away with the inspiration behind Pankeequa's theatrical experiments or too sentimental about his Enlightened gesture of holding a mirror up to each of the two cultures, it is perhaps salutary to sketch the context in which these genial entertainments were taking place, reminding ourselves about aspects of what was known as the Canton System, or China trade.[16] Canton (Gangzhou), inland and upriver on the bottom south-east coast of China, was the only Chinese port in 14,500 kilometres of coastline that was open to Europeans. All foreign ships were required to stop first at Macao, a small settlement acquired by the Portuguese in 1557, where they were obliged to hire a pilot licensed by the Chinese government. The ships were examined and, with the guidance of the pilot (who had acquired written permission or a 'chop'), the vessel could proceed up river to Whampoa, an island twenty-one kilometres below Canton, where it would anchor so that the loading and unloading of cargo could take place. Foreign sailors had to stay with their ships at all times, and only the captains and 'supercargoes' – the foreign traders – went up the river to Canton, where they were confined to a row of 'factories' or residential warehouses set up along the Pearl River outside the city gates, from where (strictly speaking) they were forbidden to venture into the city itself. No guns or arms of any kind were permitted and a handful of officially sanctioned Hong merchants were responsible for the behaviour of the foreigners with whom they traded. The

---

16 For my account of the China System and, later, on the merchant Pankeequa, I am indebted to the accounts of a number of scholars, especially Weng Eang Cheong, *The Hong Merchants of Canton: Chinese Merchants in Sino-Western Trade, 1684–1798* (London: Routledge, 1997); Paul Van Dyke's two detailed studies, *The Canton Trade: Life and Enterprise on the China Coast, 1700–1845* (Hong Kong: Hong Kong University Press, 2005) and *Merchants of Canton and Macao: Policies and Strategies in Eighteenth-Century Chinese Trade* (Hong Kong: Hong Kong University Press, 2011); Li Chen, *Chinese Law in Imperial Eyes*; and John L. Cranmer-Byng and John E. Wills, Jr., 'Trade and Diplomacy with Maritime Europe, 1644-c. 1800', in *China and Maritime Europe 1500–1800: Trade, Settlement, Diplomacy, and Missions*, ed. John E. Wills, Jr. (Cambridge: Cambridge University Press, 2011), 183–254.

supercargoes resided at the factories during the trading season (August–March), after which they were obliged to retire to Macao. Foreign women were not allowed in or near Canton, though they could reside on the coast in Macao and await the return of their husbands at the end of the trading season.

There were occasions when all of these proscriptions were honoured in the breach, but compared with trade with other nations the system was a severely restricted one – Westerners, writes Li Chen, 'were far from being considered peaceful and trustworthy in the Chinese official discourse since the early seventeenth century'[17] – bringing tensions and grievances into the community of foreign traders:

> They complained about slow unloading of ships, stealing from boats on the river, and the petty exactions of customs officials, constant themes of European merchants in Chinese harbours from the 1660s to the 1860s. They also complained of 'very unhandsome Chops [= proclamations] which have lately been affixed in public parts of the City and Suburbs accusing us of Crimes, the mention of which, is horrible to us: to them we attribute the frequent insults we meet in the Streets.'[18]

For all these complaints by foreign traders about the various constraints under which they operated, however, the truth is that, as traders, they had a good deal more freedom than the Chinese merchants with whom they dealt. Not only had 'the growing militancy of the British ... already come to influence the mentality of the local Qing officials',[19] but the official policy of the central government of attracting more ships to swell the imperial revenues meant putting in place practices and conditions that favoured foreign traders over Chinese merchants. The foreigners had equal access to a variety of markets, for example, and the assurance of the Chinese government that they would not be cheated. We are accustomed to thinking of the officials – the Hoppos or Customs

---

17 Li Chen, *Chinese Law in Imperial Eyes*, 75.
18 Cranmer-Byng and Wills, 'Trade and Diplomacy with Maritime Europe, 1644-c. 1800', 226–27.
19 Chen, *Chinese Law in Imperial Eyes*, 49.

superintendents, the provincial governors-general – as distrustful and concerned only with limitation and imposition, but they were also charged by the Chinese government with protecting foreign traders, which meant ensuring that the Chinese merchant community bore responsibility for any fraudulent practices that took place in the long supply chain between the growers and producers and foreign traders themselves. The Chinese merchants were obliged to restore goods or money lost in dishonest exchanges, whereas the 'Chinese merchants', to quote Paul Van Dyke, 'had no support from government in recovering losses from foreigners who failed to live up to their agreements'.[20]

Still, there were strict limits imposed on the mental and physical movements of foreigners in eighteenth-century Canton and 'direct contact between the foreign traders and the Chinese government was forbidden'.[21] While we are sketching a context for William Hickey's Canton experience, moreover, we also need to take into account the language barrier. Inter-cultural communication of the kind I am investigating was precisely proscribed under the Canton System. Just as only certain pilots were licensed to ferry foreigners up to Whampoa, and only certain compradors licensed to provide for the foreign traders, only certain 'linguists' were licensed to interpret and translate.[22] As Pankeequa's imitation of an English play makes very clear, the language of the merchant trade was the blunt instrument of Southern China Coast pidgin. 'This factor nonetheless served administrators well', writes Van Dyke, 'because they wanted only as much contact with and understanding of foreigners as was needed to carry on commerce'; 'Social and political interests kept pressure on the Chinese to only learn pidgin English, nothing more'.[23]

It was, in fact, a capital offence for a Chinese to teach a foreigner the Chinese language, and there was no encouragement and no opportunity for the Chinese themselves to learn a foreign language. (As Peter Kitson reminds us, Lord Macartney did at least negotiate

---

20 Van Dyke, *Merchants of Canton and Macao*, 217.
21 D. E. Mungello, *The Great Encounter of China and the West, 1500–1800*, third edition (Lanham: Rowman & Littlefield, 2009), 7.
22 Li Chen, *Chinese Law in Imperial Eyes*, 74–76.
23 Van Dyke, *The Canton Trade*, 92.

permission for the Chinese to teach their language to the East India Company employees in his otherwise unproductive mission.[24]) Only ten years before Hickey's arrival, the Mandarin-speaking James Flint's bold journey up the Chinese coastline in an attempt to petition the Beijing government for a relaxation of the tight trading practices had exposed a depth of paranoia that led to the formalisation of protective laws designed to confine (though not inhibit) foreign trade, and at the same time to prevent spying.[25] Flint was imprisoned for three years and Flint's Chinese collaborator, Liu Yabian – 'a native of Szechuan, who had composed this petition for them' – had been executed.[26]

Pankeequa

If the Chinese merchants were constrained by the conditions of trade, however, they seem to have been adept at managing (and manipulating) the system, and none more so than Pankeequa. The Pankeequa whom Hickey met, for example, appears to have mastered both Spanish and English,[27] at least to some extent, and after years of relative obscurity to have assumed a position of authority and consolidated wealth. As it happens, Pankeequa as a personality and a name is, quite literally, co-extensive with the Canton System itself, as was his firm, Tongwen Hang. Beginning trading in the 1730s and flourishing by the 1750s, the name Pankeequa was still trading affluently when the system was winding down 100 years later,[28] and still holding sumptuous feasts for foreigners, fellow merchants and government officials in the 1830s, even though the original Pankeequa – William Hickey's Pankeequa – had died in 1788. On his death he had been succeeded by one of

---

24 Kitson, *Forging Romantic China*, 81.
25 Van Dyke, *The Canton Trade*, 92.
26 Fu Lo-shu, *A Documentary Chronicle of Sino-Western Relations (1644–1820)*, in 2 vols (Tucson: University of Arizona Press, 1966), 1, 222–23; 2, 546.
27 At the famous *Lady Hughes* trial on 8 January 1785, Pankeequa was the interpreter – see Chen, *Chinese Law in Imperial Eyes*, 34.
28 The firm, Tongwen Hang, traded from 1736 to 1814 or 1815, when the name was changed to Tongfu Hang and it continued trading until 1843, when the Cohong was disestablished.

2 Cultural Cross-Dressing in the House of Pankeequa

his sons, who became Pankeequa II (1755–1820), and then by his grand-nephew, as Pankeequa III (1791–1850).

At the time Hickey was amusing himself at the English factory in 1769, Pankeequa was president of the Cohong of ten houses charged with exclusive control over foreign trading through Canton. Indeed, it was Pankeequa, along with another merchant, Swequa, who had proposed the establishment of the notorious 'Cohong' of Chinese merchants to subsume and weaken a triple alliance formed between three other trading firms in the wake of the death of the merchant Beaukeequa in September 1758.[29] The Cohong decided among themselves 'all particulars of trade' – including prices, the 'dodgins' or weights used when measuring products, exchange rates, the amount of the advances that would be sent to the inland producers, the interest rates on advanced money, and so on. And it was the Cohong against which the foreign East India companies protested so often and so vociferously.

Pankeequa was one of two or three merchants who dominated the China trade from 1760 until his death in 1788, after which the House of Pankeequa (Tongwen Hang, later Tongfu Hang) continued to dominate until well into the nineteenth century. The first Pankeequa became immensely wealthy and immensely influential, a major part of his role as president of the Cohong being to bestow gifts on the Hoppo, the governors-general, and all the government officials who passed through Canton. Pankeequa was master of productive gift-exchange – a tradition that was carried on under the same name by his descendants. 'Ten years after Phuankhequa's death in 1788', writes Weng Eang Cheong, 'the firm was the only one left of all those established before 1790; it was, moreover, the most prosperous house and Phuankhequa II the wealthiest merchant in Canton'.[30]

Pankeequa's entertainments, as recorded in the diary of William Hickey, along with comparably elaborate dinner entertainments, were by no means uncommon in eighteenth-century Canton – we could assemble an anthology of similar anecdotes and recollections by foreign traders and visitors. The invitation to foreigners to dine at a merchant's residence was a sign of the merchant's affluence – of his having made it – the

---

29   Van Dyke, *Merchants of Canton and Macao*, 55.
30   Cheong, *The Hong Merchants of Canton*, 164.

sumptuousness and sensation of the occasion arguably having as much to do with self-advertising and self-aggrandising as with transnational sympathy or hospitality. In spite of this, however, and in spite of all the restrictions and proscriptions imposed by the Qing government and privately and publicly resented by the East India trading companies – and we might want to pause, at this moment, to ask ourselves what businessman has not protested against what he saw as any inhibition on his freedom to make more money? – the impression we receive from reading William Hickey's diary is not one of mutual distrust and exploitation or of xenophobia on the streets of Canton. Far from it. 'Despite all the government restrictions', as Li Chen has written, 'transcultural adaptation and accommodation in southern China' existed at a social level, 'and the contact and collaboration between foreigners and local Chinese ... continued to grow beyond the authorized extent and scope'.[31] Certainly beside the more impatient and often quite savage reflections of eighteenth- and nineteenth-century British writers on Chinese customs and habits, particularly though not exclusively those of what we might provocatively entitle the Macartney era, Hickey's sociable, admittedly masculinist passage through the expatriate culture of the China trade, and through Canton itself, betrays all the endearing traits of the *homme moyen sensual*: Tom Jones in Canton.

Indeed, Hickey has a reputation as 'an English rake', to quote Andrew Coe, 'shipped east in 1769 to find his fortune – and to keep his hell-raising escapades from further blotting the family name. Unfortunately, he was more interested in fast living and sleeping with Chinese prostitutes than knuckling down to work'.[32] Beside the virulent contempt of George Anson, however, the labile ambivalence of Thomas Percy, the arrogant partiality of John Barrow, and the sustained polemic of Francis Jeffrey, with their litany of indictments of Chinese culture – infanticide, cruelty, misogyny (including foot binding), concubinage, homosexuality, cultural arrogance, isolationism – Hickey's generous account of his sojourn in Canton and of his cultural interactions (and escapades) with his hosts comes as a salutary relief.[33] Nothing so

---

31 Li Chen, *Chinese Law in Imperial Eyes*, 76.
32 Andrew Coe, *Chop Suey: A Cultural History of Chinese Food in the United States* (Oxford: Oxford University Press, 2009), 14.

ambitious or altruistic in Hickey's case as the 'Enlightenment comparativist ideology' of a Joseph Banks (Kitson),[34] just an openness and receptivity, an ideological (even interpretative) innocence, which is alien to the suspicious, often demonising cultural comparisons that so quickly modulate into the form of cultural one-upmanship that had come to mark comparative reflections on different cultures. 'The chief aim will be to shew this extraordinary people in their proper colours', writes John Barrow in his *Travels in China*, for example, 'not as their own moral maxims would represent them, but as they really are':

> to endeavour to draw such a sketch of the manners, the state of society, the language, literature and fine arts, the sciences and civil institutions, the religious worship and opinions, the population and progress of agriculture, the civil and moral character of the people, as may enable the reader to settle, in his own mind, *the point of rank which China may be considered to hold in the scale of civilized nations.*[35]

The full title of Barrow's account of China and the Chinese serves to underline his intentions and might function as symbolic of the obsessive ranking of civilisations being carried on as the European world was exposed to more, and more alien, global cultures: *Travels in China, Containing Descriptions, Observations, and Comparisons, made and collected in the course of a Short Residence at the Imperial Palace of Yuen-Min-Yuen, and on a subsequent Journey through the Country from Pekin to Canton, in which it is attempted to appreciate the Rank that this extraordinary Empire may be considered to hold in the Scale of Civilized Nations.* For Barrow, China, as it turned out, was 'worn out with age and disease'.[36]

---

33 See William Christie, '"Prejudice against prejudices": China and the Limits of Whig Liberalism', *European Romantic Review*, 24:5 (2013), 509–29.
34 Kitson, *Forging Romantic China*, 136.
35 John Barrow, *Travels in China* (London: T. Cadell and W. Davies, 1804), 3–4 (emphasis in the original).
36 Barrow, *Travels in China*, 222.

Saree Makdisi offers the standard account of Romantic Orientalism in his *Making England Western*:

> the Orient had become essential to virtually every attempt to articulate a sense of selfhood or subjectivity. For the sense of self that was articulated in the 1790s and on into the nineteenth century was increasingly predicated on a sense of Occidental identity, a feeling of superiority over a supine and unmanly Eastern other. Hence an ongoing series of contrasts between the manly, honest, sober, virtuous Occidental self and the effeminate, luxurious, lazy, indulgent Eastern other permeates all forms of discourse in the Romantic period.[37]

Makdisi cites Byron and Blake as the exceptions that prove the rule, though with regard specifically to China, opinion was a good deal more divided than Makdisi suggests. Popular reviews argued along ideological (and other) lines, offering sometimes starkly contrasting opinions of Chinese civilisation, some of them harking back to the peak of China's reputation in the West in the seventeenth century.[38] There can be no doubt that, if we trace commentary over the closing years of the long eighteenth century, it certainly does seem that the collision so often cited by scholars as 'inevitable' was shaping up. 'Although we must avoid looking at these years in the light of the great crisis in the next century', argue John Cranmer-Byng and John Wills, 'it seems clear that after 1780 the Qing empire and maritime Europeans, including some new types fresh from the plunder of Bengal, were increasingly on a collision course'.[39]

But the ideological (and racist) unanimity often presumed by postcolonial studies did not exist. The extent to which the clash appears as inevitable depends on whether we focus on the exceptions or the

---

37 Saree Makdisi, *Making England Western: Occidentalism, Race, and Imperial Culture* (Chicago: Chicago University Press, 2013), 13.
38 See William Christie, 'China in Early Romantic Periodicals', *European Romantic Review*, 27:1 (2015), 1–13.
39 Cranmer-Byng and Wills, 'Trade and Diplomacy with Maritime Europe, 1644-c. 1800', 223.

rule, and even here the case is not clear cut. One consequence of treating 'the vast land of China as a unit', according to Fairbank, is that 'regional differences and the forms of localism have not yet been much studied'.[40] And it is not just the differences among the regions that have been neglected, but also what Li Chen calls 'the frequently conflicting agendas and priorities of the Qing central and local governments'.[41] On the other hand, European sea traders clearly found much in common with 'the enterprising traders of Fujian and Guangdong', to quote Wang Gungwu, who 'set out to take great risks overseas while being constrained by rulers and mandarins who held an orthodox agrarian worldview that was firmly rooted in the soil'.[42] A similar tension between agrarian aristocracy and commercial enterprise could be found throughout Western nations undergoing an extensive and uneven cultural and economic transition themselves. Certain classes and professions (scholars are an obvious case in point) have always found greater affinity with the individuals in their inter- and transnational networks than they have with their own compatriots considered simply *as* compatriots.

When Lord Macartney arrived in December 1793, he, too, engaged with 'Pan-ke-qua' as one of 'the principal Hong merchants' – Pankeequa II: 'a shrewd, sensible, sly fellow', according to his journal.[43] Pankeequa was also the focus of a meditation of Macartney's that precisely identified dress and language as the twin inhibitions to effective cross-cultural communication and commerce (in all senses of the word):

> We no doubt labour under many disadvantages here at present, but some of them we have it in own power to remove. Instead of acting towards the Chinese at Canton in the same manner as we do towards the natives at our factories elsewhere we seem to have adopted a totally opposite system. We keep aloof from them

---

40 Fairbank, 'Introduction: the old order', 9.
41 Chen, *Chinese Law in Imperial Eyes*, 47.
42 Wang, *Anglo-Chinese Encounters since 1800*, 44.
43 Lord [George] Macartney, *An Embassy to China; being the Journal Kept by Lord Macartney during his Embassy to the Emperor Ch'ien-lung 1793–1794*, ed. J. L. Cranmer-Byng (London: Longmans, Green, & Co., 1962), 207.

as much as possible. We wear a dress as different from theirs as can be fashioned. We are quite ignorant of their language … We therefore almost entirely depend on the good faith and good nature of the few Chinese whom we employ, and by whom we can be but imperfectly understood in the broken gibberish we talk to them. I fancy that Pan-ke-qua or Mahomet Soulem would attempt doing business on the Royal Exchange to very little purpose if they appeared there in long petticoat clothes, with bonnets and turbans, and could speak nothing but Chinese or Arabic.[44]

What Macartney is implicitly recommending is cultural cross-dressing in the interests of more effective commerce, though the allusion here is surely to Joseph Addison's well-known celebration in *Spectator* no. 69 of the Royal Exchange as a cosmopolitan phenomenon supervening on differences and divisions between cultures – from which Macartney implicitly demurs:

> There is no Place in the Town which I so much love to frequent as the *Royal-Exchange*. It gives me a secret Satisfaction, and, in some measure, gratifies my Vanity, as I am an *Englishman*, to see so rich an Assembly of Country-men and Foreigners consulting together upon the private Business of Mankind, and making this Metropolis a kind of *Emporium* for the whole Earth … I have often been pleased to hear Disputes adjusted between an Inhabitant of *Japan* and an Alderman of *London*, or to see a Subject of the *Great Mogul* entering into a League with one of the *Czar* of *Muscovy*. I am infinitely delighted in mixing with these several Ministers of Commerce, as they are distinguished by their different Walks and different Languages: Sometimes I am justled among a Body of *Armenians*: Sometimes I am lost in a crowd of *Jews*, and sometimes make one in a Groupe of *Dutch-men*. I am a *Dane*, *Swede*, or *French-Man* at different times, or rather fancy my self like the old Philosopher, who upon being asked what Country-man he was, replied, That he was a Citizen of the World.[45]

---

44   Macartney, *An Embassy to China*, 210.

2 Cultural Cross-Dressing in the House of Pankeequa

James Wathen

One such citizen of the world was James Wathen. Throughout the 200-year history of trade relations between China and Britain in the lead-up to the Opium Wars of 1839–42, we can always find voices, like Hickey's, of openness and sympathy, and gestures of understanding and friendship that do not end with the Macartney era. Still on the theme of cultural cross-dressing and the House of Pankeequa, I want now to take up the narrative twenty years after Macartney in 1812, when Pankeequa II, now retired, entertained the visiting tourist and artist Mr James Wathen, 'an unconnected individual, who has made the India and China voyage', according to the *Asiatic Journal*, 'neither for commerce, nor for any other purpose of gain, but with the sole desire of gratifying a liberal curiosity'.[46] In his account of his voyage, Wathen recalls 'the honour of an invitation' to a dinner 'which Pon-qua-qua gave to the gentlemen of the factory, and some of his own friends':

> The party were only about thirty in number, who sat down to an elegant dinner dressed in the mixed style, English and Chinese. It was here I made my first essay in the use of the chop-sticks, instead of knives and forks. They were too [sic] long pieces of ivory, of about the thickness of a large quill, and tipped at the ends with silver. A couple of these are held in the right hand, between the fingers and thumb, something like the manner in which we hold pens in writing; and with these the Chinese pick up their meat out of their little tureens with the greatest ease and quickness. ... After a great many trials and consequent failures, to the great amusement of my English friends, (and indeed I could see that the Mandarins present could scarcely refrain from laughing at my awkwardness,) I gave up the chop-sticks, and took

---

45 *Selections from* The Tatler *and* The Specator *of Steele and Addison*, ed. Angus Ross (Harmondsworth: Penguin, 1982), 437–40 (437).
46 *The Asiatic Journal and Monthly Register for British India and Its Dependents*, 2 (October 1816), 369–78 (369).

to the knife and fork, with which I contrived to make an excellent dinner on some roast beef, and ham and fowls.[47]

Forty-three years after Hickey, in other words, the House of Pankeequa is still entertaining visitors in the same fashion, and still challenging those visitors to inhabit its culture by adopting the simple utensils of its daily rituals. Wathen admired Pankeequa II, 'who possessed a fine open countenance, displaying traits of benevolence and sensibility' and received him 'most cordially; insisting upon performing the ceremony of *ching-ching* with me, *for Josse*. This was done by his taking both my hands within his, and gently pressing them. We were now sworn friends'.

> Pon-qua-qua conducted us through an elegant suite of rooms, most richly furnished; tables of the most costly wood, some of them inlaid with marble, cabinets, and ornaments, couches, and sophas, placed and disposed, with the most finished taste, upon superb carpets of the most lively colours, graced every apartment. The library, full of Chinese books, was kept in the neatest order. And what rendered these fine rooms the more striking to a stranger, was an immense banian-tree, planted many ages since, spreading its huge branches over the greatest part of them. – This noble tree grew in the garden, and had seats beneath it, where the generous host and his visitors generally sat to converse, while they waited for dinner. On my expressing my admiration for this fine tree, the Mandarin told me that it was planted by one of his ancestors, and that he could not take too much care of it in that account. The piety of the Chinese towards their progenitors is proverbial.[48]

Reading Wathen's account of Pankeequa's sumptuous household – he goes on to mention an aviary, a greenhouse and an orchard, while other visitors tell of a museum along with the fine library Wathen mentions here, with historical drawings lining the walls and an extensive collection

---

47 James Wathen, *Journal of a Voyage, in 1811 and 1812, to Madras and China* (London: J. Nichols, Son, and Bentley, and Black, Parry, and Co., 1814), 200–1.
48 Wathen, *Journal of a Voyage*, 199–200.

2 Cultural Cross-Dressing in the House of Pankeequa

of antique maps, 'ancient copper and bronze articles, principally vases, urns, house and field utensils, & pottery, old china ware'[49] – we are reminded of another text being rewritten and published at exactly the same time, Jane Austen's *Pride and Prejudice*, specifically of Elizabeth Bennet's tour of Pemberley. The same excellent taste, the same balance of nature and built environment – the same willing deference to tradition and specifically to one's father. By all accounts, Pankeequa II was indeed a man of extensive taste and erudition. He wrote poetry (according to Fa-Ti Fan there were 'several more literary aspirants among his family') and was in correspondence with Sir Joseph Banks, supplying botanical specimens to Kew Gardens via Banks' intermediary, John Reeves.[50] More to the point in an essay on cross-cultural encounters, Pankeequa's generosity and hospitality towards the supercargoes and foreign visitors was universally recognised and appreciated, as was his uncharacteristic curiosity about European affairs:

> In the course of conversation the old gentleman was quite inquisitive as regards foreign countries & shewed that he knew something of the wars and revolutions, which have, of late years, convulsed all Europe. He was particular in his inquiries concerning England, of whose greatness and power the Imperial Court at Pekin, as well as a few of the better informed Mandarin Hong merchants here, are evidently very jealous, though they affect to have no fears. This arises in part from their knowledge of the rapid & continual conquests by the British, making westward of China, all over India.[51]

Wathen returned frequently to the home of Pankeequa on Honam Island during his brief stay in Canton, sketching the various rooms and offering his delighted host sketches of his house with himself in

---

49 From the journals of Bryant Parrott Tilden, selectively transcribed in Lawrence Waters Jenkins, *An Old Mandarin Home* (Essex Institute Historical Collections, April, 1935), 8.
50 Fa-Ti Fan, *British Naturalists in Qing China: Science, Empire, and Cultural Encounter* (Cambridge, MA: Harvard University Press, 2004), 33, 44.
51 Jenkins, *An Old Mandarin Home*, 9.

situ. 'At Macao and Canton', reflects the *Asiatic Journal*, 'Mr. W[athen] acquired some acquaintance with the Chinese of those places, and here, as everywhere, we find (what constitutes a marked and most amiable feature of this traveller's book,) a never-failing disposition to take a kindly and liberal view of his fellow creatures'.[52] It is this 'disposition to take a kindly and liberal view of his fellow creatures' that is missing from what, at the turn of the nineteenth century and in the wake of the humiliation of the failed Macartney mission, was fast becoming the educated English man and woman's reflex response to China and its culture. In telling that story, however, it is salutary to remember the few who went to China 'not to convert, trade, rule or fight', in the words of the sinologist Arthur Waley, 'but simply to make friends and learn'.[53]

And it was not just the Chinese in China who caught the attention of travel writers from the West. One reviewer of Wathen's book writes that it provides a view 'calculated to afford a light and yet lively idea of ... their respective people, our own people among them', clearly identifying the Englishman or the Scot in Canton – the 'expatriate' – no less than the Chinese, as an object of ethnographic interest for the domestic British reading public. Just as there is no one China or one Chinese culture, the British and the Chinese can be 'other' (alien or foreign) to themselves, as well as to other nations. This was especially true of the different classes and regions within Britain, as Saree Makdisi has argued persuasively, but it was also true of Britons abroad, who could displace the 'Oriental' as a source of fascination for the English-speaking reader.[54]

Bryan Parrot Tilden

In the interests of symmetry, I want to close my historical account of these Canton dinner party encounters with a similar event from the travel writing of an American businessman, Bryan Parrot Tilden, from whom I have already quoted. Tilden visited Pankeequa III in Canton

---

52   *The Asiatic Journal*, 2:378.
53   As quoted in Wang, *Anglo-Chinese Encounters since 1800*, 7–8.
54   Makdisi, *Making England Western*, 20 and ff.

2 Cultural Cross-Dressing in the House of Pankeequa

for the first time in the 1820s, sixty years after Hickey and fifteen years after Wathen:

> I have had much pleasant intercourse with the venerated Puankhequa and this time have had considerable business with him, making purchases of silks, and teas. He lately did me a signal honor by giving me a genuine Chinese *chopstick* dinner at his Honam residence leaving to me the choosing of any seven or nine American guests for him to invite. ... Pankeiqua discussed the merits and qualities of each dish or mess – and then politely requested us to follow his example and help ourselves, and now began the fun of exposing our awkwardness – we barbarians – having only chop sticks and the spout-like spoons to do it with ... Finally, seeing our distress, the old gentleman ordered plates and English knives, forks, and spoons. These treacherous chop sticks are round at one end, and square at the others and we untutored barbarians ignorantly made use of either.[55]

Reading these narratives of cultural interaction it is hard to think of the gulf between China and Britain as insuperable or the collision between them as inevitable, whatever that might mean philosophically. Indeed, 'The ties of trust and goodwill that bound the Hongists and the fanquis [= foreigners]', as Amitav Ghosh suggests in his novel *River of Smoke*, could be 'all the stronger for having been forged across apparently unbridgeable gaps of language, loyalty and belonging'.[56] These cross-cultural gestures and occasions did suffer a gradual attrition, however, and there is a later, this time elegiac, entry in Tilden's diaries written during his fifth trading tour to China in 1833–34:

---

55 As quoted in May-bo Ching, 'Chopsticks or Cutlery? How Cantonese Merchants Entertained Foreign Guests in the Eighteenth and Nineteenth Centuries', in *Narratives of Free Trade: The Commercial Cultures of Early US-China Relations*, ed. Kendall Johnson (Hong Kong: Hong Kong University Press, 2012), 99–116 (103–5). See also Jacques M. Downs, *The Golden Ghetto: The American Commercial Community at Canton and the Shaping of American China Policy, 1784–1844* (Hong Kong: Hong Kong University Press, 2014), 36ff.
56 Amitav Ghosh, *River of Smoke* (New York: Farrar, Straus and Giroux, 2011), 323.

As partly before remarked, strangers do not now receive such friendly invitations from the Hong merchants, as they did some fifteen years ago. The old social conversation, and intercourse, with occasional invitations to their interesting dinner entertainments have nearly ceased, and they but seldom see us except on business; all which unfortunate state of affairs, is altogether in consequence of the frequent misunderstandings between the British and the Chinese authorities, and whenever troubles are abroad, we poor fanquis suffer all alike. Even we quiet trading Americans – though estimated as No. 1 first chop fanquis customers, are nevertheless treated 'all same same' as Englishmen.[57]

Kipling's grim prediction that East and West would never meet metaphorically was in part the result of an historical and social alienation. Just how inevitable that differentiation and alienation were is another question entirely. 'It is ironic that the same argument of fundamental difference is repeated in China', writes Zhang Longxi, 'by those who would see the West as the reverse image of the East'.[58]

Thomas Manning and John Bell

I began with the Chinese dressing up as British sailors and will end with two Britons dressing as Chinese: two stories, two characters. The first is Charles Lamb's eccentric friend, Thomas Manning. It was not enough that he cultivated the longest beard in a period before facial hair became the rule, but when he joined the diplomatic mission of Lord Amherst to the court of the Chinese emperor in Beijing in 1816, Manning had to be dissuaded from wearing Chinese dress. Manning's qualification for joining the Amherst mission was that he was almost certainly the most distinguished of a generation (the first) of distinguished Chinese-speaking English linguists. George Thomas Staunton, who, along with John Francis Davis and the Protestant missionary glimpsed

---

57 Ching, 'Chopsticks or Cutlery?', 112.
58 Zhang Longxi, *Unexpected Affinities: Reading Across Culture* (Toronto: University of Toronto Press, 2007), 14.

2 Cultural Cross-Dressing in the House of Pankeequa

in Wathen's narrative, Robert Morrison, could be said to have rivalled Manning in his knowledge of Mandarin, recalled on Manning's death in 1840 the 'delight with which the learned Chinese heard him quote Confucius, and other ancient sages, in argument with them'.[59]

Manning's interest in China and in the Chinese language had begun while he was studying mathematics at the University of Cambridge, where a lifelong antipathy to oaths and tests – and to bureaucracy more generally – meant that, instead of taking a degree, he published a two-volume *Introduction to Arithmetic and Algebra* (1796–98) and studied medicine. In 1802, Manning went to Paris to work with the French mathematicians and study Chinese under the noted German sinologist Joseph Hager, and in 1806 he set off for the East India Company's trading factory at Canton to perfect his Mandarin, using his medical qualifications as a passport. On the way to Canton, Manning made several unsuccessful attempts to penetrate the interior of China from the West. Then, having lived for some time at Canton and assisted with the translation work of the Company, he returned to Calcutta and after several months set off for Tibet in 1811, where he became the first Westerner to arrive – cross-dressed in Tibetan costume this time – at the holy city of Lhasa. Allowed to stay in Lhasa for five months, Manning was even granted an audience with the seven-year-old Dalai Lama, but his aim had been to use Tibet as a gateway into China and make his way from there to Beijing. Again, however, access was denied him. The Amherst mission five years later was the first opportunity he had to access the Chinese capital.

For all his obvious accomplishments, Thomas Manning remains an elusive figure in the history of cultural relations between Britain and China, largely because he published so little and his correspondence is so teasingly unforthcoming on the subject of his Eastern travels.[60] But that, to some extent, is because he lived his understanding of China – dressed, ate, talked, enacted and performed it. Unlike the Eastern escapades of Sir Richard Burton later in the nineteenth century,

---

59 As quoted in Kitson, *Forging Romantic China*, 176.
60 Manning's records of his trip to Lhasa and audience with the Dalai Lama were reproduced in Clements Markham, *Narrative of the Mission of George Bogle to Tibet and of the Journey of Thomas Manning to Lhasa* in 1879.

Manning's Orientalism was never part of an elaborate program of self-publication and self-mythologising. There is little that is Orientalist (in Edward Said's sense) about Manning's attitudes to China: 'he remains an idiosyncratic and eccentric figure capable of cross-cultural understandings and sympathy', writes Peter Kitson, 'devoid of any obvious racial stereotyping'.[61]

My second exemplary cross-dresser is the Scottish physician John Bell who accompanied the Russian embassy of Leoff Vasilich Ismailov to Beijing on behalf of Peter the Great in 1719–22 and (like Wathen) published his account forty years later, as *Travels from St Petersburg in Russia to Various Parts of Asia* (1763). Bell wrote of his experiences, not with naive idealism, but with a generosity of understanding and spirit:

> On the 18th, all our gentlemen dined with my Chinese friend, named Siasiey, where we met with a friendly reception, and a sumptuous feast. After dinner, our hospitable landlord put about his cups very freely. At last, he took me by the hand, and desired I would let the ambassador return and remain with him; and he would give me my choice of which of his wives and daughters I liked best. I could not but return my friend hearty thanks for his obliging offer; which, however, I thought it proper not to accept.[62]

Bell found the Chinese to be not just hospitable but 'honest, and [to] observe the strictest honour and justice in their dealings'. Indeed, as Jonathan Spence confirms, 'Bell's overall judgments on the Chinese were positive and seemed to promise good prospects for the future of trade and diplomacy', before adding a clinching anecdote:

> Given the general aura of Bell's comments, it is perhaps not as surprising to us as it seemed to Bell's Scottish neighbors that years

---

61 Kitson, *Forging Romantic China*, 177–78. See also Laurie McMillin, *English in Tibet, Tibet in English: Self-Presentation in Tibet and the Diaspora* (New York: Palgrave, 2001), 55–70, and Felicity James, 'Thomas Manning, Charles Lamb, and Oriental Encounters', *Poetica*, 76 (2011), 21–36.
62 John Bell, *Travels from St. Petersburg in Russia to Various Parts of Asia* [1763], ed. J. L. Stevenson (Edinburgh: Edinburgh University Press, 1965), 167–68.

after his return to his native land, he could be seen riding over the rain-drenched moors wrapped in the Chinese robes he had acquired while on his embassy.[63]

'Vain trifles as they seem', writes Virginia Woolf, 'clothes have, they say, more important offices than merely to keep us warm. They change our view of the world and the world's view of us'.[64]

---

63 Jonathan D. Spence, *The Chan's Great Continent: China in Western Minds* (New York: W.W. Norton & Co., 1999), 51.
64 Woolf, *Orlando*, 179.

3
The *Lady Hughes* Affair, Extraterritoriality, and the Limits of Liberalism

Q. S. *Tong*

> Law in general is human reason, inasmuch as it governs all the inhabitants of the earth; the political and civil laws of each nation ought to be only the particular cases in which human reason is applied.
> —Montesquieu, *The Spirits of Law*[1]

> The Public execution is to be understood not only as a judicial, but also as a political ritual. It belongs, even in minor cases, to the ceremonies by which power is manifested.
> —Michel Foucault, *Discipline and Punish*[2]

International law, or what was known as 'the law of nations', emerged in the second half of the eighteenth century and was quickly accepted as the norm of international relations in Europe. In his pioneering work *The Law of Nations* (1758), Emer de Vattel defines it as 'the science which teaches the rights subsisting between nations or states, and the

---

1   Baron de Montesquieu, *The Spirits of the Laws*, trans. Thomas Nugent (New York: Hafner Press, 1949), 6.
2   Michel Foucault, *Discipline and Punish: The Birth of the Prison*, trans. Alan Sheridan (New York: Vintage Books, 1995), 47.

obligations correspondent to those rights'. What Vattel sets out to do in the book is to establish nations' 'rights and obligations' and their sovereign equality and thereby envisage a new international order in the context of expanding global commercial networks in the eighteenth century.[3] Therefore, the principle of the 'law of nations', insofar as Vattel is concerned, rests on the acceptance of national sovereignty as the foundation of international relations; whether poor or rich, small or big, weak or strong, states are full and complete bodies politic, and mutual respect for each other's sovereignty must be an accepted point of departure for agreement over, and establishment of, any form of effective international governance.

In this part of the world, too, the need for international law was increasingly urgent with the expansion and development of global trade. Following the establishment of the Canton System in 1759,[4] the British Empire began to contemplate introducing further institutional structure to consolidate its commercial presence and expand its interest in China. The dramatic increase in the volume of bilateral trade entailed a sharp increase in conflicts and disputes between the two countries. It was during this period that the idea of 'extraterritoriality' was actively considered and debated. The *Lady Hughes* incident in 1784 was a decisive event that determined the British attitude to 'the extraterritoriality question',[5] though it is not till the end of the First Opium War that British extraterritoriality was formalised in the Nanking Treaty (1842) and its supplemental treaties.[6]

---

[3] Emer de Vattel, *The Law of Nations, Or, Principles of the Law of Nature, Applied to the Conduct and Affairs of Nations and Sovereigns, with Three Early Essays on the Origin and Nature of Natural Law and on Luxury*, edited and with an introduction by Béla Kapossy and Richard Whatmore (Indianapolis, IN: Liberty Fund, 2008), 67, 85.

[4] See James Hevia, *English Lessons: The Pedagogy of Imperialism in Nineteenth-Century China* (Durham, NC: Duke University Press, 2003), 51.

[5] G. W. Keeton, *The Development of Extraterritoriality in China* 2 vols. (New York: Howard Fertig, 1969), 1:41.

[6] See Edward Hertslet, *Treaties, etc., between Great Britain and China, and between China and foreign powers: and orders in Council, rules, regulations, acts of parliament, decrees, and notifications affecting British interests in China, in force on the 1st January, 1896* (London: Harrison & Sons, 1896).

3 The *Lady Hughes* Affair, Extraterritoriality, and the Limits of Liberalism

Extraterritoriality is 'the extension of jurisdiction beyond the borders of the state',[7] an imposition of an alien jurisdiction on the local one, typically through coercion or by force. It is constituted as a sort of legal superstructure, a rule within or above the local rule, a public refusal to comply with the judicial system within which it was created, and a denial of the host state's legal sovereignty. As far as the host state is concerned, it is a dent on its legal integrity, a partial surrender of its legal sovereignty. Extraterritoriality was, therefore, manifestly a contradiction to the principle of the law of nations, a rejection of the very notion of Westphalian sovereignty, on the basis of which 'the law of nations' grew into a normativity and played an increasingly important role in the management of international disputes and conflicts.

How should extraterritoriality be legitimated and justified in conjunction with the principle of the law of nations? How would legal liberalism, which underscores the law of nations, come to terms with extraterritorial privileges? In what ways could imperial legal governance be justified as consistent with the modern legal systems? I will begin with the *Lady Hughes* affair that took place in 1784 and proceed to offer a set of comments on how the incident set off discussions of the implementation of British jurisdiction within the Qing empire and on the implications of extraterritorial establishment for Qing's understanding of its own sovereignty.

The Lady Hughes Affair and Divergences in Legal Practice

Commenting on what he called the 'Chinese problem' in 1857, Thomas De Quincey claimed that the year of 1785 was a turning point in the history of Sino–British relations. 'Up to the year 1785', he wrote, 'it is not worth while to trace the little oscillations of our Canton history'. The *Lady Hughes* incident, which occurred at the end of the previous year, offered 'a memorable one for our English instruction'.[8]

---

7   Wesley R. Fishel, *The End of Extraterritoriality* (New York: Octagon Books, 1974), 2.
8   Thomas De Quincey, 'The Opium and the China Question', in *The Works of Thomas De Quincey* (London: Pickering & Chatto, 2001), 11: 550.

The significance of the incident is acknowledged and reiterated by the historians. Jonathan Spence, for example, asserts that the *Lady Hughes* dispute was one of the two cases that 'made the greatest impact on Western thinking and forced a serious reconsideration of how to deal with the Qing at the international diplomatic level'.[9] One might think of other moments, instances or incidents in the troubled history of Sino–British relations in the late eighteenth and nineteenth centuries, such as the dispute over the court ceremony of kowtow during the Macartney embassy, but the *Lady Hughes* incident was, arguably, the most significant early example of civilisational clashes between Britain and China, foreshadowing major conflicts between the two empires in the nineteenth century. The incident nearly triggered off what Samuel Shaw, the supercargo of *Empress of China*, the first American merchant ship to visit China in 1784, called the 'Canton War',[10] and it made clear Britain's intention and willingness to shape and direct a major dispute with military force, well before the Opium War. The *Lady Hughes* incident presented an unprecedented challenge to the Qing empire, in its legal institution, its governmentality and its sovereignty.

On 24 November 1784, the *Lady Hughes*, a merchant ship owned by the British East India Company at Whampoa, was firing a salute, which incidentally hit a Chinese chop boat lying alongside it, killing one person and injuring two seriously, one of whom died the following day.[11] The local Qing officials demanded the surrendering of the gunner and insisted on his trial by the local government at Canton. Shortly after the homicide, the principal Secretary of the Canton Customs

---

9   Jonathan Spence, *The Search for Modern China* (New York: W. W. Norton, 1991), 126–27. The other incident, the *Emily* affair, occurred much later, in 1821. The *Emily* was an American merchant ship. Terranova ('the New World'), a crew member on board, dropped an earthenware pitcher on the head of a Chinese seller in a boat below, and she fell into the river and drowned. The Chinese authority demanded Terranova's surrender and when denied, threatened to stop all American trade in Canton. The man was then surrendered, and he was executed the following day.
10 Samuel Shaw, *The Life and Journals of Major Samuel Shaw* (Boston: W.M. Crosby and H.P. Nichols, 1847), 186.
11 'Chop boats' were licensed local lighters to transport the cargoes from foreign ships to the foreign warehouses after the Canton Customs measured them and collected port taxes.

3 The *Lady Hughes* Affair, Extraterritoriality, and the Limits of Liberalism

Commissioner (the Hoppo), together with a local official and the Hong merchants, visited W. H. Pigou, chairman of the British East India Company's Council of Supercargoes, de facto British representative during the East India Company's monopoly over Sino-British trade till 1834. Though it was agreed that 'some form of public examination was necessary to satisfy the Laws of [China]', the two sides disagreed over how the gunner should be tried.[12] Remembering the 1780 case in which a French suspect was publicly strangled without 'the form of a trial', Pigou refused to surrender the gunner to a Chinese court and proposed to set up a mixed and independent tribunal in the British factory, to be attended by a jury consisting of both British representatives and Chinese mandarins.[13] In his second meeting with the Chinese authorities, Pigou claimed that the Company possessed no judicial authority over the country ships such as the *Lady Hughes*, which were owned by private traders and it could only play the role of 'mediators'.

Pigou's proposal for a separate, though not entirely independent, court for foreign offences in China was unprecedented. To conduct a judicial hearing, in front of a mixed jury, within the settlement of foreign traders, would be, in practice, a partial concession of Qing judicial sovereignty over foreign offences and a tacit recognition of foreign factories as semi-independent juridical space. It was proto-extraterritoriality. Not surprisingly, the Qing authorities rejected the request and insisted upon the surrender of the accused to the Qing tribunal in the city of Canton. Failing to secure the gunner, the local authorities took the supercargo of the *Lady Hughes* into

---

12 See Hosea Ballou Morse, *The Chronicles of the East India Company Trading to China, 1635–1835*, in 4 vols (Oxford: Oxford University Press, 1926), volume 2, 99; hereafter this reference will be cited as *CEIC* parenthetically in the text.
13 A 'factory' was the earliest modern European colonial formation, 'unlike either the Roman military garrisons or the Greek free civic commonwealths of maritime emigrants, which had been multiplied in the ancient world. It was a trading "factory," or agency, commissioned for the king's mercantile profit, or for that of persons to whom this royal privilege was granted', a commercial station at which 'mercantile residents purchase from the natives of neighbouring lands what these can bring for sale'. Richard Acton, *Our Colonial Empire* (London: Cassell, Petter, Calpin & Co., 1881), 31–32.

custody on 27 November, and the Chinese army swiftly laid siege to the foreign factories:

> the Avenues leading to the Quay were barricaded & filled with Soldiers, the Linguists & Merchants were fled & their Hongs deserted by every person who could throw light on this transaction, & the communication between Canton & Whampoa suspended by order of the Hoppo. (*CEIC* 2, 101)
>
> Everyday life was suspended; the foreign traders were trapped in their factories, unable to return to their ships at Whampoa or leave Canton. On November 30th, the gunner was surrendered to the Chinese; on December 6th, the Chinese embargo on trade was lifted; on December 7th, the *Lady Hughes* sailed for Bombay. On January 8th, the gunner was strangled. (*CEIC* 2, 105)

The death sentence on the gunner of the *Lady Hughes* posed a serious challenge to the modern notion of legal justice that had been developed in the second half of the eighteenth and much of the nineteenth centuries.[14] One issue that emerged in the aftermath of the *Lady Hughes* affair was the question how to define, establish and carry out legal justice which must be ethically just. The dissonance between the Qing authorities and the British over how to interpret homicide in the case of the *Lady Hughes* was no less than a clash between two imperial legal cultures and judicial procedures. Brought to the fore was what the British considered to be the Qing legal and moral failure, in that its juridical practice had failed to recognise and acknowledge an individual's right to live. By the end of the eighteenth century, the English legal system had already evolved into one of liberal jurisprudence which incorporated such foundational modern ideas as individual rights and liberty. '[The] primary and principal object of the law', asserts Blackstone in *Commentaries on the Laws of England* (1753), 'are rights and wrongs';[15]

---

14 For a general survey of Western legal theory, see John Kelly, *A Short History of Western Legal Theory* (Oxford: Clarendon Press, 1992), especially Chapter 7, 'The Eighteenth Century'.
15 William Blackstone, *Commentaries on the Laws of England in Four Books*, 1 [1753], 93. And this is for the protection of the right of personal security.

3 The *Lady Hughes* Affair, Extraterritoriality, and the Limits of Liberalism

and such distinction is crucial for the protection and security of personal rights, foremost among which was the right to enjoy an uninterrupted life and unviolated personal property:

> The right of personal security consists in a person's legal and uninterrupted enjoyment of his life, his limbs, his body, his health, and his reputation, and any forceful interruption of such security is deemed barbaric ... Life is the immediate gift of God, a right inherent by nature in every individual.[16]

The death sentence imposed on the gunner of the *Lady Hughes*, who had accidentally and unintentionally killed two Chinese, could only be interpreted as a violation of such legal humanism, and as a negation of the legal ethics undergirding the modern theory of law and judicial practice. In response to the death sentence, the supercargoes of British ships wrote collectively to the Council:

> As a compliance conformable to these notions [of Chinese justice] seems to us so contrary to what Europeans deem humanity or justice; & if we voluntarily submitted to it, must [*sic*] appear to all, that we gave up every moral & manly principle to our Interest. (*CEIC* 2, 106)

What had transpired in the dispute over the case, then, was not just how to handle a homicide case that involved a European subject, but also how to respond to the logicality (or, in the view of the Europeans, illogicality) of the Qing legal system and how to mediate between

---

16 Blackstone, *Commentaries on the Laws of England in Four Books*, vol. 1 [1753], 97. Blackstone evokes the example of the life of an unborn child to demonstrate the need for a distinction within homicide to be made even in the case of natural death: 'For if a woman is quick with child, and by a potion or otherwise, killeth it in her womb; or if any one beat her, whereby the child dieth in her body, and she is delivered of a dead child; this, though not murder, was by the ancient law homicide or manslaughter. But the modern law doth not look upon this offence in quite so atrocious a light, but merely as a heinous misdemeanor.' *Commentaries on the Laws of England in Four Books* 1, 97–98.

Chinese and British legal positions. However, the divergence between them was radical, deep, and seriously consequential, in particular, in the following areas of legal understanding.

1. Intention

Intention, if considered at all in the Qing legal procedure, served as a point of departure for deliberation on how a criminal act began. Law, so long as it was designed and constituted to safeguard individual rights, must take into consideration the intention of the accused, and appropriate punishment was imposed in accordance with the degree of the crime committed. Manslaughter must be distinguished from premeditated murder, and accidental killing from homicide. Whereas such distinction was crucial in consideration of legal punishment under English law, the Qing penal code seemed to have paid little attention to the perpetrator's intention and allowed for no deliberation over the distinction between accidental killing and intentional murder, as in the case of *Lady Hughes*.[17] How could the criminality of the gunner be appropriately determined with no regard to his intention in this case? Though the Qing authorities acknowledged the unintentionality of the killing, it was nevertheless stressed that the Qing penal code stipulated the death sentence for homicide, whether intentional or otherwise. This judicial ignoring of 'the intention and malice aforethought' was no less a violation of legal justice that the judicial system must defend than a rejection of the rights of the gunner who could not possibly have foreseen the accident.[18] In the end, just and fair execution of law required careful differentiation of the crime committed and

---

17   John Barrow, who accompanied Lord Macartney to China as private secretary, observed: 'the Chinese legislators ... seem to have made little distinction between accidental manslaughter and premediated murder. To constitute the crime, it is not necessary to prove the intention or malice aforethought'. John Barrow, *Travels in China* (London: Printed by A. Strahan, 1804), 367.
18   The use of firearms was not permitted in the Chinese territory, and firing of salutes was theoretically illegal. Should the gunner be charged for use of firearms, it would have been a different legal and therefore less severe sentence. It should be the captain of the ship rather than the poor gunner who should be responsible for the accident.

3 The *Lady Hughes* Affair, Extraterritoriality, and the Limits of Liberalism

consideration of appropriate punishment. George Staunton, who would take on the task of translating *Ta Tsing Leu Lee*, the Qing penal code, claimed: 'to associate guilt with imprudence, and confound wickedness with misfortune, is impolitic, immoral, and cruel'.[19]

2. The life-for-life principle

As Qing judicial procedure did not recognise intention, its legal judgement was almost entirely determined and measured by the consequences of a crime. In the case of the *Lady Hughes* incident, the death sentence was a legal imperative because two Chinese lives were lost. 'It is a maxim of the Chinese law', wrote Samuel Shaw, 'that blood must answer for blood; in pursuance of which, they demanded the unfortunate gunner'.[20] For Shaw, therefore, that legal demand by itself was a death sentence without trial; the gunner would be a sacrifice to the 'barbarous' law that required life for life.[21] To comprehend this apparently incomprehensible legal practice, the supercargoes of the East India Company asked the Qing government to supply a summary of its penal code in relation to homicide. They were given an extract of relevant parts from the Qing penal code, which provided detailed information on capital punishment. In the document, there were altogether six points, of which the first three are as follows:

> 1. A man who kills another on the supposition of theft, shall be strangled, according to the law of homicide committed in an affray. 2. A man who fires at the another with a musquet, and kills him thereby, shall be beheaded, as in cases of willful murder. If the sufferer be wounded, but not mortally, the offender shall be sent into exile. 3. A man who puts to death a criminal who had been apprehended, and made no resistance, shall be strangled, according to the law against homicide committed in an affray.[22]

---

19   Quoted in Barrow, *Travels in China*, 378–79.
20   G. W. Keeton, *The Development of Extraterritoriality in China*, vol. 2, Appendix II, 174.
21   'The War with China', *Monthly Chronicle*, 1840, 418.
22   Other causes for capital punishment include: '4. A man who falsely accuses an innocent person of theft (in cases of greatest criminality) is guilty of a

Considering these clauses, and within the Qing government's long-established legal practice, the *Lady Hughes* verdict would appear less illogical, irrational or unjust. It had been made manifest to the European communities in Canton that the death sentence could not be avoided in a case where a native Chinese was killed. 'In this clear and decisive manner', observed John Barrow, 'are punishments awarded for every class of crimes committed in a society; and it was communicated to the English factory from the viceroy that no consideration was left in the breast of the judge to extenuate or exaggerate the sentence, whatever might be the rank, character, or station of the delinquent'.²³

The Chinese juridical procedure worked differently from that to which British traders were accustomed: it involved no jury, no lawyer, no pleading. Although the death sentence would need to be ratified by the emperor, foreign criminals in cases of homicide would be swiftly executed, as in the case of the gunner of the *Lady Hughes*. Apparently, 'some cases occurred many years ago ... whereon the emperor Keën Lung [Qianlong] declared that, *in order to intimidate foreigners*, the local government of Canton should require *life for life*, without regard to the extenuating circumstances which the Chinese laws admitted when natives only were concerned'.²⁴ It was reported that the emperor

---

capital offence; in all other cases the offenders, whether principals or accessories, shall be sent into exile. 5. A man who wounds another unintentionally shall be tried according to the law respecting blows given in an affray, and the punishment rendered more or less severe, according to the degree of injury sustained. 6. A man who, intoxicated with liquor, commits outrages against the laws, shall be exiled to a desert country, there to remain in a state of servitude.' Barrow, *Travels in China*, 369, note.

23 Barrow, *Travels in China*, 369.
24 Anonymous, *Address to the People of Great Britain, Explanatory of Our Commercial Relations with the Empire of China* (1836) (Cambridge: Cambridge University Press, 2013), 35. That Qianlong insisted on the death sentence of the gunner was believed to be influenced by domestic considerations: 'In 1784 a group of Muslims had rebelled in the interior for the second time in five years. Although Qianlong almost certainly grasped the distinction between Muslims and Christians, he could see some similarities too; both, for example, answered to a temporal authority beyond the emperor's control. He was afraid that the Muslim uprising would soon lead to unrest among Christians. In addition, at the time of the *Lady Hughes* incident, he had recently ordered that all Christian missionaries operating in

3 The *Lady Hughes* Affair, Extraterritoriality, and the Limits of Liberalism

Qianlong thought the sentence to be lenient as it demanded only the gunner's life for two Chinese lives.[25] Years later, in 1834, speaking about the Chinese law, perhaps not without irony, the author of 'Homicides in China', published in *Chinese Repository*, said: 'The Chinese considered homicide as a *debt*; and a debt which can only be paid *in kind*, by the creditor … He who kills another must forfeit his own life. This is the general rule; and in Chinese law the exceptions are few'.[26] As far as the author is concerned, the Chinese had 'a prejudice against foreigners' and 'their pride urges them to require the life of a foreigner, whenever the death of a native has been caused (no matter how) by his agency or instrumentality', even though the 'law of reason, of nature, and of nations, does not admit of this'.[27]

3. Collective responsibility

What aggravated Chinese judicial practice was the stipulation of collective legal responsibility for a crime in the Qing penal code. It would seem to British traders that the Qing legal machinery took a community as collective subject for legal responsibility, in addition to an individual legal subject. This non-distinction between individuals and communities, in the context of Canton trade, was in practice the

---

the provinces be suppressed. So far as he was concerned, he was acting entirely in accordance with Chinese law, and he saw no reason to do otherwise.' Joanna Waley-Cohen, *The Sextants of Beijing: Global Currents in Chinese History* (New York: W.W. Norton & Company, 1999), 101.
25 See also *CEIC* 2, 105.
26 'Homicides in China', *The Chinese Repository* 3:1 (1834), 38. The same punishment would have been meted out on a Chinese person who had committed homicide. In the same year of 1785, for example, in an affray between English and Chinese, an English sailor was killed. Several Chinese persons were arrested and six weeks later the guilty person was executed. Auber commented on this case: 'This circumstance evinces the equal administration of sanguinary laws of that extraordinary people, and at the same time holds out a fearful warning to those who have intercourse with them, of what they are to expect, if even through ignorance and misfortune they happen to fall under the operation of those laws' (*CEIC* 2, 108); Keeton, *Development of Extraterritoriality in China* 1, 42–43.
27 'Homicides in China', *The Chinese Repository* 3:1 (1834), 38.

confusion of a subject of one nation and the nation he or she was from. Staunton was evidently frustrated by the fact that a Western individual was considered in Qing China to be a representative of his/her country: 'The peculiar circumstances under which foreigners are received in China are, in fact, such, that the body or nation suffers from individual offences, almost equally, whether those offences are subjected to punishment, or permitted to escape with impunity'.[28] No British traders would be prepared to accept that they must be legally responsible for their subordinates' or colleagues' breach of the Chinese law:

> Accustomed as they were, under English law, to the personal responsibility of every individual for his own proved wrongdoing, they yet knew that by Chinese custom and law every subordinate was held responsible for his own subordinates; and they knew further that the Chinese authorities had never admitted the validity of their own waiver of control over those on the country ships. (CEIC 2, 101)

The practice of collective legal responsibility was a major cause of concern and disquiet for the British in the *Lady Hughes* incident; it posed a direct threat to the safety of the entire British community in Canton. Before the gunner was surrendered, Supercargo Smith of *Lady Hughes* was detained as a hostage, and the British were advised to 'substitute a Servant or some person of less consequence in his place' if they were concerned about his safety (CEIC 2, 106).

> We think it fair, therefore, to consider these facts as proofs that the [Chinese] Government exercise over us the same absolute and Tyrannical power as towards its own subjects – that in the case of death a man must be given up to them – that it does not admit of

---

28 He believed that such non-distinction between individual and the nation as a whole would promote nationalistic resistance to foreigners. 'The latter event naturally tends to render foreigners objects of hatred and aversion, while the former invariably entails upon them humiliation and disgrace.' George Thomas Staunton, 'Considerations upon the China Trade' (1813), in *China and our Commercial Intercourse with that Country* (Cambridge: Cambridge University Press, 2012), 153.

3 The *Lady Hughes* Affair, Extraterritoriality, and the Limits of Liberalism

a culprit's having escaped, for in that case a substitute must suffer; or if he be refused the Supra Cargo of the Ship or Chief of the Nation must answer for his crime; & to complete the rigor of this Law, it does not allow of Manslaughter and Life only can atone, for what in Europe is thought rather a Man's misfortune, than his crime. (*CEIC* 2, 106)[29]

Should the gunner or a substitute for him be handed over to the Canton government? It would be not only a disgrace to Britain's national pride but a challenge to their notion of justice, liberty and freedom. The British were caught in a dilemma:

> As a compliance conformable to these notions seems to us so contrary to what Europeans deem humanity or justice: & if we voluntarily submitted to it, must appear to all, that we gave up every moral & manly principle to our Interest ... We know therefore of no alternative but that whenever we shall find ourselves so situated as not to be able to satisfy the Chinese without giving up to execution an innocent person, to retire if possible, to our Ships, where only we can consider ourselves secure from compulsion ... The indignities we personally suffer; the vexations and impediments in our business; we have been taught by gradual encroachment to bear: but if the Trade be once lost; & the necessities of England oblige her to regain it; we apprehend it can be done only by a submission that must be disgraceful; or by the use of force, which however successful, must be productive of very serious calamities. (*CEIC* 2, 106)

Collectively, therefore, the British felt that '[o]ur personal safety [is] not altogether free from danger ... as they [Chinese officials] are to exact

---

29 John Barrow, in *Travels in China*, recorded a similar incident: 'about the beginning of the last century, a man belonging to Captain Shelvocke had the misfortune to kill a Chinese on the river. The corpse was laid before the door of the English factory, and the first person that came, who happened to be one of the supercargoes, was seized and carried as a prisoner into the city, nor would they consent to his release till the criminal was given up, whom, after a short inquiry, they strangled'. Barrow, *Travels in China*, 368.

Responsibility from whatever person they think proper to charge with it' (*CEIC* 2, 101). The execution of the gunner filled the supercargoes with dismay, and in writing to the court they expressed their apprehension for the future: 'We feel our situation to be such that if any accidental death happen in future, we think we shall not be able to extricate ourselves from a state of Personal danger, without doing that which must for ever disgrace us, or abandoning this important commerce' (*CEIC* 2, 105). There seemed the need to define the scope of law for the protection of the entire community of British traders:

> As repeated experience shews the utter Impossibility of avoiding the Inconvenience to which we are constantly subject from the imprudence, or willful misconduct of Private Traders and the accidents which may happen on board their ships, it were to be wished that the powers if any which we really possess over them were clearly and explicitly defined, or if no law or construction of law now existing allow of such powers, how far the Absolute Commands of the Government under whose jurisdiction we are, will justify our compliance and how far in such case the Commanders and Officers of the Hon'ble Company's ships are bound to obey our orders, at present equally destitute of power to resist the unjust Commands of Government and to carry them into effect we know of no alternative but retiring to our ships for Protection. (*CEIC* 2, 104–5)

At about the same time the *Lady Hughes* incident took place, some of the European nations were going through major legal reforms. Legal discrimination and juridical determination had developed into a generally accepted understanding in Europe at the end of the eighteenth century. Speaking of the abolition of torture and execution as a public spectacle in the late eighteenth century, Foucault argues that the historical transformation of Western legal practice began when it recognised the importance of its rejection of excessive and indiscriminate application of punishment. He quotes a typical statement on unregulated judicial cruelties by the chancellery in 1789: 'Let penalties be regulated and proportioned to the offences, let the death sentence be passed only on those convicted of murder, and let

3 The *Lady Hughes* Affair, Extraterritoriality, and the Limits of Liberalism

the tortures that revolt humanity be abolished'.[30] The contrast between Qing China and Europe in their understanding of juridical punishment could not be more manifest, and in the case of the *Lady Hughes*, therefore, to imagine anything less than a head-on confrontation developed out of such radical differences would be not just naive, but profoundly unhistorical.

'Queen's Foreign Jurisdiction' and the Contradiction of Sovereignty[31]

The protection of foreign commercial interests was a major challenge in the absence of a well-established and transparent juridical procedure in the Qing jurisdiction. The East India Company did much to protect British subjects and interests, and 'by means of the powers, either directly vested in them, or indirectly arising out of their situation, [it had] hitherto, in every instance of difficulty, actively interposed, either for the preservation or the restoration of harmony'.[32] Therefore,

---

30 Michel Foucault, *Discipline and Punish: The Birth of the Prison*, trans. Alan Sheridan (New York: Vintage Books, 1977), 73.
31 Francis Piggott makes a distinction between 'exterritoriality' and 'extraterritoriality', by suggesting that the former is 'the privilege of Ambassadors and their suites' and the latter is 'the Treaty privileges under which Consular jurisdiction has been established in the East'. He further explains thus: 'The two privileges rest on different grounds; the one is granted by courtesy, the other by Treaty: they differ in degree; the one being almost complete and uniform, while the other is partial and varies in different Oriental States: they differ too in the resulting relations to the home Government, and the manner in which laws may be passed affecting those who enjoy the privileges. But they have this fundamental fact in common; the ordinary consequences of residence in a foreign country do not attach, jurisdiction being waived, in great or less degree, by the Sovereign Authority of that country.
 'But the government of subjects who enjoy exterritorial privileges must be by means of laws which are an exception to the general rule that laws are territorial in their application: these laws must have an extra-territorial force.'
 See Francis Taylor Piggott, *Exterritoriality. The law relating to consular jurisdiction and to residence in Oriental countries* (Hong Kong: Kelly & Walsh, Limited, 1907), note 3.

a more institutionalised form of protection was desired by the British. Discussions of extraterritorial protection of its citizens in China would lead to the formal constitution of extraterritoriality in the mid-nineteenth century. It inspired discussion of how the Qing legal codes diverged so radically from what was commonly practised in nineteenth-century Europe and how European traders should be legally protected in China. In the midst of the *Lady Hughes* incident, the supercargoes sought for such judicial privileges: 'Mr. Pigou and his colleagues on the Council then outlined a project of extraterritorial jurisdiction' (*CEIC* 2, 107).

> The Privilege with respect to their administration of justice should be, we think, that in case of Murder, the perpetrator should be tried by us, in the presence of a Chinese Magistrate; that if he be found guilty, he should be delivered up; but if innocent that we should be allowed to protect him – Should the act prove to be only Manslaughter that they agree to some adequate punishment, such as imprisonment for a year, or whatever else may be previously regulated between us: – that in case the delinquents have really escaped, no substitute shall be demanded; but that they will trust us in making the most diligent search for him; or assisting them to do it ...[33]

In practice, what this desired privilege entailed would be the partial and specific appropriation of China's legal authority with which a judicial space was created, managed and run, not by the Chinese laws, but in accordance with those practised at distant home. Legal extraterritoriality was, therefore, an autonomous space independent of the country in which it was situated, a partial or semi-colonial space. The notion of extraterritoriality was a crucial development in the asymmetrical bilateral relations between China and Britain. However,

---

32 George Thomas Staunton, 'Considerations upon the China Trade' (1813), in *China and our Commercial Intercourse with that Country* (Cambridge: Cambridge University Press, 2012), 153.

33 Quoted in Earl H. Pritchard, *The Crucial Years of Early Anglo-Chinese Relations, 1750–1800* (New York: Octagon Books, 1970), 229.

3 The *Lady Hughes* Affair, Extraterritoriality, and the Limits of Liberalism

though expressed and formulated in the late eighteenth century, extraterritorial legal privileges were yet to be fully formalised. The *Lady Hughes* case would be the last one where the British handed over a British subject for trial in a Chinese court. Intermittently, legal disputes emerged in the following decades, until the signing of the Treaty of Nanking (1842) and its supplemental treaty in July 1843: 'General Regulations on the Five Ports of Canton, Armoy, Foochowfu, Ningpo, and Shanghai' (中英五口通商章程), which completed the classical model of extraterritorial legal arrangements and thereby formally marked the beginning of China's partial loss of its legal sovereignty and the beginning of its semi-colonial history.[34]

The introduction of extraterritorial privileges was both an extension of domestic legal and judicial systems and a serious contradiction to the spirit of modern law developed in conjunction with modern liberalism. What would extraterritoriality be, if not an imposition on the other whose legal sovereignty must be denied, rejected and violated? On what grounds, theoretical or practical, could a liberal state such as Britain be in a position to constitute and practise its own legal system within the judicial limits of another sovereign country? How to defend extraterritoriality, as it was manifestly a contradiction to the new liberal internationalism, as formulated and articulated in Vattel's *Law of*

---

34 Some of the articles in the Supplemental Treaty would be amended and embodied in the Treaty of 1858. Article 13 of the former was amended to read in the latter thus: 'Chinese subjects who may be guilty of any criminal act towards British subjects shall be arrested and published by the Chinese authorities, according to the laws of China.
'British subjects who may commit any crime in China shall be tried and punished by the Consul, or other public functionary authorised thereto, according to the laws of Great Britain.
'Justice shall be equitably and impartially administered on both sides.'
Edward Hertslet, *Treaties, etc., between Great Britain and China, and between China and Foreign Powers* (London: Harrison & Sons, 1896), 21. Extraterritoriality had since been a prominent inclusion in what China called 'unequal treaties' she had signed with foreign powers including the United States and France. For a list of the treaties, see Fishel, *The End of Extraterritoriality in China*, Appendix I 'Treaty Clauses bearing on Extraterritoriality', 225–32.

Nations? In what ways should we understand this imposition of an extraterritorial legal system as a war of civilisations?

By the end of the eighteenth century, as mentioned above, international law had already evolved into a major regulatory system in governing and managing international relations. First, as a conceptual framework, and then as a legal imperative, the law of nations could work only if it was recognised and accepted by those states which also wished to be protected by it, on the condition that member states' sovereignty, territorial and legal, was fully respected. Vattel's *The Law of Nations*, published in 1758, had a simple but powerful message in its application of liberalism to the constitution of a state's sovereignty. The international community of states or 'family of nations' should be considered the same as individuals within a nation. If individuals were equal and free in a society, states should be equal and free, too, in the international community of nations. A smaller, weaker and poorer state was no less equal and free. This model of international law, almost an intuitive analogy of legal equality among individuals in a liberal state, articulates the foundational conception in Vattel's international law: that of national sovereignty. A nation, like an individual, has every right to enjoy its freedom and liberty:

> Nations being free and independent of each other, in the same manner as men are naturally free and independent, the second general law of their society is, that each nation should be left in the peaceable enjoyment of that liberty which she inherits from nature. The natural society of nations cannot subsist, unless the natural rights of each be duly respected. No nation is willing to renounce her liberty: she will rather break off all commerce with those states that should attempt to infringe upon it. (Vattel 74)

Therefore, the classical formulation of international law might be considered to be an extension of modern legal liberalism, a replica of domestic law on an international scale. 'The state is treated at the international level', writes Stephen Krasner, 'as analogous to the individual at the national level. Sovereignty, independence, and consent are comparable with the positions that the individual has in the liberal theory of the state. States are equal in the same way that individuals

3 The *Lady Hughes* Affair, Extraterritoriality, and the Limits of Liberalism

are equal'.[35] Vattel affirmed, in the same terms, the moral foundation of such equality in international relations:

> Since men are naturally equal, and a perfect equality prevails in their rights and obligations, as equally proceeding from nature, – nations composed of men, and considered as so many free persons living together in the state of nature, are naturally equal, and inherit from nature the same obligations and rights. Power or weakness does not in this respect produce any difference. A dwarf is as much a man as a giant; a small republic is no less a sovereign state than the most powerful kingdom. (Vattel 75)

Vattel's liberal assertion of the undifferentiated equality among nations constitutes the ethical foundation of the notion of national sovereignty. 'The basic rule for international legal sovereignty is', therefore, 'that recognition is extended to entities, states, with territory and formal juridical autonomy'.[36]

> Every nation that governs itself, under what form soever, without dependence on any foreign power, is a *sovereign state*. Its rights are naturally the same as those of any other state. Such are the moral persons who live together in a natural society, subject to the law of nations. To give a nation a right to make an immediate figure in this grand society, it is sufficient that it be really sovereign and independent, that is, that it govern itself by its own authority and laws. (Vattel 83)

In essence, therefore, international law is 'the law of sovereigns: free and independent states are moral persons' (Vattel 85). Non-intervention and non-interference would be the foundation of the law of nations. Christian Wolff wrote in the 1760s that '[t]o interfere in the government of another, in whatever way indeed that may be done is opposed to the natural liberty of nations, by virtue of which one

---

35   Stephen D. Krasner, *Sovereignty: Organized Hypocrisy* (Princeton, NJ: Princeton University Press, 1999), 14.
36   Krasner, *Sovereignty*, 14.

is altogether independent of the will of other nations in its action'.[37] For Vattel, this principle should be generally applicable, not only to European states, but also to non-European ones.

The key problems in the conception of international law include what order must be established among sovereign states on the basis of just, equal and accepted rules and how such an order could be maintained and managed.[38] Central to the modern theory of sovereignty was, as Ross Johnston says, 'the idea that a sovereign power was legally omnipotent within its own territory but was legally powerless within the territory of another state – *extra territorium ius dicenti impune haud paretur*'.[39] In view of the liberal theory of the state in the international system, extraterritoriality presented a striking contradiction to the foundational conception of international law and would demand justification of its constitution and practice in such a faraway place as China. In the context of British liberalism and its shaping influence on aspects of British domestic social life in the nineteenth century, the very idea of extraterritoriality was a rejection of its core values. Justification of extraterritoriality and, indeed, of its jurisdictional imperialism constitutes an important part of Britain's larger imperial project, which would present the British Empire as the bearer of the civilisational standard. The liberal theory of international law would be quickly footnoted with the caveat that the law of nations could be applicable only to civilised nations such as European ones, but not to those uncivilised or half civilised. Thus the problem of imperialist governance and colonial rule was facilely moved into a different category of consideration, as Antony Anghie says:

> European states were sovereign and equal. The colonial confrontation, however, particularly since the nineteenth century when colonialism reached its apogee, was not a confrontation between two sovereign

---

37 Quoted in Krasner, *Sovereignty*, 21.
38 Antony Anghie, *Imperialism, Sovereignty and the Making of International Law* (Cambridge: Cambridge University Press, 2004), 15.
39 W. Ross Johnston, *Sovereignty and Protection: A Study of British Jurisdictional Imperialism in the Late Nineteenth Century* (Durham, NC: Duke University Press, 1973), 13.

states, but rather between a sovereign European state and a non-European society that was deemed by jurists to be lacking in sovereignty – or else, at best only partially sovereign.[40]

In the imperial redefining of international relations, sovereignty was not inherent in a nation, and it was a right that should be respected only when it had met certain conditions, foremost among which was its constitutional recognition and acceptance of equality, freedom and popular rule. According to such a definition of sovereignty, non-European countries could be hardly considered full sovereign states. Their exclusion from the category of Westphalian sovereignty would be an example of what Krasner has called 'organized hypocrisy'.[41]

Justification and Legitimacy: The Limits of Liberalism

The very notion of the 'Queen's foreign jurisdiction' was a contradiction and illogicality in the theoretical underpinning of the British Empire. Indeed, it is such an irony that the argument for extraterritoriality should be included in the development of a liberal theory of jurisdiction and of a conception of justice as fairness as the foundation of the social practice of liberalism. The most frequently employed, if somewhat banal, justification for the introduction of extraterritorial protection in China was that the Qing penal code was the product of a pre-modern legal system and had yet to be enlightened. One of its most controversial aspects was its lack of proper attention to a judicial procedure in which evidence was of absolute necessity to prove whether or not someone was guilty. In the Qing laws, said George Staunton with despair, 'We shall look in vain, for instance, for those excellent principles of the English law, by which every man is presumed innocent until he is proved guilty; and no man required to criminate himself'.[42] Under British law, the *Lady Hughes* case might have been defined as

---

40 Anghie, *Imperialism, Sovereignty and the Making of International Law*, 5.
41 Krasner, *Sovereignty*, 40.
42 George Thomas Staunton, *Preface to Ta Tsing Leu Lee; Being the Fundamental Laws, and a Selection from the Supplementary Statutes, of the Penal Code of*

one of negligent homicide or unintentional manslaughter, and it was a violation of the spirit of law to make no distinction between murder and accidental homicide. The death sentence imposed on the gunner of the *Lady Hughes* would be an unfair and unjustifiable punishment; his execution was comparable to a 'judicial murder',[43] a state-sanctioned killing that could have no moral justification.

Furthermore, the partiality and arbitrariness of Chinese legal practice was manifest in its procedure, which was, rather than depersonalised, ultimately subject to the emperor's will. According to Morrison, the sentence first passed on the gunner of the *Lady Hughes* was 'bastinado and transportation', but the Qianlong emperor overturned the sentence and ordered the execution of the gunner. Qianlong's reply to the governor of Canton was that the governor had acted contrary to law; that he should have required 'life for life': 'If ... you quote only our native laws, and according to them sentence to the bastinado and transportation, then the fierce and unruly dispositions of the foreigners will cease to be afraid, it is incumbent to have life

---

China, trans. George Thomas Staunton (London: Printed for T. Cadell and W. Davies, 1810), xxiv.

43 Anonymous, *Address to the People of Great Britain, Explanatory of Our Commercial Relations with the Empire of China* [1836] (Cambridge: Cambridge University Press, 2013), 82. If extraterritoriality was established to replace the 'uncivilized' and 'barbaric' local laws, the removal of extraterritorial privileges would depend on the reforming and perhaps abandonment of those laws. Britain promised in 1902, and the US and Japan in 1903, that they would 'surrender their extraterritorial rights when the state of the Chinese laws, the arrangements for their administration, and other considerations, warranted them in so doing. As a result, the Imperial Law Codification Commission (Hsien Ching Pien Ch'a Kuan) was established and drafts of Criminal, Commercial and Procedural (Civil and Criminal) Codes were prepared'. Secretary of State for Foreign Affairs, *Report of the Commission on Extra-territoriality in China* (London: Printed and Published by His Majesty's Stationery Office, 1926), 26. During World War II, it was no longer morally and practically possible to maintain extraterritorial privileges in China, which was now an ally of Britain and the US. 'On October 10, 1943, realizing that their special privileges were now worthless, and aware of the psychological value to the Chungking government of their relinquishment, the United States and Britain jointly declared their willingness to give up extraterritorial rights at once'. Fishel, *The End of Extraterritoriality in China*, 217.

3 The *Lady Hughes* Affair, Extraterritoriality, and the Limits of Liberalism

for life, to frighten and repress the barbarians'.⁴⁴ Law was thus turned into a political instrument by which the emperor could exhibit and exercise despotic power, to intimidate, scare and shock 'the foreigners'. Ceremonial and performative, the laws of the Qing Dynasty had a politico-diplomatic role to play. For example, the local government's demand for a substitute for the gunner of the *Lady Hughes* after being told of his absconding was a performative act to complete ceremonially the judicial procedure, to reassert the legal authority and political power of the government, and to reconfirm the inviolability of the authority of the Qing Empire and the need for submission to that authority by foreigners residing in China.

On the British side, the *Lady Hughes*, too, was symbolically important. The surrendering of the gunner was viewed as a national disgrace, and it entailed considerable criticism of the East India Company as unfit to represent the British Empire.⁴⁵ It was, as far as the British were concerned, a violation of Britain's sovereignty. For Qing legal practice seemed to have no respect for Western nations' sovereignty: foreigners were *man ee* or barbarians.⁴⁶ For those trading

---

44 Quoted in R. Montgomery Martin, *China, Political, Commercial, Social* (London: James Madden, 8, Leadenhall Street, 1847), vol. 2, 16. John Barrow made the following observations: 'If a man should kill another by an unforeseen and unavoidable accident, his life is forfeited by the law, and however favourable the circumstances may appear in behalf of the criminal, the Emperor alone is invested with the power of remitting the sentence, a power which he very rarely if ever exercises to the extent of a full pardon but, on many occasions, to a mitigation of the punishment awarded by law'. Barrow, *Travels in China*, 368.
45 Nearly half a century later, in an article published in *Dublin Review*, the *Lady Hughes* case was considered to be a failure of the East India Company which prioritised trade over national pride: 'The East India Company possessed but the single virtue of mercantile integrity; its factors were otherwise quite unfitted to be the representatives of a great empire. Stooping to all compliances, for the sake of their trading interests, they fostered the overweening pride of a semibarbarous people, as in the scandalous instance of the surrender of the gunner of the *Lady Hughes*, in 1784, to the certain death that awaited him (the Chinese code requiring the sacrifice of life, for even the unintentional homicide of a native), as in the more recent case of the *Topaz*, where they permitted the miserable Hong merchants to relieve their embarrassment by falsehood' (444–45). *Dublin Review* vol. xvi (March & June 1844).

and residing in China, the word *man ee* was a legal designation, and a symbolic expression of rejection and exclusion written into the Qing penal code:

> The spirit of the 225th section of the Leu Lee, or Penal Laws of China, is that all barbarians are enemies to China – that she allows no free nor friendly intercourse with other countries – that she wishes to keep her affairs secret from foreigners that all, except such as are licensed by government, who trade with foreigners are traitors.[47]

The Qing government, like the British Empire, viewed itself as an imperial sovereignty. Competing claims to civilisational superiority, which misguided their self-understanding and self-perception, were translated into different languages of legal practice with serious consequences. In his defence of individual liberty, J. S. Mill argues for the sovereignty of the subject which must be in full control of itself. If liberal international law was, as discussed above, an extension of domestic law, international liberalism should then be applicable to those states which were in full control of themselves. In *On Liberty*, one may recall, Mill famously defends the principle of liberty as a condition for the mental development of human beings, but he acknowledges that its practice has its limitations and restrictions. It applies only to 'human beings in the maturity of their faculties, excluding children and young people below the age of maturity as defined by the law', for immature minds are 'still in a state to require being taken care of by others' and should be 'protected against their own actions as well as against external injury'. 'For the same reason', Mill further argues, in the backward states of society 'the race itself may be considered as in its nonage'.[48] Elaborating on the practical impossibility of the principle

---

46 Anonymous, *Address to the People of Great Britain, Explanatory of Our Commercial Relations with the Empire of China* [1836] (Cambridge: Cambridge University Press, 2013), 79.
47 Anonymous, *Address to the People of Great Britain*, 78.
48 J. S. Mill, *On Liberty*, ed. David Bromwich and George Kateb (New Haven, CT: Yale University Press, 2003), 81.

3 The *Lady Hughes* Affair, Extraterritoriality, and the Limits of Liberalism

of liberty in an underdeveloped, non-liberal and undemocratic society, Mill states:

> Despotism is a legitimate mode of government in dealing with barbarians, provided the end be their improvement, and the means justified by actually effecting that end. Liberty as a principle, has no application to any state of things anterior to the time when mankind have become capable of being improved by free and equal discussion. Until then, there is nothing for them but implicit obedience to an Akbar or a Charlemagne, if they are so fortunate as to find one.[49]

China fits in with his conception of a despotic state; indeed, it offers a warning example of how a highly developed civilisation may be corrupted by itself:

> China ... [is] a nation of much talent, and, in some respects, even wisdom, owing to the rare good fortune of having been provided at an early period with a particularly good set of customs, the work, in some measure, of men to whom even the most enlightened European must accord, under certain limitations, the title of sages and philosophers. They are remarkable, too, in the excellence of their apparatus for impressing, as far as possible, the best wisdom they possess upon every mind in the community, and securing that those who have appropriated most of it shall occupy the posts of honor and power. Surely the people who did this have discovered the secret of human progressiveness, and must have kept themselves steadily at the head of the movement of the world. On the contrary, they have become stationary – have remained so for thousands of years; and if they are ever to be farther improved, it must be by foreigners.[50]

China's social, political and legal institutions were customised into non-developing institutions, not just because they were solidified

---

49 Mill, *On Liberty*, 81.
50 Mill, *On Liberty*, 135–36.

through and by time, but also because, dialectically, such temporal solidification constituted and rigidified part of the Chinese mind. The principle of liberty was not applicable to a country like China as it was not to those individuals who were undeveloped or not fully developed mentally. Its only hope to be revitalised was in the foreigners whose liberal ideas and institutions could bring about positive political and legal changes. Mill was not concerned with British extraterritoriality in China, but it is within the logic of his theory that the principle of liberty could not be practised within Chinese society and that the introduction of extraterritoriality would be a British intervention which might bring about some real changes to the country's legal institutions. In accordance with the principle of such liberalism, therefore, the question was not whether it is right or wrong to establish extraterritoriality in China, but how to employ it as an effective legal instrument to promulgate the British idea of justice.

Coda

Kafka's short story 'In the Penal Colony' is an allegory of how the colonial penal code is being invented and represented as it is being practised. At the heart of the story is a sophisticated 'apparatus' that tortures the condemned and inscribes the crime on his body. The apparatus is a remarkable invention that exemplifies modern technological achievement. And what has been exported to the penal colony from the metropolis, in the name of civilisation, is embodied in, and by, this apparatus. Its perfectly controlled and precisely calculated performance of torture turns the horror of execution into a spectacle, aesthetically appealing to at least the colonial 'officer' who is in charge of the machine and execution. Concealed beneath the facade of the machine's technological modernity is its barbarity, a modern form of barbarity. The 'beauty' and 'perfection' of the machine signifies the triumphant return of modernity's previous life – the dark ages – and its perfect fusion of legal barbarity and technological modernity exemplifies the consummation of imperialist civilisational achievement. The spectacular display of the machine's performance, in its dehumanised, slow and controlled torturing of the body of the

3 The *Lady Hughes* Affair, Extraterritoriality, and the Limits of Liberalism

condemned, has suppressed the massive amount of violence in the empire's extraordinary project to inscribe and materialise its law in the object – be it a person, a tribe or a country. Historically, the penal colony is needed for the purification of domestic legal sovereignty by dislocating and relocating the unpunishable under the domestic legal system; it is an autonomous jurisdictional space where what has not been possible at home may be carried out without being noticed, scrutinised or criticised, and where no liberal judicial procedure would be required to give out a sentence. The crime of the condemned is not announced; it is inscribed in his body by this fantastic killing machine; torture as punishment is the norm in the penal colony. The apparatus embodies a total rejection of the modern liberal theory of law. It is invented precisely because liberal legal theory needs to be rejected.

Perhaps unlike the establishment of extraterritoriality, the creation of the penal colony would meet with no local resistance and would demand no special moral justification. It is simply an extraterritorial prison. The very idea of extraterritoriality, on the other hand, is an acknowledgement of a different sovereignty whose consent must be procured, by whatever means, before its constitution. However, both the penal colony and extraterritoriality were imperialist inventions, and both are colonial instruments by which the imperial legal space might be effectively expanded. Extraterritoriality, which played a crucial role in extending and sustaining colonial practice, especially in global trade, was justified by the argument of liberalism's responsibility to disseminate and promulgate legal and judicial modernity, an argument that was supported by military power and legal rhetoric of sovereign dignity. The incoherence between its apparent liberalism and the way it was implemented by force is, of course, part of the schizophrenia of imperialist capitalism. Though presented as a model of legal liberty, freedom and equality, extraterritoriality, like Kafka's penal apparatus, will turn around and break its proclaimed commitment to liberal ideas. In its claimed universal applicability, its legal liberalism, like Kafka's apparatus, delivers a cruel and scary message of injustice, inequality and non-freedom. The combination of its barbarity and its liberality is so perfect that the former has been effectively suppressed. True liberal governance is not exportable.

The penal colony and extraterritoriality were fully functioning judicial spaces: the former is that of extraterritorial punishment and the latter of extraterritorial legal privileges, and they provided support for imperialist ideology and its pitiless practice of discipline, punishment and panopticism.[51] If domestic social control is sustained through institutions, medicine, and legal normatives, international control is developed through similar organisational instruments such as extraterritorial laws and penal colonies to safeguard trade and to maintain and demonstrate the desired imperial legal order in faraway places. In the end, writes Michael W. Doyle, empire is

> a relationship, formal or informal, in which one state controls the effective political sovereignty of another political society. It can be achieved by force, by political collaboration, by economic, social or cultural dependence. Imperialism is simply the process or policy of maintaining an empire.[52]

In the context of imperial expansion, the conception of equality could only be achieved by means of unequal relationships; sovereign inequalities among nations, states or peoples, then and now, are as common and widespread as inequalities among classes in a modern liberal state. Admittedly, extraterritoriality is an historical and imperial legal practice, but its underlying universal claims continue to play an active part in international politics today. In 1999, John Rawls, in his *Law of Peoples*, posits that the principles of liberal democracy should be globally constituted. This is important for world peace, because, Rawls asserts, 'since 1800 firmly established liberal societies have not fought one another' and 'liberal democratic societies have only engaged in war against nondemocratic societies'.[53] As far as Rawls is concerned, this is sufficient evidence of what he calls 'democratic peace' and stability. To build a realistic international utopia of peace, it is essential, Rawls

---

51 See Kafka, 'In the Penal Colony' and Kyle McGee, 'Fear and Trembling in the Penal Colony'. http://www.kafka.org/index.php?aid=290.
52 Michael W. Doyle, *Empires* (Ithaca, NY: Cornell University Press, 1986), 45.
53 John Rawls, *The Law of Peoples* (Cambridge, MA: Harvard University Press, 2002), 51.

3 The *Lady Hughes* Affair, Extraterritoriality, and the Limits of Liberalism

argues, to extend liberal 'public reason' to non-liberal societies through peaceful means. But whose liberal 'public reason' would be the best model for international duplication? By what means should 'liberal societies' deal with 'non-liberal' ones and 'civilise' them with the said liberal public reason? Rawls recognises that there can be 'decent' non-liberal peoples. For him, toleration of 'hierarchical people' and 'hierarchical society' must be observed; war and aggression are not permissible. 'No state has a right to war in the pursuit of its *rational*, as opposed to its *reasonable*, interests.'[54] It is not clear, however, how such toleration as a political position could be sustained. What would happen if these hierarchical societies could no longer be tolerated? What if a democratic society engages in war against a non-democratic state, though in the name of democratic values, such as the US invasion of Iraq? Should the notion of public reason be first embodied and established in some institutional form for the prevention of such war? These do not seem to be Rawls' concerns. *The Law of Peoples* proposed by Rawls, resonant with Vattel's *The Law of Nations*, is reminiscent of the arguments developed in the age of imperialism for the need to define international law for the rest of the world, and it serves as a grim reminder that more than two hundred years away from the *Lady Hughes* dispute, we have a long way to go before the achievement and constitution of global equality and justice.

---

54 Rawls, *The Law of Peoples*, 91.

4
Once Upon a Time in 1784: American Mercantile Biographies and the Romance of Free Trade Imperialism

Kendall A. Johnson

> For the historical student the Lives of the Merchants of the world, and the history of the enterprises of trade, if thoroughly investigated, would throw much light upon the pages of history.
> — Freeman Hunt, Preface, *Lives of Merchants*, vol. 1 (1855)[1]

In the antebellum United States, biographical accounts of China traders helped lend the year 1784 retrospective global historical significance with implications for China's relationship to global modernity. Life stories of American merchant princes registered the promise of *free trade* after the US broke out of Britain's mercantile world system during the Revolutionary War. Their biographies also registered the contradictory meanings of the phrase during the First (1839–42) and Second Opium War (1856–60) as sectional antagonism in the US led to the US Civil War.

Key among the American China trade biographies was *The Journals of Major Samuel Shaw, the First American Consul at Canton, with a Life of the Author* (1847), edited by the influential minister,

---

1 Freeman Hunt, 'Preface', *Lives of American Merchants* (New York: Richard C. Valentine, 1855 and 1858), iii.

editor and historian Josiah Quincy. A well-connected but threadbare veteran, Major Shaw was the supercargo of the *Empress of China* that embarked from New York in 1784. His journals document the *Empress's* progress to Macao and the negotiation of the Qing Dynasty's regulatory Canton System in sailing up the Pearl River towards Guangzhou.[2] From the island of Whampoa, Shaw paid duties to Mandarin officials and connected with cohong merchants who would broker the payload of ginseng in purchases of tea at Canton. Upon returning to New York in 1785, the voyage made a respectable profit of about twenty-five per cent. After setting up his own company, Shaw made additional voyages to Canton, where he served as the first US Consul to China, an appointment that President George Washington renewed after his election. On a subsequent voyage, Shaw visited Bengal and witnessed the country trade in opium that enabled Britain's East India Company (EIC) to control market networks between East India and South China. He died on his fourth voyage in 1794. Quincy's book rescued the veteran Major Shaw from obscurity, casting him for readers in the 1840s decade of Manifest Destiny as a diplomatic hero who hoped to make the nation's inaugural fortune in China. It mapped Major Shaw's Revolutionary War service onto his determination to become a China trader and his honourable service as a diplomat.

Quincy's 1847 resuscitation of Major Shaw is difficult to appreciate outside certain contexts: the First Opium War, the resulting unequal Treaty of Nanjing (1842) between Britain and China that recast the terms of Western trade with China and annexed Hong Kong, and the Treaty of Wangxia (1844) that was the first between China and the US. After the First Opium War, Shaw's premature demise became the beginning of a national success story as his diplomatic reputation for honesty, courage and determination became the harbinger of merchant princes' success as New York's John Jacob Astor, Philadelphia's Stephen

---

2   Regarding the voyage of the *Empress*, see Philip Chadwick Foster Smith, *The Empress of China* (Philadelphia: Philadelphia Maritime Museum, 1984). In regard to the regulations of the Canton System, see Paul A. Van Dyke, *The Canton Trade: Life and Enterprise on the China Coast, 1700–1845* (Hong Kong: Hong Kong University Press, 2005) and John D. Wong, *Global Trade in the Nineteenth Century: The House of Houqua and the Canton System* (Cambridge: Cambridge University Press, 2016).

4 Once Upon a Time in 1784: American Mercantile Biographies

Figure 4.1 Frontispiece to Samuel Shaw and Josiah Quincy, *The Journals of Major Samuel Shaw, The First American Consul at Canton: With a Life of the Author* (Boston: Wm. Crosby and H.P. Nichols, 1847). Courtesy of the Rare Book and Manuscript Library, Van Pelt-Dietrich Library Center, University of Pennsylvania.

Girard and Boston's Thomas H. Perkins and others made their fortunes to become the storied merchant princes of the United States. As these merchants won their fortune, the debate over the legality and ethicality of opium smuggling pervaded newspaper accounts in Britain and the United States.

Despite the Opium Wars, American national biographies in the 1850s presented these merchant princes as courageously independent successors of Shaw. Uncorrupted by imperial monopolies or the project of colonial land acquisitions in China or India, they had showcased new potential for American free trade in the global co-ordination of speculative enterprise through their private companies. In 1855, the New York-based editor Freeman Hunt presented Colonel Thomas H. Perkins as the reigning profile of mercantile courage in *Hunt's Merchants' Magazine and Commercial Review*. Perkins' biographer, son-in-law and business associate, Thomas G. Cary, traced Perkins' development from his first voyage to Canton in the late 1780s to his later philanthropic largesse in Boston. In the first decades of the nineteenth century, Perkins and his brothers founded companies to co-ordinate a network of trade connecting Boston to Canton, Saint-Domingue, the Pacific Northwest, and finance capitals in Europe and Britain.

However, various aspects of Perkins' commercial strategies contradicted the spirit of Major Shaw and the anti-imperial connotations of early American free trade. During the First Opium War, American merchants' neutrality generated opportunities to move freight, facilitating continued importation of opium in violation of Chinese law. Furthermore, the pursuit of trade in the Far East ran parallel with speculative imperialism in the far west of North America, where state and federal initiatives attempted to remove native peoples in territorial extension supported by new rounds of compromise regarding slavery. In the decades leading to 1860, Southern states insisted that American principles of free trade validated their sovereignty, a claim that contributed to secession and the US Civil War during which the optimism of the China trade faded in the national biography.

By looking at antebellum national biographies related to the China trade, this essay considers how Quincy and other biographers such as Hunt and Cary structured their subjects' experiences into national romances of individual accomplishment while layering meanings of *free trade* to distinguish the United States from European imperialism. To set a point of historical reference for generic development, the essay begins with the early American historian Jeremy Belknap who overlooked his contemporary Major Shaw in showcasing Christopher Columbus as the most important hero of progressive commerce. From Belknap, the essay considers how biography developed as a genre to enable Quincy's resuscitation of Shaw in 1847 and Freeman Hunt's presentation of Perkins in *Hunt's Merchants' Magazine* through the *mercantile biography*. The essay concludes with consideration of how biographies tackled the 'opium question' that troubles the equation of American freedom with free trade in a decade that included the Second Opium War and the US Civil War.

American Biography and the Spirit of Columbus

For the minister and early historian Jeremy Belknap writing in the decade after the Revolution, Christopher Columbus and his discovery of America were vastly more important to an emerging sense of national American distinctiveness than Shaw and his furtive China voyages. In 1784, the US did not yet matter in the global theatre of commerce bearing on China, and it would have been odd to regard Shaw as a significant historical icon. As late as 1820, the clergyman Sydney Smith could provocatively reassure British readers (and rankle American ones) by opining on the low commercial and cultural status of the former colonies when musing over the implications of the Union's sectional compromises over slavery. In the *Edinburgh Review*, Smith wrote:

> In the four quarters of the globe, who reads an American book? Or goes to an American play? Or looks at an American picture or statue? What does the world yet owe to American physicians or surgeons? What new substances have their chemists discovered? Or what old ones have they advanced? What new constellations have been discovered by the telescopes of Americans? Who drinks

out of American glasses? Or eats from American plates? Or wears American coats or gowns? Or sleeps in American blankets? Finally, under which of the old tyrannical governments of Europe is every sixth man a slave, whom his fellow-creatures may buy and sell and torture?[3]

Across the world, historical seas of global commerce that had led to Britain's maritime pre-eminence, the *Empress of China* voyage was a mere drop in a proverbial bucket. For most of the eighteenth century, China had raked in vast amounts of Spanish colonial silver by regulating Western demand for tea through its Canton System that designated the southern harbour of Guangzhou as the sole port open to the British and most other European traders. US merchants of the 1780s were left to strategise over what they could possibly trade at Canton where the controlling commodity and currency was silver.

For Sydney Smith and his readers, the year 1784 might have mattered for marking Britain's defeat of the Dutch in the Fourth Anglo-Dutch War (1780–84), after which the EIC secured control over areas formerly held by the Dutch East Indies Company (VOC). By exporting opium from colonial Bengal, the EIC took control of Batavia (Jakarta) and the Straits Settlements of Penang, Malacca and Singapore. These defeats contributed to the VOC's bankruptcy in the 1790s and to the steady recession of Portuguese influence in the region as the British country trade in opium restructured the 'maritime "Silk Road"'.[4] In the decades after Shaw's death, the EIC increased opium production to reverse the balance of silver exchange at Canton, augmenting flows of the drug from Bengal to China in a triangle of country trade connecting the speculative financial centre of London to the opium fields, factories and auction houses in Bengal, and the markets in South China and South-East Asia.[5]

---

3   Sydney Smith, 'Rev. of Statistical Annals of the United States, by Adam Seybert', *The Edinburgh Review* 33 (1820): 69–80.

4   Leonard Blussé, *Visible Cities: Canton, Nagasaki, and Batavia and the Coming of the Americans* (Cambridge, MA: Harvard University Press, 2008), 4.

5   See André Gunder Frank, *ReOrient: Global Economy in the Asian Age* (Berkeley, CA: University of California Press, 1998) and Man-houng Lin,

4 Once Upon a Time in 1784: American Mercantile Biographies

Given that US international commerce was relatively weak, it is not surprising that, despite its title, no actual American citizens appear in Belknap's two-volume *American Biography: Or, an Historical Account of Those Persons Who Have Been Distinguished in America, as Adventurers, Statesmen, Philosophers, Divines, Warriors, Authors, and Other Remarkable Characters. Comprehending a Recital of the Events Connected with Their Lives and Actions* (1794, 1798). Nevertheless, Belknap's book influenced the national historical implications of biography for decades after through republication, including four successive editions before the Civil War by the highly reputable Harper & Brothers (in 1841, 1846, 1851 and 1855).[6] Belknap's influence also registers in the enduring heroism of Columbus, to whom Washington Irving devoted extensive attention in the 1820s.[7] Biographers in the 1850s would continue to adapt themes and methods from Belknap's biographical chronicle.

Belknap blazed a path for national biography by appreciating British colonial history as a prelude to focusing on New England. Thus national historiography carried expansive world-historical implications for understanding the past and the future. In regard to practical influence, Belknap was crucial to founding the Massachusetts Historical Association (1791), incorporated by the State of Massachusetts in 1794. His early biographies of eighteenth-century British non-conformist ministers Isaac Watts and Philip Doddridge reflect the religious sensibility of political and cultural connection to Great Britain. After Watts and Doddridge, he delved into a regional sense of identity by spending twenty years on the three-volume *The History of New Hampshire* (1784, 1792, 1792). Belknap moved to the

---

China Upside Down: Currency, Society, and Ideologies, 1808–1856 (Cambridge, MA: Harvard University Press, 2006).

6   The teacher and Episcopal priest F[ordyce] M[itchell] Hubbard, who contributed to Jared Sparks' *The Library of American Biography*, edited the later editions into three volumes with notes; see F. M. Hubbard, 'William R. Davie', *Library of American Biography*, volume five of the 2nd Series, ed. Jared Sparks (Boston: Hilliard, Gray and Co. 1834–48).

7   Washington Irving published *A History of the Life and Voyages of Christopher Columbus* (1829) and *Voyages and Discoveries of the Companions of Columbus* (1831).

state and collected 'manuscripts scattered here and there in the possession of individuals' bearing on the topic.[8] He assessed the veracity of received historical accounts and the reliability of sources that he designated as primary, acknowledging longstanding disagreements and recent controversies with footnotes signalled with an asterisk, plus sign, or vertical double-plus sign. His care with citation earned Belknap praise from contemporaries and subsequent generations of scholars for championing a mode of historical scholarship that cultivated dialogue among scholars.

After his history of New Hampshire, Belknap turned to his final work: *American Biography*. Belknap looks deep into the classical past and far across a global geography of maritime trade in order to adumbrate an emerging spirit of national distinctiveness. He chronicles centuries' long durations of time across vast geographies in order to discern the origins of an inchoate American commercial ambition.[9] The grand scale of his history matches the depth of antiquarian textual sources, among which are classical writers such as Herodotus and Pliny, the accounts by Columbus' son Ferdinand Columbus, and Puritan histories of New England. As particularly informative, Belknap singles out Richard Hakluyt's *Voyages and Discoveries* and Samuel Purchas' *Pilgrimage, or Relations of the World and the Religions Observed*, commenting that complete sets of each were respectively available at the Massachusetts Historical Society and Harvard College library.[10]

Although Belknap encouraged scholarly attention to US archives, his *American Biography* does not include an actual US citizen in its chronicle of great individual explorers. The United States emerges from a transhistorical global scale of commercial experimentation by which

---

8   Jane Belknap Marcou, *Life of Jeremy Belknap, D.D., the History of New Hampshire from His Correspondence and Other Writings, Collected and Arranged by his Grand-daughter* (New York: Harper and Brothers, 1847), 128.
9   See Giovanni Arrighi, *The Long Twentieth Century: Money, Power, and the Origins of Our Times* (London: Verso, 1994).
10 Jeremy Belknap, *American Biography: Or, An Historical Account of Those Persons Who Have Been Distinguished in America, as Adventures, Statesmen, Philosophers, Divines, Warriors, Authors, and other Remarkable Characters. Comprehending a Recital of the Events Connected with their Lives and Actions.* 2 vols (Boston: Isaiah Thomas and Ebenezer T. Andrews, 1794, 1798), vol. 1, 409.

4 Once Upon a Time in 1784: American Mercantile Biographies

Portuguese explorers ventured around Africa to India and China, while Columbus discovered America on the westward way to the Indies. Such innovative trajectories of commerce set the stage for British colonisation of the Americas that led, in time, to an American Revolution that affords the premise of Belknap's biographical study. The rise of the United States extends the Columbian goal of expanding trade to the East Indies in a westward course of empire. In illustration of this westward course, the two volumes of *American Biography* comprise a 'Chronological Detail of Adventures and Discoveries made by the European Nations, in America, before the Establishment of the Council of Plymouth, in 1620 that begins with the Norman explorer Biron (1001 AD) and ends with William Penn in the 1680s'. In a pattern that subsequent biographers would repeat, the first volume's 'Preliminary Dissertation' reviews classical history to align the progress of scientific inquiry with a proleptic sense of national destiny, ciphering the dawn of the United States in cyclically progressive currents of adventuresome exploration emanating from an imperial Europe vexed with the corruption of greedy Catholics and aristocrats, while on the cusp of religious reformation personified in the scientific ambition of Columbus. British colonialism follows through on the Columbian promise that Spanish avarice had betrayed. Belknap thus infers national distinctiveness in a historical glance *backward* as he discerns various styles of corporate enterprise that blend science and Protestant faith into a commercial spirit heralding the distinct nation of the US.

In idealising maritime exploration as an innovative mode of scientific inquiry, Belknap overlooks the original Silk Road and situates the seat of modern commercial power in a proto-European Mediterranean zone of trade. Looking to the historical print record, he lends great significance to the 'circumnavigation of Africa by the Ancients', as the 'first navigators' of the 'Phenicians' [*sic*] extended their commercial influence 'beyond the pillars of Hercules' south along the west coast of Africa and north to Britain, from where they imported lead and tin – this already suggesting the 'probable consequence' of populating 'Some Part of America'.[11] However, he denigrates the westward reach and significance of proto-European exploration

---

11 Belknap, *American Biography*, vol. 1, 5.

(Phoenician), thus preserving the individual importance of Columbus, who in his scientific curiosity prefigures the durable colonisation of the Americas by Britain, and to a lesser extent France and Holland. Columbus hovers above the volumes as a tragic hero whose Enlightenment curiosity and scientific abilities were undercut by the 'licentiousness of the Spaniards' and the 'avarice of his fellow adventurers'.[12] Spain's subsequent explorers, such as Ferdinand de Soto, are inconsequential and nefarious, driven by an 'inextinguishable thirst for gold' to be cruelly violent towards Indians.[13]

In the spirit of Columbian experimentation, Belknap highlights Britain's ability to manage aggression through royal charters, like those granted by Queen Elizabeth to the early adventurers Walter Raleigh and Richard Grenville, and eventually through monopoly charters such as the charters of the Virginia Company under King James. The corporate model of the first Virginia Company (1606) enabled the adventurer John Smith to direct his resolution and courage in managing the 'disorderly, factious, disappointed set of men' colonising Virginia. It also gave him the political framework to stand up to the savagely 'native lords of the soil' in setting terms of mutual recognition that in Belknap's narrative lead to land transfer through treaty and contract.[14]

By facilitating permanent colonisation in the Americas, these monarchial charters and monopolies enabled Britain to shape human history in a way more profound than Spain. But the early British patents and charters were flawed in concentrating managerial power among those far away from the colonial site to whom the monarch had delegated authority. Ultimately Virginia suffered as the Virginia Company divided management from colonial experience; those wrangling for authority in London sidelined Smith in Virginia and forced his return to England. However, Belknap sees Britain's forms of corporate organisation progressing in New England where adaptations of the Virginia Company of Plymouth led to Edward Winslow's account of 'the confederation of the [New England] Colonies', a confederation that parliament passed in 1649 in order 'to promote the civilization

---

12   Belknap, *American Biography*, vol. 1, 107, 108.
13   Belknap, *American Biography*, vol. 1, 186.
14   Belknap, *American Biography*, vol. 1, 299.

of the Indians, and their conversion to Christian religion'.[15] Belknap died before finishing *American Biography*, but a sense of progressive optimism pervades the second volume, which concludes with William Penn, whose Pennsylvania evinces Britain's tendency to respect indigenous inhabitants by trying to purchase land, even as these savages threatened the colonial hearth.

Throughout Belknap's *American Biography* the East Indies lingers as an ultimate destination of colonial accomplishment in a westward horizon of Columbian ambition. As mentioned, Belknap sets up Columbus as the primary world-historical 'enterprising adventurer' who embraces science in navigating the seas 'by experiment'; in his experimental courage, Columbus pivots between Catholicism and Protestantism to pave the way for British charters that will enable colonial heroism in pre-national New England.[16] Reaching the East Indies is a pervading motivation behind John Cabot's quest for a north-west passage in finding 'a way to India by the west', an endeavour that had 'long been a problem with men of science as well as a desideratum in mercantile interest'.[17] In these grand spatial and geographical arcs of commercial extension, *American Biography* presents the United States as one of the 'grandest of these experiments' that fixes a standard of 'freedom' and invites 'the distressed of all countries to take refuge under it'.[18]

Belknap influenced many scholars who adapted biography to express greater degrees of national distinction through presentation of a life story. Two decades after *American Biography*, the Philadelphia-based biographer and portrait collector Joseph Delaplaine presented an explicitly national group of citizen patriarchs in *Repository of the Lives and Portraits of Distinguished Americans* (1815, 1817). While not as influential as Belknap's work, this two-volume book (actually one volume in two parts) reflects the developing logic by which biographies purported to represent national type through the life narrative of an individual. Delaplaine cross-references visual and verbal portraits to

---

15 Belknap, *American Biography*, vol. 2, 305.
16 Belknap, *American Biography*, vol. 1, 20.
17 Belknap, *American Biography*, vol. 2, 150.
18 Belknap, *American Biography*, vol. 1, 36.

generate a representative effect in the portrayal of those 'distinguished Americans' whom readers throughout the world should recognise. Those whom he showcases are 'exalted personages who directed, in their day, the destinies of the world' and who are connected to each other based on the pride of 'consanguinity' and 'love of country'.[19] Like Belknap, Delaplaine prefaces his presentation of American statesmen with profiles of Columbus and Vespucci, 'Not only because the discovery of this quarter of the globe gave a new aspect to the whole civilized world, but because our revolution forms a cardinal era in the progressive condition of man, this republic must present to after ages one of the greatest spectacles in the history of the world'.[20] Columbus occupies the 'loftiest station on the scale of greatness', especially because the 'effects of this discovery [of America]' have 'not been experienced in their final amount' until the nation of 'America' is 'destined to become the arbiter of the earth'.[21] Vespucci is next before a distinguished sequence of American citizens, including Dr Benjamin Rush (practitioner, teacher, philosopher, writer, physician), Fisher Ames (statesman, orator, legislator), Alexander Hamilton (colonel, legislator, financial and political philosopher on par with Cicero) and George Washington (general, president). The second book includes Peyton Randolph, Thomas Jefferson, John Jay, Rufus King, De Witt Clinton and Robert Fulton. Major Shaw is not among them.

Subsequent biographers, such as Quincy and Hunt, would borrow from Delaplaine in using a portrait to complement a life story. Delaplaine's *Repository* registers generic innovation in the extent to which he pursues visual illustration in a referential circuit of verbal and pictorial correspondence that equates individual life narrative to national kind or type through the concept of 'character'. He writes in the Preface:

---

19 Joseph Delaplaine, *Repository of the Lives and Portraits of Distinguished Americans*, 1 volume in two parts (Philadelphia: William Brown, 1815, 1817), vol. 1, iii; vol 1, i.
20 Delaplaine, *Repository*, vol. 1, ix.
21 Delaplaine, *Repository*, vol. 1, 1.

4 Once Upon a Time in 1784: American Mercantile Biographies

Figure 4.2 Portrait of Columbus, Joseph Delaplaine's *Repository of the Lives and Portraits of Distinguished Americans* (Philadelphia: William Brown, 1815), 2 volumes; vol. 1, no page.

> In the pages of the *Repository* pains have been taken and heavy expenses incurred, to remedy the defect that exists in the writings of the ancient biographers. The engravings which those [these] pages contain, besides being sufficiently elegant and ornamented, are correct and striking likenesses of the distinguished characters they are intended to represent. While the text shall communicate to remote posterity what, at a former period, the leading men of America thought and performed, the portraits accompanying it will give a view of their features and general aspect, their costume and air. Thus by the combined operations of the type and the graver will a correct image of the whole man be exhibited to view.[22]

On a practical level, portraiture augments the size of an audience by capturing readers' attention with a glance at a picture. Considering fully Delaplaine's allusion to ancient biographies could take one back to the translations of Theophrastus and Petrarch and the caricatures of Hogarth, but the point is that Delaplaine foregrounds a sense of national American type that coheres in the wake of Columbian adventure, as he sets references between individual and national characteristics. In pictorial terms, he wants the reader to sense the depth of a unique personal character, elucidated in verbal descriptions of life narrative (and vice versa). On the basis of this cross-referential sense of the visual and the verbal, the biographical individual becomes representative, as readers identify with him as a fellow American, civilised Western Christian, or fellow human being dedicated to the Columbian project of globally expansive commerce. The cross-referential premise of Delaplaine's presentation of national type converts concern over a portrait's accuracy into a challenge: can readers apprehend a national type by co-ordinating the layers of verbal and pictorial representation related to an individual? Delaplaine thus presents 'the portraits of that glorious band of patriots, heroes, and sages, who have America to the realms of freedom' so that they will 'be viewed with pleasure by enlightened men in all countries, but to the remote ages be contemplated with pride and transport by the grateful

---

22 Delaplaine, *Repository*, Preface, iii.

citizens of this republic, as models by which to shape their conduct, and as examples whom it will be their glory to emulate.'[23]

Delaplaine's method also suggests the rise of commercial themes in national biography. Delaplaine deepens the referential layers by promising an expanded edition with '*fac similies* of the hand writing of all the distinguished men of our country'.[24] Looking ahead to the frontispiece portraits of the biographies of Major Shaw (Figure 1) and Thomas H. Perkins (Figure 4), one notices beneath the images hand-written signatures that could not but evoke the act of signing contracts and trade agreements in an age when international commerce was becoming even more important to biographers hoping to express the distinctive and even exceptional contours of national American commerce.

The Life of Major Samuel Shaw and Spirit of 1784

In the 1830s and 1840s, Jared Sparks and Josiah Quincy continued developing the historical authority of biography in ways that enabled the reintroduction of Major Shaw to the world as an honourable diplomat and aspiring China trader with national significance. Both Sparks and Quincy served as president of Harvard College, earning high scholarly reputations in New England during a volatile era of waning federalist influence as John Adams' generation faded after the presidency of his son John Quincy Adams and the rise of Jacksonian Democracy in the late 1820s. In their conception of biography, the life of the person depicted served instructive ends, in regard both to filling out the picture of national history and to aiding readers in their paths of personal development.

In the 1830s, Sparks became the major force in the development of national biography. As Scott Caspar writes in *Constructing American Lives: Biography and Culture in Nineteenth-century America*, 'Sparks considered biography a branch of history, with a mission akin to the

---

23 Delaplaine, *Repository*, Preface, vii.
24 Joseph Delaplaine, *Prospectus of Delaplaine's National Panzographia, for the Reception of the Portraits of Distinguished Americans* (Philadelphia: William Brown, 1818), 16.

state historical societies founded in these years: preserving America's fast-fading past, separating documentary "truth" from unreliable "tradition" or lore before it was too late'.[25] A founding editor of the *North American Review*, Sparks edited the writings of George Washington and Benjamin Franklin and then oversaw two major series entitled the 'Library of American Biography' that ran to twenty-five volumes.[26]

The China trade was a relatively minor theme in the 'Library of American Biography' series, although Sparks wrote a biography of an early proponent of the Northwestern fur trade named John Ledyard.[27] Sparks became particularly interested in Major Shaw while editing the diplomatic record for the US Congress in the 1820s for the seven-volume *Diplomatic Correspondence of the United States* (1833–34).[28] As a result, Shaw's name circulated among those looking for a signpost of early China–US diplomatic relations and caught the eye of US missionaries in Canton who published on Shaw in the September 1836 issue of their monthly periodical *The Chinese Repository*.[29] These missionaries worked with China traders such as Charles King and David Oliphant, who decried the trade of opium as immoral and a violation of the principle of free trade as the First Opium War approached.[30]

It was not until five years after the First Opium War that Shaw received full biographical attention when Sparks' colleague Josiah

---

25 Scott E. Caspar, *Constructing American Lives: Biography and Culture in Nineteenth-century America* (Chapel Hill: University of North Carolina Press, 1999), 4.
26 Caspar, 16. The First Series ran from 1834–38; the Second Series ran from 1844–47.
27 See Jared Sparks' *The Life of John Ledyard, the American Traveler; comprising Selections from his Journals and Correspondence* (Cambridge, MA: Hilliard & Brown, 1828).
28 Jared Sparks (ed.), *The Diplomatic Correspondence of the United States of America, from the signing of the Definitive Treaty of Peace, 10th September 1783, to the Adoption of the Constitution, March 4, 1789.* 7 vols (Washington, DC: Frances Preston Blair, 1833–34).
29 Shaw's writings also surface in William Jay's biography of his father, *The Life of John Jay* (1833); see Kendall A. Johnson, *The New Middle Kingdom* (Baltimore, MD: Johns Hopkins University Press, 2017), 37–38.
30 See Johnson, *The New Middle Kingdom*.

4 Once Upon a Time in 1784: American Mercantile Biographies

Quincy published *The Journals of Major Samuel Shaw*. Shaw might have faded into the past if his adopted nephew, Robert Gould Shaw, had not preserved his writing as he made a fortune in the China trade. Quincy did more than save Shaw from the dustbin of history. Quincy formulated these writings into a *bildungs* with nationally representative implications. Quincy's notion of biography represents Shaw as a 'character' to imply a 'true self' that is fundamental to the private and public layers of identity.[31] Accordingly, an individual's 'reputation' derives from personal 'habits of industry, temperance, piety, and so on' that shape a 'true self' that gets revealed on the 'public stage' through the biography.[32] The frontispiece to Quincy's book captures the position of the reader in relation to the self-referential circuit of Shaw's signature, portrait and life story. The unfinished status of the sketch (Figure 1) suggests that Shaw's legacy is still unfolding and that readers can participate in extending the national reputation that Shaw had established in the nation's initial foray into the China trade.

Shaw never made his fortune. But Quincy touted Shaw's honesty, determination and courage in securing the foundation of an honourable national character in China. Shaw represents the early national promise of the China trade and his premature death and failure to make a fortune give Quincy's readers a chance to appreciate how far their nation has come as they take the baton. Shaw also provides a practical sense of the China trade that is more logistically nuanced than the long arcs of commerce Belknap charts in *American Biography*. In 1784, US merchants faced the question of what to trade in Canton. After the encouraging returns on the *Empress of China* payload, Shaw predicted in reports to the Secretary of Foreign Affairs, John Jay, that the root ginseng, indigenous to North America and North-East Asia, would prove as lucrative in the China trade as Spanish-controlled silver mines of Mexico and Peru. On subsequent voyages, ginseng disappointed Shaw, as furs and sealskins became the lucrative commodity. Eventually it was opium.

---

31 Samuel Shaw, *The Journals of Major Samuel Shaw, the First American Consul at Canton, with a Life of the Author by Josiah Quincy*, ed. Josiah Quincy (Boston: Wm. Crosby and H. P. Nichols, 1847), 6.
32 Shaw, *Journals*, 7.

Judging from Shaw's journals of the first two voyages, he was never deeply involved in the opium trade, despite being attuned to the competitive advantage that the British derived from it. Quincy's biography directs readers to appreciate Shaw for his determination and honesty in establishing a creditable reputation in Canton as a diplomat and businessman – a reputation upon which subsequent American speculation depended. In this light, his hyperbolic description of ginseng's potential profitability seems inspirationally optimistic rather than naive and misinformed. As Quincy writes, it is to the benefit of future generations that Shaw gave the Chinese inhabitants of Canton 'the first impression of the character and resources of a new nation'; Shaw's 'intelligence, business talent and fidelity to his duties and engagements, his amenity of manners and gentlemanly bearing, greatly contributed to establish, in that remote country, confidence and respect for the American people'.[33]

Shaw definitely noticed the potential power of opium in British strategies to control trade across a maritime zone stretching from India to China. He notes that the 'English derive considerable advantages' from the movement of the drug from India to China – advantages not just in regard to trade at Canton, but also in regard to leveraging control over markets through the straits between contemporary Indonesia and Malaysia.[34] British investment in opium developed despite the fact that China had declared opium 'contraband' and prohibited its admission 'to their ports, under any condition'.[35] Shaw estimated that two thousand chests were making their way into South China each year; by 1832 the estimates are nearly twenty-two thousand and, by 1839, on the eve of the First Opium War, more than forty thousand.[36] Shaw's observations on opium never materialise into Shaw's dealing in opium in the account Quincy gives of this reputable American trader.

Locking in on Shaw as a paradigm of personal integrity, Quincy also overlooked Belknap's motif of corporate form – a motif that would

---

33 Shaw, *Journals*, 128–29.
34 Shaw, *Journals*, 169.
35 Shaw, *Journals*, 238.
36 Carl A. Trocki, *Opium, Empire and the Global Political Economy: A Study of the Asian Opium Trade 1750–1950* (London: Routledge, 1999), 95.

4 Once Upon a Time in 1784: American Mercantile Biographies

come back into view in subsequent biographies that appreciated the rise of American merchants against the fall of the EIC. In the words of the eminent early twentieth-century trade historian Hosea Ballou Morse:

> The Americans were the 'free-traders' of the day, in the sense in which the word was then understood; in their country there were no privileged corporations to exercise any monopoly, trade was open to all on equal terms, and the merchants and sailors of Boston, Salem, and New York asked only a fair field and no favour.[37]

Over the course of his voyages Shaw became more sophisticated in his approach to the China trade, especially after seeing the EIC development of country trade between India and China. As Mira Wilkins notes, after Shaw's first voyage he started Shaw & Company in Canton to act 'on behalf of merchants who lacked familiarity with the East'.[38] *Pace* Sydney Smith, British manufacturers and private merchants had taken note of American success in criticising mercantilist policies. *Free trade* became a mantra of those advocating the repeal of corn tariffs that shielded landed aristocrats from market competition and of others seeking to revoke the EIC charter that locked private British merchants out of trade opportunity.

By the 1850s, the term 'free trade' took on even more implications as editors such as Freeman Hunt introduced new American heroes of the China trade in *Hunt's Merchants' Magazine and Commercial Review*. It went from embracing Quincy's presentation of Major Shaw's biography as evidence of national commercial integrity to using Shaw to foreshadow the success of American merchants. As articles that appear alongside these men's lives register, the controversy over opium trade threatened to disrupt the alignment of free trade with American success in China.

---

37 Hosea Ballou Morse, *The International Relations of the Chinese Empire* (1910–13), 3 vols (London: Longmans, Green, 1910–18) vol. 1, 87.
38 Mira Wilkins, 'The Impacts of American Multinational Enterprise on American-Chinese Economic Relations, 1786–1949', *America's China Trade in Historical Perspective*, eds. Ernest M. May and John King Fairbank (Cambridge, MA: Harvard University Press, 1986), 279–80 (260).

Thomas H. Perkins and the Mercantile Biography

Upon publication, Quincy's biography of Major Shaw fit perfectly in *Hunt's* because it provided a direct link back to the founding generation in promising a bright future for trade with China. In 1848, Charles H. Glover reviewed the biography for *Hunt's*, writing that 'Like most men of his time, [Shaw] acted various parts in the changing drama of life. In his youth, an active and gallant soldier; in his manhood, a sagacious and enterprising merchant'.[39] Shaw's image was featured as the frontispiece to the volume. However, by the 1850s, Hunt was celebrating a new China trader named Thomas H. Perkins. When the two-volume *Lives of Merchants* came out in the late 1850s, Perkins was featured first and Shaw was relegated to the middle of the second volume.[40]

Throughout his editorship, Freeman Hunt celebrated commerce as a nationally inspiring force through something he called the 'mercantile biography'. Whereas Sparks and Quincy represented the elite scholarly circle that Belknap had envisioned fostering in the 1780s, Hunt approached publishing as a business to make money on topics related to national and international commerce. Born outside Boston and raised by his mother in impoverished circumstances, he rose from delivering newspapers to publishing the popular Mrs. Hale's *Ladies' Magazine* before editing and directing the company that published the *American Magazine of Useful and Entertaining Knowledge*. In 1839, he became the influential editor of the eponymous New York-based *Hunt's*, which he edited until his death in 1858 just before the US Civil War.[41]

Hunt never attended university, but was well versed in the classical symbols of empire that pervade Belknap's *American Autobiography*. The image on the cover of *Hunt's* (Figure 3) adapts classical iconography to an era of Manifest Destiny in depicting national commerce as a connecting principle that joins the international high seas to the

---

39 Charles H. Glover, 'The Life of Major Samuel Shaw, the First American Consul at Canton (with a portrait)', *Hunt's Merchants' Magazine* 18:1 (January 1848), 31–42 (32).
40 *Lives of American Merchants* (1858), vol. 2, 201–22.
41 Frank Luther Mott, *A History of American Magazines*, 5 vols (Cambridge, MA: Harvard University Press, 1933–68), vol. 1, 696–98.

4 Once Upon a Time in 1784: American Mercantile Biographies

Figure 4.3 Cover page of Freeman Hunt's *The Merchant's Magazine and Commercial Review* (August 1839).

footholds of eastern coastal port cities and to the inland frontier of the continental hinterlands. The Roman God Neptune (protector of sailors) sits atop pillars that echo those of Hercules designating the known extent of the world during the Holy Roman Empire. But these columns no longer mark the classical bounds of empire at the Strait of Gibraltar. Rather they stand at a port opening to the westward expanse of the American 'plus ultra', marking a gateway for circulating traffic that flows out, through and into the nation. Neptune reclines on cargo crates and a ship funnel bellows smoke to power a steam vessel situated at the head of a line of sailing ships. His paredrae sit below, framed by the pillars. On the right is the goddess Venilia, patroness of homeward winds that push ocean waves towards the shore; she looks up to Neptune, holding a staff that is attached to a thread of yarn, suggesting that the flows of global commerce weave through plots of pastoral domesticity. On the left is Neptune's regal spouse, the goddess Salacia, holding a sextant and with an anchor leaning behind her. Her symbols imply outward-bound seafaring adventurers whom she protects as she looks down to survey a landscape of national industry connecting sea to harbour and to inland continental development. To complement this neoclassical iconography, *Hunt's* offered a compendium of articles addressing the legal, statistical, diplomatic, historical, practical and historical dimensions of commerce.

The 'Introduction' to the first issue links development of the continental Far West to ongoing international commerce in a gale force of national commercial optimism. Hunt avers that 'commerce is now the most honorable pursuit in which a man of talent and enterprise can engage' and analogises trade to a new 'lever of Archimedes', with 'the intelligence, enterprise, and wealth of the merchants and bankers' as 'the fulcrum' that will 'move the world', as they 'determine the questions of peace or war, and decide the destinies of nations'.[42] He continues:

> Essentially and practically a trading people, the commerce of the United States has been pushed, by the enterprise of her citizens, to every part of the habitable globe – her ships penetrate every ocean, and her canvas whitens every sea, bringing home the varied productions of every soil and climate, and while rewarding individual enterprise and exertion, adding to the store house of general knowledge, and increasing the prosperity of the country.[43]

---

42 *Hunt's Merchants' Magazine*, July 1839, 2.

Hunt feminises the United States as the conventional motherland but swaps the terrestrial rhetoric of virgin land for that of a national maritime hive. The patriarchal frontier husband yields to the adventuring merchant, whose ships penetrate every ocean and whose commercial thrust 'whitens every sea'. The immense reach of the commercial activity – to the four quarters of the world – dilates the world-historical importance of national identity while concentrating ambition in nationally representative individual men. 'Enterprise' connotes democratic principles by motivating 'citizens' as individuals to seek wealth attained in a world market of ports. This individual wealth propels the westward movement of Manifest Destiny.

As Hunt established a broad classical perspective on commerce, he used biography to focus implications of national distinctiveness in new national patriarchs. The magazine regularly featured the 'mercantile biography' that Hunt described as follows:

> In devoting a portion of the Magazine to Mercantile Biography, we are influenced by a desire to exhibit the strong points of character which have distinguished the patriarchs of commerce, as furnishing examples to the young merchant of the present and future times, and as a stimulus to the attainment of the enviable distinction which they have acquired.[44]

Hunt's included a mercantile biography each month from 1839–41 and frequently thereafter for the next two decades. In paying respect to a national legacy of merchant patriarchs, Hunt hoped to inspire younger generations to heed practical advice as they looked to the stars of global commerce with self-reliant determination. He writes in July 1839: 'Wherever the minds of the young are to be formed, and an incentive given to those who, after the present busy actors in our crowded marts of commerce are removed, are to occupy their places, they will find us inspiriting them in their career, and doing all in our power to aid the incipient merchant in his high and honorable avocation.'[45] As with

---

43   *Hunt's Merchants' Magazine*, July 1839, 1.
44   *Hunt's*, vol. 2 (1840), 407.
45   *Hunt's Merchants' Magazine*, July 1839, 2.

Delaplaine, Hunt's sense of commercial character folded verbal descriptions into visual representation and from 1840 to 1859 expensive 'steel engraved frontispieces' set merchants before the reader on a 'semi-annual basis'.[46] The mercantile biography was a constant feature of Hunt's publication project. More than a decade later, in his Preface to a two-volume collection of biographical essays pulled from his magazine called *Lives of Merchants* (1856, 1858), he again personified commerce as the prime mover of national political cultural invention and development, asserting that 'Trade discovered America in the vessels of adventurers, seeking new channels to the old marts of India; trade planted the American colonies, and made them flourish, even in New England, say what we please about Plymouth Rock; our colonial growth was the growth of trade – revolution and independence were measures of trade and commercial legislation, although they undoubtedly involved the first principles of free government'.[47] Hunt thus extends Belknap's chronicle to credit commercial ambition with provoking the American Revolution and establishing a 'free government'.[48]

Over the decade from the First to the Second Opium War, Hunt changed the image of the China trader, presenting Thomas H. Perkins as the nation's new hero. *A Memoir of Thomas Handasyd Perkins: Containing Extracts from his Diaries and Letters, with an Appendix* (1856) appeared the year after Perkins died and the year before the Second Opium War started. The authorial editor was Perkins'

---

46 Mott, *History of American Magazines*, vol. 1, 697.
47 Freeman Hunt, 'Preface', *Lives of Merchants*, vol. 1 (1855), iv.
48 Hunt was not alone in using biography to tout the national wonders of commerce. In the 1830s, Washington Irving wrote up John Jacob Astor's attempts to territorialise the Northwest through the American Fur Company and Pacific Fur Company in *Astoria, Or Anecdotes of an Enterprize Beyond the Rocky Mountains* (1836; 1849). Concurrently the Philadelphia educator John Frost spent the final decade of his life editing biographies about diverse topics related to the US; his *Lives of American Merchants* (1844) includes a chapter on Stephen Girard taken from an article that first appeared in the April 1841 issue of *Hunt's Merchants' Magazine*. Later James Parton's *Life of John Jacob Astor* (1856) extended the treatment of Astor. On Irving, see Johnson, 'Caleb Cushing and the Corporate Romance of Free Trade Imperialism in Washington Irving's *Astoria* (1836)', *Literature Compass* 14:9 (September 2017), 1–11.

4 Once Upon a Time in 1784: American Mercantile Biographies

Figure 4.4 Frontispiece of Thomas G. Cary, *Memoir of Thomas Handasyd Perkins: Containing Extracts from His Diaries and Letters. With an Appendix* (Boston: Little, Brown and Company, 1856).

son-in-law and business partner Thomas G. Cary. *Hunt's* published Cary's shorter version as a mercantile biography in the July 1855 edition and this shorter account became the first and primary chapter of the first volume of Hunt's *Lives of Merchants* in 1856.[49] Both long and short versions follow the template of Quincy and Sparks, offering Perkins' live narrative up in a Franklinesque mode for young readers to emulate: 'Each day with him was the illustration of a thought which young men, and particularly young men entering on commercial life, will find to be a safeguard against precipitation or perplexity, and against the irritation as well as the miserable shifts to which they sometimes lead'.[50] In contrast to Shaw, the lesson Perkins offers is less about honesty and more about the determination to connect the West Indies to the East Indies through lines of credit emanating from the capitals of Europe in order to establish a fortune in Boston.

Perkins conveyed the full potential of American commerce because his companies had established a position in networks of trade that Shaw merely described. Perkins was a much younger contemporary of Shaw. He first ventured to China in the late 1780s, making it to Canton via Batavia to trade for teas just as the ship *Columbia* arrived from the Columbia River of Northwest America with a payload of pelts that yielded dramatic profits.[51] Inspired by the demand for fur in Canton, Perkins returned and persuaded his brothers to commit to the trade. At the time, the Perkins brothers were concentrating their business in Saint-Domingue but after the 'insurrection began', they reoriented their trade to Canton, incorporating James & Thomas Handasyd Perkins Company in Massachusetts as a vehicle of increasingly expansive trade speculation in East Asia.[52] In 1819, they opened a commissions house in Canton called J.P. Perkins, which Perkins renamed Perkins & Sons after the death of James in 1822. This company would eventually merge with Russell & Company in the early 1830s to form the largest and most successful American trading firm in China. Perkins' nephews

---

49   Thomas G. A. Cary, 'Mercantile Biography: Thomas Handasyd Perkins', *Hunt's Merchants' Magazine* 33:1 (July 1855), 19–52.
50   Cary in *Hunt's*, 44.
51   Cary, in *Hunt's*, 26.
52   Cary, in *Hunt's*, 27.

4 Once Upon a Time in 1784: American Mercantile Biographies

John Murray Forbes and Robert Bennet Forbes made fortunes working with Russell & Company. Today, Perkins is generally remembered as a pre-eminent early national philanthropist, terms that Cary established in the 1850s. Perkins' wealth enabled him to fund the Massachusetts General Hospital's Asylum for the Insane, the Boston Athenaeum, and the Perkins Institution for the Blind.[53] Perkins also invested in one of the nation's first railroads before the industry exploded westward with the application of steam technology.

Perkins developed strategies upon which Shaw had reflected in his journals of his voyages.[54] Whereas Quincy offered Major Shaw's diplomatic reputation to mark a beginning of China–US commercial relations, Hunt and Cary offered Perkins to evince the fruition of national commerce in a global network that linked frontier settlement to West Indies trade, to European financing, and to the China trade. In presenting Perkins, Cary revels in a sense of free-trade ambition enabled by state-chartered companies through which Perkins, his brothers and nephews co-ordinated ventures in vast international commercial networks emanating from Boston. In becoming a biographical character, Perkins personifies the corporate legal instruments that facilitated intergenerational familial partnerships across the world geography of markets. The waning relevance of Shaw's diplomatic reputation echoes in the article 'Commerce with China' published in the first year of the Opium War in 1840 that summarises the longstanding history of US trade with China without even mentioning Shaw. Hunt writes:

> Our American intercourse with China commenced soon after the revolutionary war; and since that time, our commerce in tea with the Chinese markets, especially from the port of Boston, has been the source of great national convenience, and has laid

---

53 Thomas G. Cary, *A Memoir of Thomas Handasyd Perkins: Containing Extracts from his Diaries and Letters, with an Appendix* (Boston: Little, Brown and Company, 1856), 219, 222, 223.
54 See Immanuel Wallerstein, *World-Systems Analysis: An Introduction* (Durham, NC: Duke University Press, 2004) and Frank 1998.

the foundation of splendid fortunes to several merchants in that section of the country.⁵⁵

Notice that, instead of highlighting Shaw's diplomatic example of honesty and determination, Hunt mentions those 'especially from the port of Boston' who had 'laid the foundation of splendid fortunes'.⁵⁶ With them in mind the article's 'general view of the present state and future prospects of the China trade', fixes on the 'termination of the India monopoly' that 'took place on the 22d April 1834'.⁵⁷ Thus, opportunities of the China trade are those that arose in a new type of 'country trade' that grew with the EIC's de facto diminishment. In this sense, American *free trade* conveyed the flexible and nimble dynamism of merchants who learned how to turn the lack of monopoly power into an advantage and profited from the nominal neutrality of the United States during the First Opium War.

Free Trade and the Opium Question in American Biography

Whereas Shaw, according to Quincy, approached the China trade with concern over how his commercial endeavours created a reputation for the United States, Perkins succeeded in making a fortune in part by putting moral concerns aside. It is striking that Perkins' biographer Cary never mentions the word opium, neither in book form nor in the shorter 'mercantile biography' that appeared in *Hunt's* and as the lead biography of *Lives of Merchants*. In euphemistic terms, Cary describes Perkins as collecting 'a fund of information concerning trade there [in Canton] in all its branches' while on his first trip to Canton in 1789.⁵⁸ He accounts for the Perkins brothers' 'rising fortunes' by crediting profits from 'consignments' that trace back to 'Col. Perkins's' first trip to China in 1789.⁵⁹

---

55   Freeman Hunt, 'Commerce of China', *Hunt's Merchants' Magazine* 2:12 (December 1840), 465–81 (466).
56   'Commerce of China', 466.
57   'Commerce of China', 466.
58   Cary, in *Hunt's*, 26.

4 Once Upon a Time in 1784: American Mercantile Biographies

Subsequent historians explain that Perkins' ability to establish profitable market positions depended on sourcing opium from Turkey and providing trans-shipment services to British traders who invested in Bengal markets related to the drug. In their 1971 biography *Merchant Prince of Boston*, Carl Seaburg and Stanley Paterson chart the escalating involvement of the Perkins brothers' companies in the opium trade, from their decision to go 'heavily' into the trade of opium from Turkey in 1815, to warehousing opium in ships anchored in island harbours at the mouth of the Pearl River, and to refining routes 'shuttling ships back and forth between Canton, Manila, and Batavia'.[60] One can speculate why Cary omitted mention of opium in 1855, but it was crucial to maintaining the impression that American merchant princes had extended the high reputation of Shaw's diplomatic service and distinguished themselves from British traders such as James Matheson (Jardine, Matheson & Co.) and Lancelot Dent (Dent & Co.), who built immense fortunes as they capitalised on their rights to trade opium with the devolution of the EIC.

The hyperbolic 'Introduction' to Hunt's *Lives of Merchants* illustrates the full extent to which Hunt and his collaborators went in order to avoid implicating Americans in the opium trade. It is written by George R. Russell, a China trader who had engaged in the opium trade as a partner in the American company Russell, Sturgis, & Co headquartered in Manila.[61] As a teenager, Russell accompanied his

---

59   Cary, in *Hunt's*, 35.
60   Carl Seaburg and Stanley Paterson, *Merchant Prince of Boston, Colonel T. H. Perkins, 1764–1854* (Cambridge, MA: Harvard University Press, 1971), 266, 285, 300–1, 314. Also see Jacques M. Downs, *The Golden Ghetto: The American Commercial Community at Canton and the Shaping of American China Policy, 1784–1844* (Bethlehem, PA: Lehigh University Press, 1997); Charles Stelle, 'American Trade in Opium to China, Prior to 1820', *Pacific Historical Review* 9:4 (December 1940), 425–44; and Timothy Mason Roberts, 'Commercial Philanthropy: ABCFM Missionaries and the American Opium Trade', in *The Role of the American Board in the World: Bicentennial Reflections on the Organization's Missionary Work 1810–2010*, eds. Clifford Putney and Paul T. Burlin (Eugene, OR: Wipf & Stock, 2012), 27–48.
61   For the biographical information on George R. Russell, see Freeman Hunt's Preface to *Lives of American Merchants* (New York: Derby and Jackson, 1858), vol. 1, vi; and Downs, *The Golden Ghetto*, 191.

diplomat father Jonathan Russell through Belgium, Holland and France during the War of 1812. He returned to the US and studied law at Brown University before turning to the China trade. After twelve years he retired at age thirty-five, returning to Boston where he married the daughter of Major Shaw's adopted nephew Robert G. Shaw. In 1849, Russell delivered Brown University's Phi Beta Kappa address that became the Introduction to *Lives of Merchants* in 1856.

Russell's essay rehearses, with some key differences, Belknap's *American Biography* in giving a celebratory account of world commerce that contrasts American commercial virtue to the EIC's heavy-handed promulgation of opium. On the one hand, Russell appreciates the de-commissioned EIC for having facilitated Britain's rise to world maritime commercial supremacy; on the other hand, he chastises the EIC for letting convenience override conscience in the pursuit of imperial power. Like Belknap, Russell offers an overview of commerce that cycles through stages of imperial influence, moving from Egypt, to the ancient states of Phoenicia and Carthage, to Greece and Rome. Activating a primitive sense of Christian faith, Russell considers the Crusades to the Holy Land, the rise of Venice, Genoa, Pisa and Florence after the fall of Constantinople, and the Hanseatic League as expressions of commerce. Unlike Belknap, Russell relegates Columbus and elevates the importance of Portuguese mariners who doubled the Cape of Good Hope. The Portuguese 'passage round the southern cape of Africa changed the whole course of commerce'.[62] And, 'from beyond the awful barriers of old existences, the colossal shadow':

> which had obscurely told of the coming of a young world, grew into glowing life, and as it beckoned to the old, offering more than fancy had pictured to hope, familiar things were disdainfully cast aside, and the quickened impulses of humanity turned to the new and distant revelation.[63]

---

62 George R. Russell, 'Introductory Essay', *Lives of American Merchants*, vol. 1, xxviii.
63 Russell, *Lives of American Merchants*, vol. 1, xxviii.

4 Once Upon a Time in 1784: American Mercantile Biographies

What followed was a sort of commercial renaissance in which 'the whole earth lay open to enterprise'.[64] In the three centuries that followed the voyages of Portugal and Spain, Europe 'covered America with [its] population' and 'extended civilized dominion over a large part of Asia'.[65]

The commercial exploits of Portugal and Spain 'awakened England' who 'developed the commercial power on which her greatness and success were founded'.[66] In narrating the inexorable forward march of commercial progress, Russell maintains a fatalistic tone as he acknowledges abuses of power, such as '[t]he subjugation of India, by a company of [British] merchants, who, from a dark and dingy street of London, set out decrees of life and death to kingdoms and princes, and built up an empire which shames the wonders of enchantment'.[67] Russell also singles out for criticism Britain's war with China in the First Opium War, characterising it as:

> a decided case where something could be made by hard knocks, and they were given with a vigor and profusion that confounded a people [the Chinese] unaccustomed to wholesale butchery, and to the curious contrivances by which Christians manage to get rid of each other. They concluded, therefore, to smoke opium. But their compliance did not preclude an ethical commentary on the purity of an operation, which increases the revenue of one nation by introducing beggary and idiocy to another.[68]

Russell does not condone such schemes of colonial domination or naked military aggression, but rationalises them as developmental points of reference in the larger scale of civilisation's historical advancement. As civilisation progresses, military aggression becomes less frequent and less harsh. Even as Britain stooped to conquer India and smuggle opium into China, she was attaining a higher state of ethical consciousness, demonstrated by the relative restraint towards

---

64 Russell, *Lives of American Merchants*, vol. 1, xxviii–xxix.
65 Russell, *Lives of American Merchants*, vol. 1, xxix.
66 Russell, *Lives of American Merchants*, vol. 1, xxxix.
67 Russell, *Lives of American Merchants*, vol. 1, xxix.
68 Russell, *Lives of American Merchants*, vol. 1, xxxi–xxxii.

the United States during the War of 1812. Russell writes that 'She [the United Kingdom] knew that the bombardment of New York or Boston would not advance her system of free trade, and that she could not make market for her productions by destroying or ill-treating the consumers'.[69] As further evidence of progress, Russell signposts the growing 'easiness of communication' and the 'great Continental Fairs' that add 'their salutary influence' in showcasing the 'intelligence of mercantile enterprise'.[70] Thus commerce is 'wearing away' the *prestige* of military life', creating the 'current of public feeling' that is 'utterly opposed to war for national aggrandizement'.[71]

In the wake of British world supremacy, the United States emerges as virtuously ambitious, typified by the self-reliant and determined energy of individual men born of a revolutionary spirit dedicated to the expansion of maritime routes. Russell's 'American merchant' is 'a type' that is 'restless, adventurous' and an 'onward going race and people'.[72] Folding land into sea and the Far West into the Far East, Russell declares that the 'commerce of our own people is coextensive with the globe': as the 'lakes of New England awaken to life of the rivers of the sultry east', 'the white canvas of the American ship glances in every nook of every ocean'.[73]

To take the edge off the likelihood that such commercial omnipresence implies US involvement in the opium trade, Russell celebrates China as the originator of commerce, prefacing Belknap's epic cycles of proto-European and European maritime discovery by delving into a pre-textual Chinese history that universalises commerce as a feature of human progress. Russell claims that the 'antiquity of the Chinese empire' evinces commerce as a fundamental energy of human history and that 'the history of commerce would give the history of that people; for the love of trade is so much part of their very natures, is so interwoven with their being, that it seems impossible there should ever have been a time when they did not traffic with

---

69 Russell, *Lives of American Merchants*, vol. 1, xxx–xxxi.
70 Russell, *Lives of American Merchants*, vol. 1, xxxvii.
71 Russell, *Lives of American Merchants*, vol. 1, xxxvii.
72 Russell, *Lives of American Merchants*, vol. 1, xxxviii.
73 Russell, *Lives of American Merchants*, vol. 1, xxxviii.

4 Once Upon a Time in 1784: American Mercantile Biographies

each other and with their neighbors'.[74] Russell goes on to idealise the Chinese people as fundamentally and trans-historically commercial: 'The Chinese trade competes with the European wherever the latter has founded settlements in the Eastern world. His sleepless diligence overcomes every obstacle, and his love of gain is not quenched by contumely and persecution. No sooner does he put his foot among strangers, than he begins to work'.[75] Most likely influenced by the Chinese traders in Manila and other port cities he had visited and the newly arriving Chinese labourers working on the transcontinental railway, Russell extols the Chinese for their honesty, their adaptability, and their durability of body and spirit.

Russell's admiration of China is double-edged. He marvels at their invention of gunpowder and the compass, declaring that when the 'modern nations were in a state of barbarism', China 'was advanced as she is now'.[76] On the one hand, the Chinese are a primary site of commercial determination, efficiency and innovation. However, Russell freezes them in an ancient frame before the emergence of a textually informed, progressive historical consciousness, epitomised by Herodotus, who 'makes no mention of China' because there are no written records that reach that far back in time.[77] Whereas modern nations in Europe and the Americas could track their progress by how far they had risen in relation to a pre-textual Middle Kingdom, modern China had become stuck in a rut of repetition.

Russell's Orientalist conceptualisation implies another sense in which American merchants styled themselves as heroes of free trade. On the one hand, merchants such as Perkins had survived the monopolist power of the EIC and shown the world the benefits of corporate competition unrestrained by centralised authority; on the other, they had endured the restrictive terms of China's Canton System with its putative monopoly of Cohong merchants. The terms of Russell's ambivalence are summed up in a curiously brief sentence that had appeared in *Hunt's* to mark the start of the First Opium War, a decade before Russell delivered

---

74 Russell, *Lives of American Merchants*, vol. 1, xii–xiii.
75 Russell, *Lives of American Merchants*, vol. 1, xiii.
76 Russell, *Lives of American Merchants*, vol. 1, xii.
77 Russell, *Lives of American Merchants*, vol. 1, xi.

his speech to the graduates of Brown University. The short editorial comment entitled 'The Opium Trade in China' reads:

> There probably was never since the existence of the world an exercise of despotic power, displayed in the promotion of a *moral* object, comparable to that recently exhibited by the Emperor of China, in the suppression of the opium trade within his dominion.[78]

The word 'despotic' in this melodramatic nugget harkens back to the revolutionary era to vilify the Qing enforcement of a ban on opium importation, while simultaneously acknowledging the moral justification of attempting to end the smuggling of opium. Accordingly, the Canton System was not about regulating trade, but arbitrarily restricting it. Its rules quarantined Western traders to a single area outside the southern port city of Guangzhou and required them to engage Cohong merchants as brokers for any trade. Some British merchants went so far as to claim that Britain's violent reaction to Qing enforcement of opium regulations was not only an appropriate but also an instructive reaction to barbaric China's rejection of free trade.[79]

Through the 1840s and 1850s, contributors to *Hunt's* debated the precise *moral* dimensions of the so-called 'opium question' alongside the frequent 'mercantile biographies'. The anti-opium China trader Charles King contributed the article 'Commerce as a Liberal Pursuit' (1840), first delivered as a lecture to Boston's Mercantile Library Association. His topical headings convey the importance of using commercial ambition to set a virtuous national example: 'Commerce is the Nurse and Companion of Freedom'; 'Commerce is the Civilizer and Refiner of Nations'; 'Commerce is Averse to Monopolies and Restrictions'; 'Commerce is the Herald of Religion'.[80] As a principle of morality, he invokes the New Testament: 'Wherever the interest and feelings of others are in question,

---

78 Freeman Hunt, 'The Opium Trade of China', *Hunt's Merchants' Magazine* 1:5 (October 1839), 362.

79 On free trade imperialism, see John Gallagher and Ronald Robinson, 'The Imperialism of Free Trade', *Economic History Review*, second series, 6:1 (1953), 1–15, and Bernard Semmel, *The Rise of Free Trade Imperialism: Classical Political Economy, the Empire of Free Trade and Imperialism, 1750–1850* (Cambridge: Cambridge University Press, 1970).

4 Once Upon a Time in 1784: American Mercantile Biographies

a reference to the brief, yet all embracing injunction, "do unto others as you would be done by," will be found to cover the whole ground of duty, and to present the all-sufficient rule of conduct".[81] Five months later, the New York lawyer E. W. Stoughton directly addressed the opium trade in an unflinching critique entitled 'The Opium Trade – England and China' (1840), writing:

> The belligerent attitude recently assumed by England towards China, has produced, and is still creating, consequences which must ere long end in the entire suspension, if not utter annihilation, of our valuable Chinese trade. In either case, the most ruinous results will fall heavily upon the interests of our wealthy and enterprising merchants, many of whom are largely engaged in it, and who are free from the slightest suspicion of having trafficked in the interdicted drug – a practice held in such abomination by the Chinese emperor.[82]

Stoughton accepts as reasonable that the Chinese emperor would attempt to enforce regulations prohibiting opium and then continues by condemning Britain's pursuit of war as more than a violation of Chinese sovereignty:

> A wholesale murder of weak and almost unresisting Chinese, has been perpetrated in their own waters, and within the exclusive jurisdiction of their maritime laws, by the armed ships of a foreign power, with whom peaceful relations had been maintained for a period of two hundred years.[83]

Stoughton concludes by yoking the future interests of American trade with China to the federal government's willingness to condemn British

---

80 Charles King, 'Commerce as a Liberal Pursuit', *Hunt's Merchants' Magazine* 2:1 (January 1840), 1–16 (3, 5, 6, 10).
81 King, 'Commerce as a Liberal Pursuit', 15.
82 E. W. Stoughton, 'The Opium Trade–England and China', *Hunt's Merchants' Magazine* 2:5 (May 1840), 386–405 (386).
83 Stoughton, *Hunt's* (May 1840), 404–5.

aggression. He notes that all '[t]he merchants of this [US] country are seriously affected by the great question here presented, and the protecting mantle of national strength should be thrown around their interests in the eastern world'; however, it is vital that 'the government of the United States' realise that it 'is bound by the most sacred obligations' to 'protest' against the British invasion of China and to decry such an 'unwarranted act of arbitrary power, committed in violation of the broad principles of eternal justice.[84] In the face of such severe condemnation, Russell's celebrations of commerce and Cary's refusal to mention opium make more sense. Meanwhile, another meaning of *free trade* cast a shadow through the pages of *Hunt's* in 'vexed questions of tariff and free-trade' relating to state rights that would lead to the US Civil War.[85]

Read through the filter of American mercantile biography, 1784 reflects a tangle of contradictions that troubles the phrase 'free trade' as biographers celebrated Major Shaw's diplomatic service in China after the First Opium War and rationalised the American merchant princes' willingness to engage in the opium trade in China on the verge of the Second. As for the significance of 1784 in China's relationship to global modernity, such contradictions seem more germane than the mere fact of the *Empress of China* arriving from New York with a payload of ginseng.

---

84 Stoughton, *Hunt's* (May 1840), 405.
85 Russell, *Lives of American Merchants*, vol. 1, xxxviii. For representative examples of the way in which sectional disputes regarding the efficacy of protectionism complicated the phrase 'free trade', see Russell, 'Introductory Essay', *Lives of American Merchants*, vol. 1, xxxviii; Horace Greeley's 'Commerce and Protection', *Hunt's Merchants' Magazine* 1:5 (November 1839), 413–18, and Samuel Beman's 'The Principles of Free Trade', *Hunt's Merchants' Magazine* 24:1 (January 1851), 53–59.

5
'What stories I shall have to tell!': Mediating China in the Writings of Charles Lamb and Thomas Manning
James Watt

The history of relations between Britain and China has often been narrated in terms of watershed events, and the Macartney embassy of 1793 has been accorded particular attention in this respect, constituting from the British perspective, as Peter Kitson has argued, a moment of national 'trauma' that in turn generated retaliatory denigration of a Chinese empire caricatured as wilfully ignorant of European modernity.[1] One shorthand way of illustrating what appears to be a significant cultural shift in British representations of China during the decades before and after the Macartney embassy is to juxtapose writings by Sir William Jones and Thomas De Quincey that compare Britain and China. The Orientalist scholar Jones presented his experience of being 'almost encircled by the vast regions of Asia' en route to India as stimulating his will-to-knowledge, and in his 'Seventh Anniversary Discourse' (1790) he referred to China as 'a celebrated and imperial land, bearing in arts and in arms ... a pre-eminence among Eastern kingdoms analogous to that of *Britain* among the nations of the west'.[2] Three decades later, by contrast, De Quincey responded to Jones by accentuating what he took to be the absolute difference of China, describing in his *Confessions of an English Opium-Eater* (1821)

---

1   Peter J. Kitson, *Forging Romantic China: Sino-British Cultural Exchange 1760–1840* (Cambridge: Cambridge University Press, 2013), 157.

a virtual encounter with the 'Asiatic' sublime that was at once terrifying and overpowering; if he were 'compelled to forego England, and to live in China, and among Chinese manners and modes of life and scenery', De Quincey wrote, he would 'go mad'.³

Critics have recently cautioned against assigning representative significance to De Quincey's opium nightmares, however, and Kitson and others have emphasised that the nature of Britons' imaginative engagement with China in the early nineteenth century extended beyond the anticipation of future conflict seemingly evident in De Quincey's work.⁴ With this point in mind, the present chapter will focus on the often frivolous writings of the Romantic essayist Charles Lamb and the sinologist Thomas Manning – the 'M' who Lamb's persona Elia refers to at the outset of 'A Dissertation Upon Roast Pig' (1822). While Lamb's exploration of broadly 'Chinese' subject matter has now been quite widely discussed, this chapter will resituate 'Old China' (1823) and 'A Dissertation Upon Roast Pig' in the context of Lamb's connection to Manning, as well as in relation to the scholarly example of Jones and the aggressive paranoia of De Quincey. Examining the letters exchanged by Lamb and Manning helps us to recognise that the two men could jokingly invoke the same received ideas about China (most notably where the practice of foot binding was concerned), but also that Manning – who, unlike Lamb, sometimes signalled a 'Jonesian' intellectual ambition – had his own stories to tell about China too. As I will show, Manning drew upon his experience of travel in Asia, as well as of working in the East India Company factory at Canton, in order to challenge any notion that China was somehow especially difficult for Europeans to apprehend. Albeit that Manning actually published very little, what he did write about China arguably invites us now to think about the lost possibilities of the decades between the Macartney

---

2   'Seventh Anniversary Discourse, on the Chinese, delivered 25th February 1790', in *The Works of Sir William Jones*, 13 vols (London: Stockdale, 1807), vol. 3, 137–61 (138).
3   Thomas De Quincey, *Confessions of an English Opium-Eater*, ed. Grevel Lindop (Oxford: Oxford World's Classics, 1985), 73.
4   Kitson, 240; see also Elizabeth Hope Chang, *Britain's Chinese Eye: Literature, Empire, and Aesthetics in Nineteenth-Century Britain* (Stanford: Stanford University Press, 2010).

embassy and the First Opium War (1839–42), during and after which British representations of China became increasingly and more consistently adversarial.

There are reasonable grounds for approaching Lamb's essay 'Old China' (first published in the *London Magazine*, like De Quincey's work) as a rewriting of De Quincey's response to Jones. It begins with a confession of sorts, as the narrator declares his 'almost feminine partiality for Old China', but in contrast to De Quincey's paranoid presentation of himself as the object of others' attention in 'The Pains of Opium' ('I was stared at, hooted at, grinned at, chattered at'), it sets up a stable spectatorial position from which the visual delights afforded by Chinese-style porcelain can be enjoyed.[5] It is unclear as to whether the 'china jars and saucers' referred to here are Chinese imports or British imitations, and for Elia, the relation of china the commodity to China the polity appears to be beside the point; his approach to China here chimes with that of Lamb himself to the explorer James Bruce's *Travels to Discover the Source of the Nile* (1790), which he viewed as a source of 'infinite delight' regardless of whether or not it told the truth.[6] Elia describes the scene that appears on an individual tea-cup in his possession as one in which 'little, lawless azure-tinctured grotesques, … under the notion of men and women, float about, uncircumscribed by any element', and his reference to this scene as 'a world before perspective' nicely captures the nature of the essay's engagement with a China of the imagination.[7]

Elia's description of Chinese figures ('old friends') who 'float about' offers an intriguing echo of a letter written by Samuel Taylor Coleridge to John Thelwall, in which he self-critically contrasted his attempts to 'raise and spiritualize my intellect' with the more relaxed strictures of the 'Brahman Creed' exemplified by the Hindu deity Vishnu, said 'to float about along an infinite ocean cradled in the flower of the Lotos,

---

5   Charles Lamb, 'Old China', in *Elia & The Last Essays of Elia*, ed. Jonathan Bate (Oxford: Oxford World's Classics, 1987), 281–86 (281); De Quincey, 73.
6   Lamb, 'Old China', 281; Kitson, 171; on Lamb and Bruce, see Nigel Leask, *Curiosity and the Aesthetics of Travel-Writing 1770–1840* (Oxford: Oxford University Press, 2002).
7   Lamb, 'Old China', 281.

and wake once in a million years for a few minutes'.[8] The benign 'world before perspective' that Lamb's persona imagines is broadly comparable to the domain of Vishnu invoked by Coleridge, and this suggestive phrase again invites us to see Lamb as responding to De Quincey, drawing attention to how Elia's vision of China is one where the relations of time and space that prove so disorientating to De Quincey are simply suspended, to amusing effect. These pleasures of the imagination may still manifest a 'condescension' towards China and the Chinese, as David Porter has argued, because even as the narrator is drawn to the appeal of 'pre-perspectival lawlessness', he provides Britons with an index of their own modernity: '[a]ccompanying such reflections, as lighthearted as they may be, is the comforting assurance that our own thoroughly rationalized, post-Renaissance visual world has advanced to the next level, and that we can recognize ourselves in this difference'.[9] Nonetheless, any concern with China, or with power relations between Britain and China, is at most oblique here, and Elia's references to porcelain come either side of a longer exchange that he has with his cousin Bridget about the change in household 'circumstances' which meant that they could sometimes 'afford to please the eye ... with trifles of this sort'.[10]

'Old China' may indeed be read as an essay with a predominantly domestic focus in which Lamb shows himself at his most irreverently Cockney. As Karen Fang has argued, 'Old China' parodies the elevated poetic register of Coleridge's 'Kubla Khan' (Elia's identification of the '*speciosa miracula*' figured on a set of china recalls Coleridge's description of Kubla Khan's pleasure-dome as a 'miracle of rare device'), and it also offers a jesting reminder of Coleridge's material debt to the manufacturers Thomas and Josiah Wedgwood, who had earlier supported his writing with an annuity.[11] The narrator states at the

---

8 Coleridge to John Thelwall, 14 October 1797, *Collected Letters of Samuel Taylor Coleridge*, ed. Earl Leslie Griggs, 6 vols (Oxford: Clarendon Press, 1956–71), vol. 1, 350.
9 David Porter, *The Chinese Taste in Eighteenth-Century England* (Cambridge: Cambridge University Press, 2010), 3.
10 Lamb, 'Old China', 282.
11 Karen Fang, *Romantic Writing and the Empire of Signs: Periodical Culture and Post-Romantic Authorship* (Charlottesville; University of Virginia Press, 2010), 53–57.

outset that '[w]hen I go to see any great house, I enquire for the china-closet, and next for the picture gallery', and for all that porcelain had long been a relatively inexpensive everyday object for people across the social spectrum, Elia here associates the Chinese taste with a leisured social elite and thus presents himself as performing an audacious act of Cockney connoisseurship. His use of a mock-heraldic idiom to describe a 'cow and rabbit couchant' on a piece of chinaware further represents an expression of the boundary-crossing aesthetic censured by *Blackwood's Edinburgh Magazine* in its series of articles on Leigh Hunt, Keats and 'The Cockney School of Poetry' (1817–25).[12]

Elia's account of his 'Chinese' reveries looks slightly different again, though, when it is read alongside Lamb's correspondence, in which he frequently presented his creative writing as a release from the demands of his daytime toil. Lamb began working as a clerk in the accountant's department at the Leadenhall Street headquarters of the East India Company (EIC) in 1792, and there are ways in which he might be regarded as a Cockney version of Sir William Jones, imagining literary composition just as Jones saw Orientalist research, as (in the latter's words) a 'relief' from 'severer employment in the discharge of publick duty'; Lamb, like Jones, seems to have conceived of a 'second self' that was not accountable to authority or responsible to other people.[13] Lamb's role at India House remained a relatively lowly one (he never sought promotion during his thirty-three-year career there), however, and unlike Jones or a more senior colleague such as Thomas Love Peacock, he did not claim to serve any larger imperial cause.[14] Instead, as in a letter to William Wordsworth in March 1822, contemporaneous with his first Elia essays, Lamb often associated paid work with a state of un-freedom: 'My theory is to enjoy life, but the practice is against it. I grow ominously tired of official confinement. Thirty years have I served the Philistines, and my neck is not subdued to the yoke. You don't know how wearisome it is to breathe the air of four pent walls without relief

---

12 Lamb, 'Old China', 281.
13 Jones to Samuel Davis, 21 September 1786, *The Letters of Sir William Jones*, ed. Garland Cannon, 2 vols (Oxford: Clarendon Press, 1970), vol. 2, 705.
14 H. V. Bowen, *The Business of Empire: The East India Company and Imperial Britain 1756–1833* (Cambridge: Cambridge University Press, 2006), 146.

day after day, all the golden hours of the day between 10 and 4 without ease or interposition'.¹⁵

While he was able to dismiss his superiors as uncultured 'Philistines', Lamb – unlike Jones – displayed no ambition to become better educated about the wider world, whether China or anywhere else. Through his correspondence with Thomas Manning, whom he first met in 1799, however, Lamb was certainly in a position to find out more about China, had he wanted to do so. One of the pre-eminent sinologists of the period, Manning might himself be assimilated to Jones, as another man of diverse talents in the EIC's employ; initially based in Canton, where he was a doctor in the English factory, Manning also spent time in Calcutta, from where he mounted an expedition to Tibet, and he later served as an interpreter on the Amherst embassy to Peking in 1816. Lamb had established a close bond with Manning by the time that the latter sailed for Canton in May 1806, and he likened his farewell to his friend to 'having shaken hands with a wretch on the fatal scaffold', although in a more playful mode he also asked him to bring back 'a sprightly little Mandarin' for the mantelpiece of the house that he shared with his sister Mary.¹⁶ Manning's response to the send-off he received from Lamb is worth quoting at length:

> I am not dead nor dying – some people go into Yorkshire for 4 years & never come to London all the while! I go to China. What's the difference to our London friends?
>
> I am persuaded I shall come back & see more of you than I have ever been able. Who knows but I may make a fortune & take you & Mary out a-riding in my Coach. There's nobody has a prior claim to you, you may depend upon it – of course you must leave room for my little Chinese wife, because poor pipsey's feet are so small she can't walk, you know!¹⁷

---

15 Lamb to William Wordsworth, 20 March 1822, in *The Works of Charles and Mary Lamb*, ed. E.V. Lucas, 7 vols (London: Methuen, 1905), vol. 7, *Letters 1821–1834*, 563.
16 Lamb to Thomas Manning, 10 May 1806, in *Works*, vol. 6, *Letters 1796–1820*, 348.
17 Manning to Lamb, 12 May 1806, in *The Letters of Thomas Manning to Charles Lamb*, ed. G. A. Anderson (London: Martin Secker, 1925), 95.

5 Mediating China in the Writings of Charles Lamb and Thomas Manning

This letter is particularly interesting because even as it indicates – most obviously via the nature of its allusion to the custom of foot binding – that Manning and Lamb shared a common bantering idiom, it also shows Manning gently challenging his friend's hyperbolical sense of the distance and strangeness of China. Lamb declared in another letter later that year, 'China – Canton – bless us – how it strains the imagination and makes it ache!', and Manning's subsequent letters to Lamb, like the letter cited above, sometimes appear intended to offer a kind of reassurance on this front, appealing to the sense of amusement about things Chinese that their addressee displayed when he requested a curio for his mantelpiece.[18] 'Ten to one but what you'll laugh when you see me again', Manning wrote to Lamb in November 1807; 'What stories I shall have to tell!', he promised a few months later.[19]

Lamb in turn frequently teased Manning, for example by asking him in March 1809 whether he liked 'the Mandarinesses' in China and was 'on some little footing with any of them', thereby carrying on the in-joke that Manning may have initiated with his reference to 'poor pipsey's feet'.[20] Lamb also kept on playing on the idea of the vast spatial distance between England and China, as in a letter that he wrote on Christmas Day 1815 in which he told Manning that while so much had happened in 'the western world' during his time away ('Empires have been overturned'), he had been wasting his time 'settling whether Ho-hing-tong should be spelt with a — or a — '.[21] David Higgins has suggested that Manning could himself be 'troubled by departure, alienation, and the crossing of boundaries', as seems to have been the case when he wrote to Lamb, prior to his leaving Calcutta for 'God knows where!' (actually Tibet) in October 1810, that, feeling '[v]ery strange in mind', he was about to travel 'out of the bounds of civilization'.[22] If Manning here described his predicament in a language

---

18 Lamb to Manning, 5 December 1806, in *Works*, vol. 6, 364.
19 Manning to Lamb, 20 November 1807 and 3 March 1808, in *Letters*, 102, 106.
20 Lamb to Manning, 28 March 1809, in *Works*, vol. 6, 397. Lamb's fixation on the bound foot is evident again in a letter to Mr and Mrs J. D. Collier, 6 January 1823, in which referring to 'a dear pigmy pig' he had just had a share in eating, he states, 'His little foots would have gone into the silver slipper. I take him to have been Chinese, and a female', *Works*, vol. 7, 192.
21 Lamb to Manning, 25 December 1815, in *Works*, vol. 6, 481.

that may have been congenial to Lamb, however, in an earlier letter, sent from Canton in April 1807, he rejected any assumption that distance from Britain was necessarily productive of disorientation. After telling his unidentified addressee to imagine him 'sitting alone in a room at the very extremity of the earth', Manning accentuated his experience of social isolation in an alien environment, '[s]urrounded … by people whose thoughts, actions, dress and affections have nothing in common with Europe', only then to add: 'you are not to suppose me unhappy, quite the contrary. I have not undertaken what is beyond my strength'.[23]

While we can only speculate about Manning's state of mind when he wrote the letters from Calcutta and Canton cited above, reading them alongside each other does at least demonstrate something of the range of registers that he employed in his correspondence. If there are ways in which Lamb might be regarded as a Cockney Sir William Jones, as I have suggested, the idiom of Manning's letter describing his life in Canton appears to be 'Jonesian' in a more straightforward manner. Like Jones during his sea-voyage to India, Manning emphasised that a situation which might have been overpowering for others actually inspired in him a sense of determination and resolve: whereas De Quincey was to declare that 'if I were compelled to live in China … , I should go mad', Manning seems to have relished the challenges that his new life presented.[24] Manning's high estimation of his own capacities is evident again in his journal of his journey to Lhasa. En route to Tibet, for example, Manning saw the possibility of 'opening a commercial intercourse between the Chinese and English through Bhutan', but also bemoaned the lack of opportunity that he had to facilitate this, complaining that the EIC ('Fools, fools, fools … !') had given him 'no commission, no authority, no instructions'.[25] Although the phrase

---

22 David Higgins, *Romantic Englishness: Local, National, and Global Selves, 1780–1830* (Basingstoke: Palgrave Macmillan, 2014), 147; Manning to Lamb, 11 October 1810, in *Letters*, 114.
23 Manning to Mr W[?], 24 April 1807, London, Royal Asiatic Society, MS TM/5/4. Thanks to Ed Weech for this reference.
24 De Quincey, 73.
25 *Narratives of the Mission of George Bogle to Tibet, and of the Journey of Thomas Manning to Lhasa*, ed. Clements Robert Markham (London: Trübner, 1879), 218.

5 Mediating China in the Writings of Charles Lamb and Thomas Manning

is a ubiquitous one, Manning's reference to 'commercial intercourse' appears consistent with the usage of the Scottish Enlightenment historian William Robertson, who, in his *Historical Disquisition Concerning the Knowledge which the Ancients had of India* (1791), sought to distinguish between the peaceful, equalising agency of commerce and the actual record of the EIC.[26] This understanding of commerce is implicit in Manning's claim that just as '[t]he Bhutanese lord it over their Hindu subjects', so, in Tibet, '[t]he Chinese lord it … like the English in India'; Manning here 'equat[es]' the Qing with the British as comparable imperial formations', in Kitson's words, while also, by presenting the Chinese as 'like the English', suggesting that the EIC constitutes the primary example of such overweening power.[27]

Manning described the object of his planned expedition to China via Tibet as 'a moral view of China; its manners; the actual degree of happiness the people enjoy', stating that he wanted to identify 'what there might be in China worthy to serve as a model for imitation, and what to serve as a beacon to avoid'.[28] Manning failed to gain permission to enter China at this time, however, and Kitson presents him as 'the man who might have been', emphasising the gulf between his ambition and ability on the one hand and his 'profound absence of published writing' on the other.[29] His more productive fellow sinologist John Francis Davis (who also accompanied Amherst in 1816) claimed that Manning was 'seldom serious' and 'did everything in his odd and eccentric way', and Manning's journal notably shifts between moments of political reflection of the kind considered above and seemingly frivolous anecdotes that remind us of Manning's earlier promise to Lamb that he would have 'stories … to tell' about his exploits.[30] Referring to the period he spent in Lhasa, for example, Manning described how, in the presence of a 'Tatar mandarin', he 'for the first time … , performed the ceremony of *ketese*' – a reference to the

---

26 See Stewart J. Brown, 'William Robertson, Early Orientalism and the *Historical Disquisition* on India of 1791', *The Scottish Historical Review*, 88 (2009), 289–312.
27 Markham, *Narratives*, 217; Kitson, 177.
28 Markham, *Narratives*, 280.
29 Kitson, 176.
30 Markham, *Narratives*, clx.

'kowtow' which came to assume such symbolic weight in the aftermath of the Macartney embassy.[31] He suggested here that his compliance with ceremonial convention was calculated to impress local officialdom (and thus improve his chances of gaining access to China), but he also indicated the pleasure with which he played the part, stating that 'if there was an option between one *ketese* and three, I generally chose to give three', and adding that he 'knelt down' before 'Tibet mandarins' as well, even though his Chinese servant 'wished this mark of respect to be paid only to Chinamen'.[32] Manning apparently wore Chinese dress (and sported an extravagant beard) when he did eventually manage to enter China as a member of the Amherst embassy, and in his journal he emphasised his ability to adapt to new environments, which he contrasted with the example of his cloth-coated countrymen in India.[33]

Although it is impossible to recover how Manning transmitted his experience of China and elsewhere after his return to England in 1819, it seems fair to say at least that he lived up to his promise of having 'stories ... to tell'. In a letter to Lamb in May 1819, for example, Manning – now established among the 'country folk' of rural Hertfordshire – presented himself as a figure whose past travels accorded him a privileged status in his new social circle: 'they all, here, think me prodigious learned'.[34] Manning's subsequent claim that 'they declare ... that I understand all the Languages in the World!' nicely captures both his enjoyment of his mediatory role and his sense of the limited knowledge, and perhaps impressionability, of his audience.[35] This letter is especially interesting for the purposes of the present chapter because it additionally demonstrates the endurance of Manning's bantering relationship with Lamb, and at the same time hints at the genesis of Lamb's essay 'A Dissertation Upon Roast Pig' (1822). After listing some of the differences between the pleasures of life in London and the country ('You cannot frame a notion of *our* delights. *You* delight in Elections; we in a Horsefair'), Manning's letter comes

---

31 Markham, *Narratives*, 258.
32 Markham, *Narratives*, 259.
33 Markham, *Narratives*, 228–29.
34 Manning to Lamb, 30 May 1819, in *Letters*, 124.
35 Manning to Lamb, 30 May 1819, in *Letters*, 125.

to the 'grosser delights' that are likewise beyond the imagining of his addressee: 'what can be more delightful than killing a pig?', he asks.[36] Manning here juxtaposes the 'benefits [that] accrue from the death of that stubborn ill-manner'd animal!' and 'the cry of a pig' during the process of slaughter, adding that 'One would think to hear him one was doing a mischief instead of a service!'[37]

The second half of 'A Dissertation Upon Roast Pig' plays on this idea of humans 'doing ... a service' to the pigs that they kill for their meat, suggesting that roasting a pig 'of tender age' actually saves it from itself: 'wouldst thou have had this innocent grow up to the grossness and indocility which too often accompany maturer swinehood?'[38] The essay acknowledges Manning in its opening sentence, when Elia tells of how the 'great lubberly boy' Bo-bo accidentally set fire to the wooden shed in which his father's herd of pigs was housed and thereafter, when he 'applied' his burnt fingers to his mouth, became the first person in the world to taste the delights of 'burnt pig': prior to Bo-bo's discovery, the narrator states, with reference to 'a Chinese manuscript, which my friend M. was obliging enough to read and explain to me', '[m]ankind ... for the first seventy thousand ages ate their meat raw, clawing or biting it from the living animal, just as they do in Abyssinia to this day'.[39] 'A Dissertation Upon Roast Pig' might thus be read as a continuation of the jokey exchanges about Chinese customs and manners sometimes evident in the correspondence between Lamb and Manning before and after the latter's arrival in Canton; that Elia's reference to how 'Confucius ... designates a kind of golden age by the term Cho-fang, literally the Cook's holiday' suggests that he may have drawn upon Manning's linguistic expertise in the composition of the essay.[40] Its tale of Bo-bo's potentially lucrative discovery alludes to the story of Aladdin (which has 'an ostensible Chinese setting' in Galland's

---

36   Manning to Lamb, 30 May 1819, in *Letters*, 120, 122.
37   Manning to Lamb, 30 May 1819, in *Letters*, 122.
38   Lamb, 'A Dissertation Upon Roast Pig', in *Elia & The Last Essays of Elia*, 137–44 (141).
39   Lamb, 'A Dissertation Upon Roast Pig', 137, 138.
40   Lamb, 'A Dissertation Upon Roast Pig', 137; Karen Fang notes that '"Cho-fang" is another Elian pun. The term is likely a transliteration of *chī fàn*, which means "to eat" in Chinese', Fang, 196 n. 48.

translation of *The Arabian Nights*), and it clearly enjoys the substantial creative licence afforded by ideas of China and Chinese antiquity.[41]

The mock-Orientalism of the essay's opening remains potentially compatible with an intellectually serious approach to China ('a moral view') of the kind that Manning had earlier presented as his goal; if we see Manning as a figure possessed of 'Jonesian' ambition, it is relevant to note that, as in the poem 'The Enchanted Fruit' (1784), his brilliant precursor sometimes offered a parodic distance on his own scholarly enterprise.[42] When Lamb's essay is read as a post-Amherst (as well as post-Macartney) text, and as a work that, like 'Old China', responds to De Quincey's *Confessions*, however, it appears a little less playful, exhibiting a casual derisiveness about China in excess of that which is evident in Manning and Lamb's exoticising references to foot binding. Elia's account of Bo-bo's 'slow understanding' of the effects of fire, for example, obliquely reflects upon the history of China, and the meaning of Chinese antiquity, more broadly.[43] After Bo-bo chanced upon the delights of roast pig, the narrator states, the Chinese deliberately burnt down their houses to achieve the same results, until 'a sage arose, like our Locke, who made a discovery, that the flesh of swine … might be cooked … without the necessity of consuming a whole house to dress it'; following this development of 'the rude form of a gridiron', we are told, '[r]oasting by the string, or spit, came in a century or two later'.[44] The figure of 'our Locke' is contrasted here with 'their great Confucius', said to have memorialised the 'seventy thousand ages' in which the Chinese 'ate their meat raw', and this hailing of Locke as a benchmark of 'improvement' clearly defines Britons' dynamic example against the apparent slowness of the Chinese to embrace technological innovation.[45] For all that it gives more space to the comic detail of Bo-bo's revelation than to any larger conclusions that might be drawn from it, the essay thus anticipates later writings – for example Dickens'

---

41   Kitson, 229.
42   Kate Teltscher, *India Inscribed: European and British Writing on India 1600–1800* (Delhi: Oxford University Press, 1995), 216–18.
43   Lamb, 'A Dissertation Upon Roast Pig', 138.
44   Lamb, 'A Dissertation Upon Roast Pig', 140.
45   Lamb, 'A Dissertation Upon Roast Pig', 137.

5 Mediating China in the Writings of Charles Lamb and Thomas Manning

'The Great Exhibition and the Little One' (1851) – that recast Chinese exceptionalism as an unaccountably eccentric defiance of the spirit of 'progress'.[46] 'A Dissertation Upon Roast Pig' in turn counters De Quincey's anxious apprehension of the 'Asiatic' sublime, since whereas De Quincey imagines a 'young Chinese' as 'an antediluvian man renewed' ('the vast age of the race and name overpowers the sense of youth in the individual'), Elia appears to purge Chinese antiquity of any threat that it might pose, such that he describes the cottage that Bo-bo burns down as 'a sorry antediluvian make-shift of a building'.[47]

After noting that 'the string, or spit' eventually replaced 'the rude form of a gridiron', the narrator airily exclaims 'I forget in whose dynasty'.[48] Together with the essay's crediting of Confucius with the authorship of a philosophical work titled 'Mundane Mutations', this seemingly insouciant display of ignorance and lack of interest might additionally be read as a comic debunking of De Quinceyan anxieties about the sublime antiquity of China.[49] Karen Fang goes further to present 'A Dissertation Upon Roast Pig' as a text that travesties the history of Chinese civilisation in order to make an implicit claim about 'British imperial destiny'. In Fang's reading the essay is marked not by the memory of unsuccessful diplomatic missions but rather by the EIC's annexation of Singapore in 1819 and the 'confident sense of … economic superiority' that this helped to facilitate.[50] Fang argues that the tale of Bo-bo's burning of his father's cottage allegorises the history of porcelain manufacture, and she contends that the role in this history of 'a sage … like our Locke' serves to foreshadow 'the imminent triumph of British domestic porcelain manufacturers' who were about to supply the EIC's Canton factory with their own version of blue and white chinaware, intended for export to Chinese consumers.[51]

---

46 Charles Dickens with R. H. Horne, 'The Great Exhibition and the Little One', in Charles Dickens' *Uncollected Writings from Household Words 1850-1859*, ed. Harry Stone, (London: Allen Lane, 1969) 319-29 (320).
47 De Quincey, 73; Lamb, 'A Dissertation Upon Roast Pig', 138.
48 Lamb, 'A Dissertation Upon Roast Pig', 140.
49 Lamb, 'A Dissertation Upon Roast Pig', 137.
50 Fang, 62.
51 Fang, 63.

Fang also acknowledges the importance of opium as 'the new commodity within British and Chinese trade' that would re-orient trading relations – and go on to generate a series of conflicts – between Britain and China. If 'A Dissertation Upon Roast Pig' anticipates the consequences of the opium trade in its 'depiction of addled Chinese consumers and the social degradation their consumption depicts', as Fang suggests, however, its staging of 'imperial destiny' and a shifting balance of power between Britain and China is less clear cut than she claims.[52] This is partly at least because of the way in which, after concluding the supposedly manuscript-derived tale of Bo-bo, the narrator so candidly returns to his own experience as an epicurean: 'if a worthy pretext for so dangerous an experiment as setting houses on fire … could be assigned in favour of any culinary object', he states, 'that pretext and excuse might be found in ROAST PIG'.[53] Elia shows himself to be no less of a glutton than Bo-bo, and as Felicity James has argued, his account of his appetite reveals 'the cruelties even apparently civilized society can contemplate in the pursuit of its own pleasure' – most notably, for example, when he poses (but does not answer) the question of whether whipping a pig to death would be justified if it 'superadded a pleasure upon the palate of a man more intense than any possible suffering we can conceive in the animal'.[54] As much as the essay can be read (like 'Old China') as a satirical riposte to De Quincey, then, its allusion to opium and the opium trade via its story about the irresistibility of roast pig invites us to read it as in its own way an addiction narrative.[55]

In his correspondence especially, Lamb can additionally be seen to display his own idiosyncratic 'anxieties of empire': Lamb here constructs what David Higgins refers to as 'an obsessively localized sense of self that is uneasy to the point of morbidity in its apprehension of the exotic'.[56] In the letter to Manning in which he stated that the idea

---

52 Fang, 62.
53 Lamb, 'A Dissertation Upon Roast Pig', 140.
54 Felicity James, 'Thomas Manning, Charles Lamb, and Oriental Encounters', *Poetica* 76 (2011), 21–38 (32). I am very grateful to the author for sending me a copy of her essay.
55 Fang, 62–64.
56 Higgins, 130.

of China 'strains the imagination', for example, Lamb questioned if the Great Wall of China actually existed, and if so whether it was 'as big as London Wall by Bedlam'; this comparison between the Great Wall and a remnant of Roman fortifications in London constitutes a seemingly less playful act of miniaturisation than that performed in 'Old China'.[57]

Lamb's 'unease' about the wider world and the pressure it exerted on his sense of self is particularly evident in his accounts of his working life and of the business of the EIC. Whereas the 'pre-perspectival' world of 'Old China' may simultaneously be regarded as pre-lapsarian by virtue of its being 'lawless' and 'uncircumscribed', Lamb's correspondence often presents commercial modernity and global trade as consequent upon the Fall of humankind.[58] In a letter to William and Dorothy Wordsworth in September 1805, Lamb referred to 'business' as 'the invention of the Old Teazer who persuaded Adam's Master to give him an apron and set him houghing', before adding that 'Pen & Ink & Clerks, and desks, were the refinements of this old torturer a thousand years after under pretence of Commerce allying distant shores, promoting and diffusing knowledge, good & c. –'.[59] Writing to Wordsworth a decade later, Lamb similarly drew attention to the gulf between the theory that commerce united the peoples of the world in peaceful and mutually beneficial interrelationship and his actual experience as a functionary of the EIC:

> I 'engross', when I should pen paragraph. Confusion blast all mercantile transactions, all traffick, exchange of commodities, intercourse between nations, all the consequent civilization and wealth and amity and link of society, and getting rid of prejudices, and knowledge of the face of the globe …[60]

---

57 Lamb to Manning, 5 December 1806, in *Works*, vol. 6, 368.
58 Lamb, 'Old China', 281.
59 Lamb to William and Dorothy Wordsworth, 28 September 1805, in *Works*, vol. 6, 317.
60 Lamb to William Wordsworth, 28 April 1815, in *Works*, vol. 6, 463. Lamb may have helped to record among other things the illegal trade by which EIC merchants exchanged Indian opium for Chinese tea, then imported to Britain.

Lamb denounced the EIC as 'the Scarlet what-do-you-call-her of Babylon' in a letter to Dorothy Wordsworth in February 1818, and although the immediate occasion for this expression of outrage was the loss of a customary right (going home early on Saturdays), his invocation of 'Babylon' here also calls up other contemporary accounts of a Britain irredeemably corrupted by its empire.[61]

In view of Lamb's attack on his superiors at India House as 'Beasts', 'Liberty takers' and 'tyrants', it is interesting to recall Manning's rather different claim that the EIC were 'Fools, fools, fools' for not making use of his talents to effect 'a commercial intercourse between the Chinese and English through Bhutan'.[62] The idea of 'commercial intercourse' cannot be regarded in straightforwardly benign terms, needless to say, and as the EIC in later decades sought to protect its lucrative export of Indian opium to China the imperative of free trade would come to be mobilised against China's defence of its own interests: in his 1857 essay 'Hints Towards an Appreciation of the Coming of the War in China' (written at the beginning of the Second Opium War), for example, De Quincey argued that China was not 'free to dissolve her connections' with Britain by banning the import of opium from India.[63] To return to Manning's reference to 'the English' as 'lording it' in India, however, it seems reasonable to suggest that Manning may have been critical of the way in which the EIC betrayed its origins as a trading corporation to assume sovereign power in India and to assert its authority elsewhere. In identifying a potential 'commercial intercourse between the Chinese and English', indeed, Manning appears to have invoked precisely the idealised – and essentially eighteenth-century – understanding of global commerce ('intercourse between nations') that Lamb derisively rehearsed in his correspondence with the Wordsworths.[64]

To conclude this chapter I want to say more about areas of divergence as well as of common ground between Manning and Lamb,

---

61   Lamb to Dorothy Wordsworth, 18 February 1818, in *Works*, vol. 6, 513.
62   Lamb to Dorothy Wordsworth, 18 February 1818, in *Works*, vol. 6, 513; Markham, *Narratives*, 218.
63   Thomas De Quincey, 'Hints Towards an Appreciation of the Coming of the War in China', *Titan* 25 (1857), 65–74 (70); Dickens refers to 'England, maintaining commercial intercourse with the whole world', and to China's attempt to thwart this, in 'The Great Exhibition and the Little One', 322.

by briefly referring to the series of 'Chinese Jests' that Manning published in the *New Monthly Magazine* in 1826. The idea of 'Chinese jests' recalls Manning's correspondence with Lamb, in which both men sometimes approached Chinese customs and manners, in particular the customary practice of foot binding, as a subject that was ripe for comic treatment. Manning also contextualised the various anecdotes that he presented, however, initially declaring that '[a]mong all the lighter productions of a literary people, there is no thing from which we can with such certainty gather their real opinions, humours, habitual feelings, and popular manners, as from a current jest-book'.[65] To some extent, therefore, Manning redefined the idea of the 'Chinese jest' by suggesting that, as slight as they appeared to be, the anecdotes he compiled offered a perspective on Chinese mentalities that was more intimate than – and at least as enlightening as – any that was provided by a more scholarly source; in a footnote he referred to the French Jesuit historian du Halde's work on China as 'accurate' but also 'unreadable'.[66] Manning said nothing about the process of fieldwork that must have been involved in his collection of his materials, but in stating that 'no people in the world can know the private practices of the Chinese so well as the Chinese themselves', he emphasised that any insight into Chinese ways of thinking had to be underpinned by linguistic proficiency as well as by travel and cultural encounter.[67]

The most common butt of Manning's Chinese jests is the figure of the incompetent – though also self-important and self-serving – doctor, as illustrated by the following vignette:

> 21. A fagot-man, carrying a load, by accident brushed against a doctor. The doctor was very angry, and was going to beat him with his fist. 'Pray, don't use your precious hand, good sir; -- kick me and welcome'. The standers-by asked what he meant. Says the

---

64   Markham, *Narratives*, 218; the ur-statement of this understanding of global commerce is Joseph Addison's description of the Royal Exchange in *Spectator* no. 69 (1711).
65   Manning, 'Chinese Jests', *New Monthly Magazine and Literary Journal* 11 (1826) 280–84; 386–92; 573–75 (280).
66   Manning, 'Chinese Jests', 386.
67   Manning, 'Chinese Jests', 282.

woodman, 'Kick me with his foot and I shall recover: once come under his hands, and 'tis all over with me'.[68]

Six of the forty jests published by Manning relate to doctors (others refer to bonzes, magistrates and mandarins), and an anecdote such as this could perhaps be read as presenting the apparent charlatanry of Chinese medical professionals as an index of a wider social backwardness. It is worth noting nonetheless that a comparably irreverent treatment of doctors in Britain is evident in the contemporary work of Thomas Hood (another friend of Lamb), who wrote a number of poems exploring the murky relationship between anatomists or surgeons and the infamous body-snatchers Burke and Hare.[69] Reading Manning's jest about the 'fagot-man' alongside Lamb's 'A Dissertation Upon Roast Pig', moreover, throws into relief the significance of what it does not say. If, as a seller of firewood, the fagot-man can be seen as a figure with an indirect connection to the combustible 'Chinese' world of Lamb's essay, the brevity of Manning's jest allows for no comic embellishment of the kind provided by Lamb. Whereas the name of Lamb's Bo-bo underscores his status as 'village idiot' and then allows for a slippage to the adjective 'booby', which describes the manner in which he 'applied' his burnt fingers to his mouth, Manning's fagot-man is unnamed and un-individuated.[70] The nature of his interaction with the doctor – addressing him as 'good sir' and inviting physical retribution for the offence of touching him – demonstrates a conspicuously sly civility, and his subsequent indictment of all Chinese doctors stages an inventive wit and a suspicion of social elites that at least some readers would probably have found congenial.

It is tempting, therefore, to regard Manning's 'Chinese Jests' as both a tribute to Lamb and an implicitly critical response to 'A Dissertation Upon Roast Pig'. If, on the one hand, Manning's collection of anecdotes approaches China under the sign of comedy just as Lamb's essays do, on the other it tellingly refuses some of the moves that Lamb's writing

---

68 Manning, 'Chinese Jests', 389.
69 See for example 'The Dead Robbery'.
70 Fang, 61; Lamb, 'A Dissertation Upon Roast Pig', 138.

makes to play the subject of Chinese customs and manners for laughs. Manning's 'Chinese Jests' might be seen indeed to effect a reconciliation of the frivolity with which he was associated by contemporaries and his own desideratum of taking 'a moral view of China', at least to the extent that these vignettes of quotidian social life are presented as illuminating the 'popular feeling' of the Chinese.[71] While Manning himself remains something of an enigmatic figure, in part because he published so little, it is significant that the China he represents in 'Chinese Jests' is not particularly mysterious or even exotic. Just as Manning challenged Lamb's sense of the strangeness of China in the letters that he wrote from Canton, so he emphatically rejected any idea of an essential Chinese inscrutability of the kind that is evident in De Quincey's opium nightmares, and which would harden as the century progressed. From his early correspondence with Lamb through to his 'Chinese Jests', Manning seems to have defined himself as a raconteur, as John Francis Davis recognised when he referred to him as 'seldom serious'.[72] As I hope to have shown here, focusing on Manning's relationship with Lamb, as well as on his more indirect engagement with De Quincey, helps us to think about how, certainly in the period prior to the First Opium War, there were 'stories ... to tell' about China other than those that were premised on antagonism and the expectation of future conflict.

---

71 Manning, 'Chinese Jests', 280.
72 Markham, *Narratives*, clx.

6
Global Contacts of Canton in the Qing Dynasty: A Discussion of Export Painting

Yinghe Jiang

Canton Port, located on the southern coastal area of China, has a long maritime history. It has been an important port city for the Chinese to interact with the outer world. Historically, Canton (now called Guangzhou) was the trade port for Chinese and foreign goods and the production base of exports. In Canton, generations of superb craftsmen serviced overseas markets, and the city has been deeply merged in the history of global development. Since the sixteenth century, there has been direct trading between the East and the West seasonally at Canton, particularly after the Canton System was implemented in the middle of the eighteenth century during the reign of the Qianlong Emperor of Manchu Qing. Canton then became the production base of many new exports with typical Western characteristics, as a number of new industries began here. Of these industries, export painting or trade painting became a complex global industry, with works destined for the European and American markets. As they were produced for Western markets, few traces remain in China; however, the creation of these paintings and the career development of their painters profoundly influenced the globalisation of Canton Port.

Canton Export Paintings and Their Creation During the Qing Dynasty

Under the Foreign Management System of the Qing Dynasty for the supervision of foreigners' actions and residency at Canton (known as the Canton System), foreigners were not allowed to leave the foreign factories during the trade season. They were only allowed to visit Hoi Tong Monastery on Honan Island and Faa Dei twice a month, where they had to be accompanied by a Chinese Hong merchant and the number of visitors was restricted. Thus, foreigners were limited strictly in terms of the places they could go. They could only stay in the Thirteen Factories, which were located on the banks of the Pearl River outside the city. The houses they lived in and warehouses they used were called 'foreign factories' by the Chinese. Tong Wen Street and Jing Yuan Street near the foreign factories, known as New China Street and Old China Street by foreigners, had many shops providing goods and services for Westerners who could visit and buy things. The American captain Samuel Shaw, of the *Empress of China*, wrote in his journal during his first voyage to Canton that 'the restrictions on European people were extremely strict, apart from the square, only some nearby streets were open to them, and these streets were occupied with shops'.[1] These shops sold all kinds of export products, as William Hunter, the American merchant who traded in Canton in 1830s–40s, wrote in his journal, 'the articles offered were of the most diversified kind, and these shops were the objective of all sailors, as in fact, there was no other kind of resort for them'.[2]

Since the mid-eighteenth century, references to new craftsmen and new products appeared in the journals of foreign visitors as these crafts became a source of fascination during their stay in Canton. William Hickey, a British man who came to Canton in 1768 for commercial purposes, wrote in his journal about the various shops and craftsmen to be found around the Thirteen Factories of Canton, noting that 'there

---

1 John Goldsmith Philips, *China Trade Porcelain* (Cambridge, MA: Harvard University Press, 1956), 14.
2 William C. Hunter, *Bits of Old China* (London: Kegan Paul, Trench, & Co., 1885), 5.

were glass painters, fan makers, ivory craftsmen, lacquer makers, jewellery makers, and many other craftsmen'.[3] John Pope, another British visitor who was in Canton in 1786, wrote about the China Streets when he was there:

> this is generally a morning walk. China Street, the only one that deserves the name of a street, is about 30 feet broad and a quarter mile long, inhabited totally by shopkeepers who deal wholly with Europeans, chiefly silk merchants, china shops, fan makers, lacquer ware and printers and such like. I have bought for you some paintings on paper, one set containing 113 paintings exhibiting all the different trades in China.[4]

M. La Vollée, a Frenchman who was in Canton in 1837, wrote about a special group of painters he encountered: 'Lamqua was the best painter in Canton, a Chinese painter. This central empire's painter was not Rubens ... China, in particular Canton, had several painters with long braids: Lamqua, Tingqua, Yinqua, and some other Quas, their paintings were popular among Chinese, and the amateurs from Europe'.[5] Through his comments, we can see the fact that, in the mid-nineteenth century, Canton Port already had a large number of professional painters who painted according to the needs of the Western market.

Osmond Tiffany, who came to Canton in 1840 from America, also wrote about a group of craftsmen around the Thirteen Factories: 'there were Ahning, Mahning, Wingshing (sculptors), Howqua (shop owners or Cohong), Luequa (considered as painters), Hipqua (lacquer makers), GonQua (ivory sculptors), and forty other businessmen'.[6] A great number of export watercolours were sold in Europe and America

---

3 Quoted in M. Jourdain and R. S. Jenyns, *Chinese Export Art in the Eighteenth Century* (London: Fletcher & Son, 1950), 12.
4 Quoted in Paul A. Van Dyke and Maria Kar-wing Mok, *Images of the Canton Factories 1760–1822, Reading History in Art* (Hong Kong: Hong Kong University Press, 2015), 87.
5 Albert Ten Eyck Gardner, 'Cantonese Chinnerys: Portraits of How-qua and Other China Trade Paintings', *The Art Quarterly* 16 (Winter 1953): 316.
6 Osmond Tiffany Jr, *The Canton Chinese or the American Sojourn in the Celestial Empire* (Boston and Cambridge: J. Munroe, 1849), 68–69.

and there are a great number of Canton export paintings in popular collections featuring works from the eighteenth and nineteenth centuries.

Western art influenced Canton through commerce, as William Langdon pointed out in 1843, writing 'the Fine Arts in China are undoubtedly far from the perfection that belongs to them in the enlightened nations of Christendom ... In paintings for foreigners, they endeavour to meet the ideas of their employers, by the introduction of light and shadow'.[7] Similar comments on those painters and their works were made by S. Wells Williams, an American missionary in Canton in 1848. Wells wrote that:

> the paintings obtained at Canton may, some of them, seem to disprove these opinions of the mediocrity attained by the artists of the country, but the productions of the copyists in that city are not the proper criteria of native uneducated art. Some of them have had so much practice in copying foreign productions that it has begun to correct their own notions of designing. These constitute, however, a very small proportion of the whole, and have had no effect on national taste.[8]

From such observations, it is clear that from the eighteenth century to the mid-nineteenth century, Canton had professional export painters who acquired Western skills to paint new artworks unique in China. Huang Shijian praised the historical value of export painters after analysing the export paintings collected in Peabody Essex Museum in the United States, arguing that 'a complete Chinese art history should contain folk Arts, including export paintings. Both the trade importing Western art works in and the communications it brought should be included ... Canton executed foreign paintings for more than a hundred years and it is worth further study, so that China and the West never skip this important page in the book of cultural communication between the East and the West'.[9]

---

7   Quoted in Craig Clunas, *Chinese Export Watercolours* (London: Victoria & Albert Museum, Far Eastern Series, 1984), 96–7.
8   Quoted in Clunas, *Chinese Export Watercolours*, 97.

6 Global Contacts of Canton in the Qing Dynasty

The export painters' humble social status limited their influence on Chinese traditional society, and the different taste between Western and Chinese fine arts also had the same limitation. Mainstream Chinese society paid little attention to those painters in Canton who painted for the 番鬼 'Fankwaes' or 'foreign devils', and their works were not included in traditional mainstream exhibitions. As art historian Craig Clunas has written, 'In Chinese terms they were artisans and not artists, players and not gentlemen. Beyond the pale socially, their craft was also beneath the notion of Chinese writers'.[10]

Since the export painters' individuality was suppressed by the guild system, their paintings were called 'guild paintings', thus it is difficult to conduct individual studies that identify the artists' personal styles and development. Export painting was a new industry, and the painters were a group of Chinese learning to paint for a Western clientele in a style completely alien to them. Both the painters and their works possess strong commercial appeal, and they are branded with Canton Port characteristics. Their creations, in a hybrid style combining Chinese and Western cultural traits, constituted the first reaction of the Chinese to Western paintings. These paintings show the transfer of different aspects of civilisation between the East and the West, revealing a neglected aspect of globalisation. The following analysis of export paintings illustrates the extent of this exchange.

---

9   Huang Shijian and William Sargent, eds, *Customs and Conditions of Chinese City Streets in 19th century, 360 Professions in China*, The Collection of Peabody Essex Museum, America (Shanghai: Shanghai Classics Publishing House, 1999), 10.
10 Clunas, *Chinese Export Watercolours*, 73.

Figure 6.1 Chinese artist, *Portrait of Mrs and Miss Revell in a Chinese Interior*, about 1780. Reverse painting on glass, 46.673 x 40.958 cm. Purchased with funds donated anonymously, 2000. AE85763. Courtesy of Peabody Essex Museum. Photo by Mark Sexton and Jeffrey Dykes.

6 Global Contacts of Canton in the Qing Dynasty

Europe's Chinese Taste in the Eighteenth Century: Portrait of Mrs and Miss Revell in a Chinese Interior

This Chinese reverse glass painting is now hanging near the entrance of the Asian Export Art Department at Peabody Essex Museum, Salem, Massachusetts, in the United States, and is astonishingly attractive. According to the museum, it was painted on a piece of glass in 1774. Utilising Western painting techniques, the work portrays two European ladies in Chinese costumes. Interestingly, Mrs Revell, the lady in the blue Han costume, is portrayed wearing lotus shoes for bound feet, while her daughter, Miss Revell, is wearing a piece of red cheongsam, and her feet are not bound. Both of them are seated at a table, on which writing brushes, vases and other items are portrayed. The setting is depicted in typical Chinese style, and the ladies are surrounded by plants, such as pine trees, bamboos, peony and lychees, which are a Lingnan speciality. Three pheasants are playing and, in the background, scenes of the shore are painted which echo the view of the Pearl River at Canton Port. This painting typifies the style, combining Chinese and Western genres in terms of form and content. According to documents from the British East India Company, the two ladies in the painting are the wife and eldest daughter of Henry Revell, an employee of the China Civil Service of Britain.[11]

The East India Company regularly traded with China. Along with the tea and porcelain going to Britain, the officials and employees of the East India Company also purchased a considerable number of goods from private traders, including various new artworks and souvenirs. This elegant painting of Mrs and Miss Revell is one such work, typifying the Chinese trend in eighteenth-century Europe.

---

11 David Howard and John Ayers, *China for the West, Chinese Porcelain & Decorative Arts for export illustrated from the Mattahdeh Collection, 1978*, (London: Sotheby Parke Bernet, 1978) 648–49.

King George III's View of Canton

Recently, an exquisite painting in the King's Topographical Collection of the British Library has been published.[12] This aquatint depicts the scenery along the Pearl River, and it shows the prosperous shores of the Pearl River and city views during the reign of the Qianlong Emperor. It has been described as Canton's equivalent of the painting 'Going up the river during the Qingming Festival' by the Chinese artist Zhang Zeduan.[13] Zhao Yi, who had been a magistrate in Canton in the reign of Qianlong, recalled the city scene in his later years, writing that 'Miles of the Pearl River was by rouge painted red; the river flows with all the prosperity of the city of Canton'.[14] Cai Hongsheng at Sun Yat-sen University has suggested this painting be named 'View of a Prosperous Canton' because the features of a port city and a trade centre are emphasised.

It was originally in the collection of King George III, entering the collection before 1824. According to Peter Barber, Head of the Map Collection in the British Library, it may have been presented to King George III by George Staunton (1737–1801) in 1796, after the Macartney mission returned to England. Another possibility, which seems more likely, is that George III sent someone to bid for the painting at the Christie's auction of the Chinese export paintings of Andreas Everadus van Braam Houckgeest (1739–1801) in 1799.[15]

The painting begins in the west side of Canton city, at the Yellow Sands of the upper reaches of the Pearl River west of Canton city, and the West Gate Battery (also called 'West Battery') at Willow Wave Harbour, and ends at Dashatou and East Water Battery (also known as East

---

12 Andrew Lo, Song Jiayu, Wang Tzi-cheng, Frances Wood, eds, *Chinese Export Paintings of the Qing Period in the British Library* (Guangdong: People's Publishing House, 2011).
13 Zhang Zeduan (张择端 1085–1145), Chinese famous painter in North Song Dynasty.
14 Zhao Yi, 'Memories of my Official Career' (追忆宦游陈迹杂记以诗), in *Ou Bei Ji* (《瓯北集》) (Shanghai: Shanghai Classic Publishing House), 4.
15 Andrew Lo, Song Jiayu, Wang Tzi-cheng, Frances Wood, eds, *Chinese Export Paintings of the Qing Period in the British Library* (Guangdong: People's Publishing House, 2011), vol. 1, 9.

6 Global Contacts of Canton in the Qing Dynasty

Battery) to the east of Canton city, downstream from the Pearl River. The painting depicts the harbour of Canton, the city of Canton, and the scenery along this section of the shore and Pearl River. In the painting, there are small and large piers, and over two hundred buildings, including various types of official and private residences, religious buildings, and Chinese and Western buildings. There are four to five hundred boats of various types, moored or going about their journeys, and six to seven hundred figures on the shore or on the boats and ships. The painting is a lively and realistic representation of the flourishing commercial port of Canton, stretching eight to nine kilometres along the riverside, around two hundred and fifty years ago.[16]

This kind of export painting is typical in its combination of Chinese and Western techniques. The painter has chosen the traditional Chinese horizontal scroll format. In this way, the painting combines Chinese cavalier perspective (also known as shifting perspective) and Western-focused perspective. The centre of the painting depicts the Thirteen Factories outside Canton city, then it extends horizontally from east to west; all the scenes on and off shore are portrayed in bird's-eye view. In order to show clear details of the river scenery, cavalier perspective is applied. This strategy avoids the weakness of focused perspective in which the near view would be too large and the far view too small for clear details. Hence, a unique effect is created by the combination of two contrasting painting techniques.

From the middle of the eighteenth century, export painters in Canton gradually started to paint the scenes of Canton Port. There are three main forms: single painting, combined painting (consisting of several painting segments), and long scroll painting, which is particularly rare. This work at the British Library is thought to be the earliest, largest and most exquisite work. Today, it is priceless in terms of both historical and cultural value. For economic colonisers of the seventeenth and eighteenth century, these paintings provide a crucial opportunity for collecting information and cultural examination.

---

16 Lo et al., *Chinese Export Paintings*, 9.

Tribute and Trade

Figure 6.2 *View of Canton* (detail), 1780s, aquatint, 920 x 74 cm, 075041, The King's Topographical Collection of the British Library, United Kingdom. Courtesy of the British Library.

The Memory of Western Countries' Voyage: Scenery of the Port

Mariners often asked local painters to paint the scenery of the port on their arrival as a way of commemorating their voyage and sharing it with their family and friends. Port scenery is undoubtedly a crucial part of Canton export painting, and it was said in Canton that 'No Englishmen goes back to Britain without a painting of Canton port scenery'.[17] Scenes of Canton Port are mostly depicted in oil and watercolour. The scene most frequently portrayed is that of the Thirteen Factories along the Pearl River outside Canton city, with other themes including the shore scenes of the Pearl River, Whampoa, Bocca Tigris and Macao. The Thirteen Factories outside the city were the only areas where Westerners were legally allowed to live and trade, thus the buildings were of distinctly Western appearance, making it a conspicuous cultural landscape. Ye Zhanyan from Qiantang in Zhejiang Province once travelled to Canton and the landscape left a deep impression on him. In his poem 'Notes when Travelling in Canton' (广州杂咏), he wrote:

> It is the west part along the river at Thirteen Factories where
> Foreign buildings of fine walls and portiere made of rhinoceros stood,

---

17   Albert Ten Eyck Gardner, 'Cantonese Chinnerys: Portraits of How-qua and Other China Trade Paintings', *The Art Quarterly* 16 (Winter 1953): 318.

6 Global Contacts of Canton in the Qing Dynasty

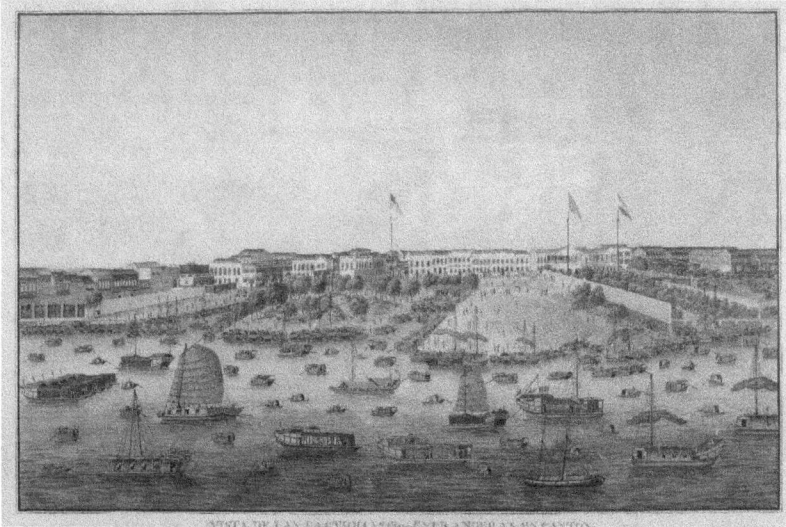

Figure 6.3 Anonymous Painter of Canton, Painting of the Foreign Factories, c.1825, Gouache on paper, 50 x 76 cm, Courtesy of Guang Dong Provincial Museum, Guangzhou, China. Photo by Liu Guzi.

> Painted flags waved in the wind and painted the sky colourful,
> Amongst which it is even hard to distinguish Japanese flag from Liuqiu's.[18]

From the mid-eighteenth century to the nineteenth century, many export paintings portraying the Canton Port and the Thirteen Factories were created by a succession of different painters and studios. These paintings record the changes undergone by the factories along the Pearl River at Canton Port and are therefore invaluable images documenting the history and development of the area.

---

18 Huang Foyi, ed., *Guangzhou City Annuals* (Guangdong: People's Publishing House, 1994), 621.

Figure 6.4 Painting of the Foreign Factories by You Qua or his Studio, Oil on canvas, c.1855, 65 x 111 cm, Courtesy of Guangdong Provincial Museum, Guangzhou, China. Photo by Liu Guzi.

Whampoa, the main anchorage for Western merchant seamen, was painted by many Westerners. On 4 January 1812, British traveller James Wathen wrote in his journal that:

> Here we had views peculiar to this wonderful country. It was from hence we saw rivers and canals, all navigable, intersecting the country, carry craft of all descriptions loaded with merchandize ... Beautiful pagodas, and superb residences of Mandarins, rose in the plain, among villages and groves. As far as the sight could discern, every open spot was cultivated with the utmost care, even to the tops of the hills and mountains. Towards the rivers and the sea, the view was not less interesting. The English and American ships at anchor; the Chinese junks, tea-boats, beautiful passage-boats, almost concealing the water in some places by their numbers, moving to and fro; the village of Whampoa, a fine expanse of country behind it, and gigantic mountains in the distance, exhibited a scene not to be parallelled in any other

country in the world. So various and so interesting did the surrounding objects appear to me, that I determined to attempt a panorama of them; and for that purpose, I fixed upon the next day to make my essay.[19]

The next day, this European did indeed bring a complete set of drawing tools and paint the panorama of Whampoa at the peak of Changzhou Mountain. As this extract demonstrates, Whampoa was attractive to Westerners, so its scenery, along with that of the tower of Pazhou, the water canals, the anchorage, the dock, even the ships anchored further away, all became subjects of export paintings.

Occasionally, the scenes of Canton Port were painted and sold in sets. Before 1840, a common set of Canton Port scenes consisted of four paintings, portraying the landscapes of Bocca Tigris, Whampoa, Macao and Canton. In 1800, Sullivan Dorr from Providence, Rhode Island, in the United States bought a set of four paintings and mailed them to his brother. This set, which Sullivan Dorr mentioned in a letter to his brother on 14 January 1800, is a typical depiction of Canton Port, with the four paintings giving detailed images of what Western merchants could see before the Opium War. The areas depicted include:

1. The Portuguese territory of Macao, which was the place along the coastal areas where Westerners left their first footprint when they reached China. It was also where they resided and stayed throughout the winter season;
2. Bocca Tigris, a crucial entrance to the Pearl River;
3. Whampoa Port, which offered anchorage for merchant vessels from the West; and, finally,
4. Canton, the Western merchants' final destination and trading zone.

Apart from common riverscapes of Canton Port, vistas of other Chinese port cities – for example, Xiamen, Sanya, Fuzhou, and later on Shanghai and Hong Kong – are all found in those port scenery paintings. As well as these, landscapes of South-East Asia, India, South Africa and even Brazil in South America are also depicted. All these

---

19   James Wathen, *Journal of a Voyage in 1811 and 1812 to Madras and China* (London: J. Nichols, Son, and Bentley, 1814), 180–81.

places had port cities that were either necessary for vessels sailing to Canton from Western Europe, or important West European colonies that had trade connections with Canton. Westerners brought depictions of their voyages with them and asked the export painters to replicate them.

The Peabody Essex Museum, for example, holds what Carl Crossman calls 'a set of four superb miniature paintings on brass of Whampoa, Jamestown (St Helena), Cape Town, South Africa, and Canton'.[20] A matching view of Cape Town, another view of Jamestown, and a view of Macao, also painted on brass, are also in the Peabody Essex Museum. 'A set of five ports, including two most unusual views of Penang and Singapore, together with three Chinese ports which have been assembled with them, are in a private collection.'[21] According to Crossman, two superb paintings are exhibited which are said to be painted in gouache and clearly signed by Sunqua. Both are views of Penang – *View of Mt Erskine & Pulo Ticoose Bay, Prince of Wales Isles* and *View of Strawberry Hill* – and 'both are based on the William Daniel hand-coloured aquatints of 1818'.[22] There are even views of Rio de Janeiro in Brazil in Canton export paintings.[23]

The Earliest Western-style Painting of the Human Body: *La Grande Odalisque*

In 1814, French painter Jean-Auguste Dominique Ingres painted *La Grande Odalisque*. In Canton, export painter Lamqua did an excellent reverse replication of *La Grande Odalisque* according to a customer's request. He then confidently signed the left bottom of the oil painting in both Chinese and English. Replications were the main form of export painting, and Lamqua possessed the engraved works of several British

---

20 Carl Crossman, *The Decorative Arts of the China Trade* (Suffolk: The Antique Collector's Club Ltd, 1991), 113.
21 Crossman, *The Decorative Arts*, 113.
22 Crossman, *The Decorative Arts*, 170.
23 Jose Roberto Teixeira Laite, 'Sunqua and Landscape of Rio de Janeiro by Chinese Painter', *Culture Review* (Chinese version) Macao (Spring 1995): 54–60.

artists, including those by portraitist Sir Thomas Lawrence. According to Osmond Tiffany, 'the walls in his [Lamqua's] Studio are decorated with his own copies of English paintings'.[24]

However, the replication of a beautiful naked woman was truly an astonishing artwork in China at that time. When the first group of Chinese ministers had been dispatched to Europe and America in the late nineteenth century, they visited Western galleries and passed by the works depicting nudes with their hands covering their eyes, finding the nudes pornographic.[25] At the beginning of the twentieth century, famous Chinese painter Liu Haisu was advocating for nude art in Shanghai, but one hundred years earlier Canton export painters had already overcome the obstacles between Eastern and Western conceptions of art and replicated such a tremendous representation of the human body. Lamqua's *La Grande Odalisque* indicates that Canton Port was at the frontier of Chinese and Western cultural exchange. Similar Western works replicated by Canton export painters include *Leda and the Swan*, and those that use Cupid and Venus as themes. Those paintings all depict beautiful and plump females in a Western style.

Forms of Port Culture: Canton Export Painters Facing the World

The modern world was created by trade. The trade connection not only united different places around the globe to form global networks out of regional ones, but also shaped the living habits and economic systems of different people. The port cities are key frontiers in this network; while expanding connections, they are the first to experiment with new trends and goods and their history reflects aspects of the world's history.

Existing studies of the history of Canton, covering the period from its connections with the Arabic world in the Tang and Song dynasties to its interactions with the West in the Ming and Qing dynasties, mainly focus on issues in the history of important people and of things relevant

---

24 Osmond Tiffany, Jr., *The Cantonese Chinese or the American's Sojourn in the Celestial Empire* (Boston: James Munroe and Company, 1849), 85.
25 Yinghe Jiang, *Western Painting and Canton Port during the Qing Period* (Beijing: Zhonghua Book Company, 2007), 111.

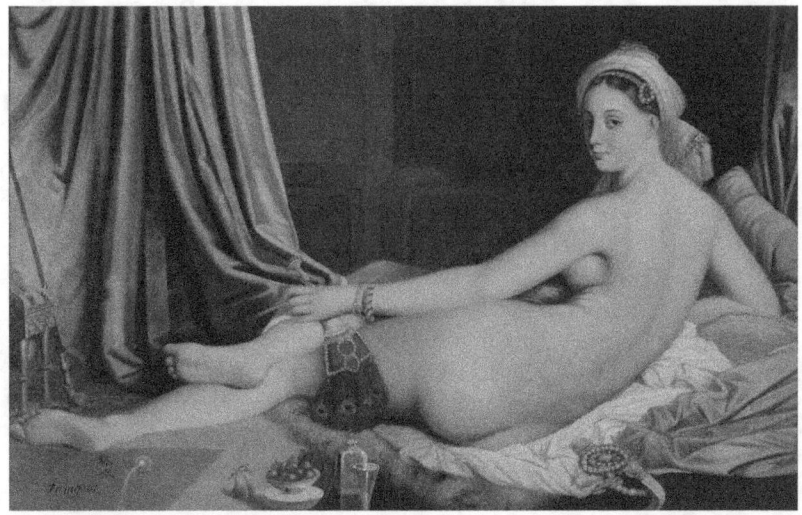

Figure 6.5 Lamqua, *La Grande Odalisque*, after 1826. Oil on canvas, 28.734 x 45.403 cm. Purchased in part with funds donated by the Asian Export Art Committee and The Meserve Fund, 2010. 2010.28.1. Courtesy of Peabody Essex Museum. Photograph by Bob Packert.

to the trade system itself. These studies have produced research examining customs officers, foreign and Chinese merchants, missionaries, and the trade, cultural and diplomatic connections relating closely to them. However, the existence of export painters in Canton in the eighteenth and nineteenth centuries compels us to look at the history of Canton from a new perspective. Their history constantly reminds us that, in order to comprehend the culture of Canton as a trade port connecting various civilisations, one fact should not be overlooked: people of different classes in this society all participated in this global phenomenon. Social historians have shown that 'the general public are the sacrifice and silent witness of history, but they are also the active subject of history'; thus, it is crucial to discover 'the lively history of the people without history: the primitives, farmers, labourers, immigrants and minorities who are conquered by others'.[26]

6 Global Contacts of Canton in the Qing Dynasty

Although history leaves us few records, through the limited number of documents we do have, and through exquisite paintings and cultural relics, we can reconstruct the interaction between China and the rest of the world. Those who were 'employed by Westerners' at Canton included not only the interpreters, compradors and pilots working for foreign merchants and ships, but also hundreds of coolies and various craftsmen offering products and services. They were marginalised in China, but they were the first and the most willing group of people to interact with foreigners and the outer world. Some of them mastered foreign languages and skills that were not accessible to common Chinese people. Despite the fact that they are not well known, they indeed brought changes to the material and spiritual culture of Chinese society. They promoted new thoughts and invited new technologies, thereby building a new world and making Canton a distinguished port city in developing new industries that were unimaginable to the inland cities.

After his studies of port cities such as Canton in China, Nagasaki in Japan and Batavia in Indonesia, Leonard Blussé named such cities 'windows of opportunity'.[27] Along with the direct interaction between East and West, these 'windows of opportunity' became the first area in the East to access Western civilisation. In China, Western civilisation first arrived at Canton and then spread to the south-eastern coast. Western culture captured the attention of various social levels and elicited different reactions; it certainly influenced the lives of common people. In traditional Chinese society, spirits and materials are clearly differentiated. Literati and bureaucrats, as representatives of authority and tradition, might learn about Western technologies or even receive foreign applicants out of curiosity. However, they were not likely to accept them, being strongly influenced by authoritative concepts that emphasised loyalty to one's native culture. Common people, like rural workers and merchants, experienced far less of a spiritual or ethical

---

26 Eric Wolf, *Europe and the People without History* (Chinese Version) (Shanghai: People's Publishing House, 2006), 2.
27 Leonard Blussé, *Visible Cities: Canton, Nagasaki, and Batavia and the Coming of the Americans* (Cambridge, MA: Harvard University Press, 2008; Chinese trans. Hangzhou: Zhejiang University Press, 2010), 1.

burden when facing Western civilisation, and they therefore showed less rejection, their options mainly based on needs and practical benefits. As Sang Bing pointed out, '[T]hose who get access to and accept Western culture first are not the enlightened gentry who acknowledged Western art and learning, but common people who lived in the coastal areas where foreign merchants and missionaries could reach. Before opium and cannons, foreign goods and religion are the two keys of Westerners for opening the door of China'.[28]

The export paintings examined in this essay were all painted in Canton in the eighteenth and nineteenth centuries and typify Canton export paintings during the Qing Dynasty. Each and every one reflects the intriguing history of foreign trade and cultural communication, combining the hard work and innovation of numerous craftsmen and indicating that Canton was more than just a trade port facing the outer world. More importantly, the hybrid culture shaped by Chinese and Western interaction made Canton a veritable melting pot of cultural exchange.

---

28 Sang Bing, 'Cultural Stratification and the Beginning of Western Learning to the East', *Journal of Sun Yat-sen University Social Science Edition* 1 (1991): 52.

7
'A desperate traffic': John Francis Davis, China, the Opium Trade and First Opium War

Peter Kitson

The case of Sir John Francis Davis' troubled involvement with the British opium trade to China is a vexed one. This essay is an attempt to outline and hopefully disentangle some of the contradictions, personal as well as governmental, that surrounded the much-disputed trade in this most ambiguous of commodities, both medicine and poison, taking as a case study Sir John Francis Davis, sinologist and diplomat. Born in 1795, Davis was the son of Samuel Davis (1760–1819), magistrate for Benares and later a director of the East India Company.[1]

---

1 K. D. Reynolds, 'Davis, Sir John Francis, first baronet (1795–1890)', in *The Oxford Dictionary of National Biography*, https://doi-org.nls.idm.oclc.org/10.1093/ref:odnb/7287 (23 September 2004). For diplomacy, trade, and commerce, see W. C. Costin, *Great Britain and China: 1833–1860* (Oxford: Clarendon Press, 1937); Nathan A. Pelcovits, *Old China Hands and the Foreign Office* (New York: King's Crown Press, 1948); Frederic Wakeman, Jr, *Strangers at the Gate: Social Disorder in South China, 1839–1861* (Berkeley and Los Angeles: University of California Press, 1966); John K. Fairbank, *Trade and Diplomacy on the China Coast: The Opening of the Treaty Ports 1842–1854* (Cambridge, MA: Harvard University Press, 1969), 108–9; 110–11; Priscilla Napier, *Barbarian Eye: Lord Napier in China, 1834, the Prelude to Hong Kong* (London: Brasseys, 1995); Peter J. Kitson, 'The Dark Gift: Opium, John Francis Davis, Thomas De Quincey and the Amherst Embassy to China of 1816', in *Writing China: Essays on the Amherst Embassy (1816) and Sino-British Cultural Relations*, eds Peter J. Kitson and Robert

In 1813, John Francis was appointed to the lucrative post of writer or clerk in the East India Company factory at Canton at the age of eighteen, where his talent for languages was quickly noted by the Company's translator, the missionary Robert Morrison, of whom he became a star pupil.² Davis was able to master Chinese relatively quickly, becoming proficient enough to serve as an interpreter, with Morrison and others, on Lord Amherst's embassy to Beijing in 1816, the second royal embassy to reach the Chinese capital. He became a fellow of the Royal Society in 1821 and also a key member of the Royal Asiatic Society, founded by George Thomas Staunton in 1823, where his scholarly papers on Chinese literature were read. He was also a member of the Oriental Translation Committee that funded the publication of several of his translations. His scholarly study of

---

Markley (Cambridge: D.S. Brewer, 2016), 56–82; Will Peyton, 'John Francis Davis as governor and diplomat on the China Coast' (1844–1848)' *The International History Review* 39 (2017), 903–26; Gerald Graham, *The China Station: War and Diplomacy 1830–1860* (Oxford: Clarendon Press, 1978). For Davis as governor of Hong Kong, see Christopher Munn, *Anglo-China: Chinese People and British Rule in Hong Kong* (Richmond: Curzon, 2001), 65. 115; G. B. Endacott, *A Biographical Sketch-Book of Early Hong Kong* (Hong Kong: Hong Kong University Press, 2005), 27; John M. Carroll, *Edge of Empires: Chinese Elites and British Colonials in Hong Kong* (Cambridge, MA: Harvard University Press, 2005). For Davis and sinology, see James G. St Andre, 'The Development of British Sinology and Changes in Translation Practice: The Case of Sir John Francis Davis (1795–1890)', *Translation and Interpreting Studies* 2.ii (2007), 3–42, and 'Modern Translation Theory and Past Translation Practice: European Translations of the *Haoqiu zhuan*', in *One into Many: Translation and the Dissemination of Classical Chinese Studies*, ed. Leo Tak-hung (Amsterdam: B.V. Rodopi, 2003), 39–66; Peter J. Kitson, *Forging Romantic China: Sino-British Cultural Exchange, 1760–1840* (New York: Cambridge University Press, 2013), 98–125; Dongshin Chang, *Representing China on the Historical London Stage: From Orientalism to Intercultural Performance* (London: Routledge, 2015), 97–139; Lawrence Wang-chi Wong, '"Objects of Curiosity": John Francis Davis as Translator of Chinese Literature', in *Sinologists as Translators in the Seventeenth to Nineteenth Centuries*, eds Lawrence Wang-chi Wong and Bernhard Fuehrer (Hong Kong: Chinese University Press, 2015), 169–204.

2   Susan Reed Stifler, 'The Language Students of the East India Company Canton Factory', *Journal of the North China Branch of the Royal Asiatic Society* 69 (1938), 46–82; James St André, 'Modern Translation Theory', 51.

7 John Francis Davis, China, the Opium Trade and First Opium War

Chinese was motivated by the 'necessity' for the British to study and understand Chinese. Davis was also instrumental in initiating the Hong Kong branch of the Royal Asiatic Society in 1847.[3] Knowingly, he writes that with the 'extension of our Indian frontier to the northward and eastward' this necessity will increase if Britain is placed in relations of a 'far more weighty and important nature, than such as are simply commercial'.[4] He never saw himself simply as a disinterested scholar of China or its literature and culture, and viewed his translations of Chinese literature as closely related to the ongoing development of British commercial interests in the region – after all, knowledge was power in his view.[5]

Davis' promotion to be the last president of the Company's select committee at Canton in 1832 and thereafter his appointment as joint commissioner in China with Lord William Napier in 1834, after the abolition of the Company's monopoly of the China trade, marks a major change in the focus of his work and career. Critical of Napier for his unwillingness to compromise with Chinese forms and customs, Davis was appointed to the post of chief superintendent after Napier's death that year. His ingrained Company loyalties and evident discomfort with an unfettered private trade with China (and his disdain for those involved) led to persistent conflict with the more aggressive opium traders, who accused him of pusillanimity in his dealings with the Chinese. After three months of their hostility he resigned from the post in 1835. With his accumulated fortune he purchased the estate of Hollywood Tower in the village of Compton Green, close to Bristol, in 1839, thus establishing himself as an English country gentleman.

---

3   C. F. Beckingham, 'A History of the Royal Asiatic Society, 1823–1973', in *The Royal Asiatic Society: Its History and Treasures* eds. Stuart Simmonds and Simon Digby (London: Routledge, 2002), 17. For British sinology, see T. H. Barrett, *Singular Listlessness: A Short History of Chinese Books and British Scholars* (London: Wellsweep Press, 1989); Kitson, *Forging Romantic China*.
4   J. F. Davis, 'Eugraphia Sinensis; or, the Art of Writing the Chinese Character with Correctness', *Transactions of the Royal Asiatic Society* (London, 1826) 2:ii, 304–12 (306–7).
5   J. F. Davis, *Chinese Novels translated from the originals to which are added proverbs and moral maxims, collected from their classical books and other sources* (London: John Murray, 1822), 2–3.

Only one thing was missing – a baronetcy. In 1844, at the suggestion of Staunton, he was offered the governorship of Hong Kong, the territory ceded to Britain by the 1842 Treaty of Nanjing, succeeding Sir Henry Pottinger, and gaining a substantial salary and a knighthood to boot.[6]

As well as a key political actor in the region, Davis established himself as *the* major British expert on China after Robert Morrison's death and Staunton's retirement; his *The Chinese: A General Description of the Empire of China and Its Inhabitants* (1836) became the standard work on China, frequently revised over his lifetime. His *Sketches of China* (1842) recorded his travels in China as a member of the Amherst embassy of 1816, written from the perspective of the First Opium War. Davis published his *Vocabulary, Containing Chinese Words and Phrases Peculiar to Canton and Macao* (1824) as well as several contributions to the Royal Asiatic Society. He contributed numerous translations of Chinese literary texts to the new British sinology, including: (with Morrison) *Translations from the Original Chinese* (1815); *San-Yu-Low; or the Three Dedicated Rooms* (1815); *Laou-seng-urh or, 'An Heir in His Old Age'* (1817); *Chinese Novels* (1822); *Hien Wun Shoo. Chinese Moral Maxims* (1823); *Han Koong Tsew or the Sorrows of Han* (1829); *Poeseos Sinensis commentarii: on the Poetry of the Chinese* (1829); and *The Fortunate Union* (1829). He returned to England in 1848 and continued to publish works on China into the mid and later century, including his *China During the War and Since the Peace* (1852) and *Chinese Miscellanies: a Collection of Essays and Notes* (1865). Throughout his life, first as a Company man, and then as a servant of the British crown, Davis was a key agent of British foreign policy in China. He wrote and acted during a period of increasing political instability in China – or 'the late unsettled state of the empire', as he describes it.[7] Interest in Davis' work as translator and sinologist has increased in recent years, yet this literary and cultural study of China largely ceased with his major translation of the novel *Haoqiu zhuan* as *The Fortunate Union* in 1829. His major study, *The Chinese*, appearing first in 1836, represents the apex of his writing about China and its history, literature and customs. His *Sketches of China* (1842) revisits his diplomatic

---

6   George Thomas Staunton, *Memoirs*, 93–94, 194.
7   Davis, *Chinese Novels*, 9.

experience with the Amherst embassy of 1816 and the focus of his *China During the War and Since the Peace* (1852) is more precisely on the diplomatic, military and economic aspects of Sino–British relations, including the First Opium War, and his experience as governor of Hong Kong.[8]

The central issue facing Davis was that of establishing the British right of entry into the city of Canton, which, despite the terms of the Treaty of Nanking (1842), had not thus far been granted, the Chinese arguing that the populace was too hostile to the British to be controlled. In April 1846, he agreed with the senior Chinese official and his opposite number, the governor-general of the Liangguang, Qiying (Keying), to delay British entry into the city in exchange for an agreement not to alienate the Zhousan islands. Davis later described Qiying as 'by far the most remarkable person with whom Europeans have ever come in contact in that part of the world'.[9] Nevertheless, attacks on the British in Canton multiplied, and in April 1847 Davis decided to retaliate by sending an armed force to capture the Bogue (Humen) ports and occupy the Canton factories.[10] In response, Qiying reached a rapid agreement with Davis to open Canton in two years' time and to punish those who had offended the British, conceding the right to build warehouses and churches.[11] Despite the apparent success of this venture, Davis was censured for his actions at home

---

8   Kitson, 'Dark Gift'; Tamara S. Wagner, 'Sketching China and the Self-Portrait of a Post-Romantic Traveler', in *A Century of Travels in China* (Hong Kong: Hong Kong University Press), 13–26.
9   J. F. Davis, *China During the War and Since the Peace*, 2 vols (London: Charles Knight, 1852). 1. 520. Further references to this edition will be given by short title and page reference within the text. For Qiying, see Mao Haijian, *The Qing Empire and the Opium War: The Collapse of the Heavenly Dynasty* (Cambridge: Cambridge University Press, 2016), 394–402, 410–13, 424–32, 435–39, 450–55, 457–64, 474–86, 504–8.
10   Davis' account is given in *China During the War*, 2.150–81. See John King Fairbank, 'The Manchu Appeasement Policy of 1843'. *Journal of the American Oriental Society* 59 (1939): 469–84; For Davis and the history of Hong Kong, see Endacott, *Early Hong Kong*, 23–29; Christopher Munn, *Anglo-China: Chinese People and British Rule in Hong Kong, 1841–1880*; John M. Carroll, *Edge of Empires: Chinese Elites and British Colonials in Hong Kong* (Cambridge, MA: Harvard University Press, 2015).

and resigned two years before his term of office was completed in November 1847, although he did not leave his post until the following March. Furthermore, an 1847 parliamentary select committee inquiry into British commercial relations with China, without naming Davis, succeeded in condemning his administration of Hong Kong and upholding the views of the British merchants who consistently opposed his policies.[12] G. B. Endacott judged that the conduct of Davis, though uniquely qualified for the post, 'aroused such strong local opposition … that when he left the Colony just less than four years later, he was regarded with hatred and contempt. He was the most unpopular governor in the colony's history'.[13] Davis returned to England in 1848 and again took up residence at Hollywood Tower, where he lived until his death in 1890, his career as a diplomat at an end.

Davis and Opium

As both a commentator on, and actor in, Chinese affairs, Davis' position regarding opium is deeply conflicted and paradoxical. It seems he was never really comfortable with the opium trade and very much disliked the private traders whom it involved, such as William Jardine and James Matheson, who famously made their fortunes dealing in the drug. When he gave evidence to the House of Commons in its report into the affairs of the East India Company in 1830, his responses were somewhat perfunctory, distancing himself and the Company from the smuggling of opium into China by the private traders, both British and American. He was aware that the private merchants were licensed by the Company in India but insisted that the select committee in Canton did not recognise the traders, who stay outside the river and 'lurk amongst the islands for the purpose of smuggling opium'. When confronted with the fact that the chests of opium sold in China bore

---

11   J. Y. Wong, *Deadly Dreams: Opium, Imperialism and the Arrow War (1856–1860) in China* (Cambridge: Cambridge University Press, 1998 [2002]), 84–219; Peyton, 'John Francis Davis', 911–13.
12   Munn, *Anglo-China*, 42–52.
13   Endacott, *Early Hong Kong*, 25.

the Company mark, he claimed he had never seen a chest of opium and thus was unable to 'speak to it'. He admits that the opium sold to China was grown by the Company in India, which grants licences to private traders to carry it to China as the Company 'enjoys a monopoly of the growth in China', but argues that as the Chinese are unaware of the fact, it was not really an issue. When confronted with the question as to whether the select committee was 'cognizant of the fact that that contraband article is brought to China under the license' of the Company's government in India, he responds somewhat abruptly that 'they cannot be ignorant of a fact so generally notorious to Englishmen'. So awkward and evasive was Davis' exchange with his interlocutors that it was frequently cited by anti-opium campaigners in the 1840s.[14]

Davis was fully aware of the intricacies of the tea and opium trade, yet he is somewhat disingenuous about it. As early as January 1835, he was warning the then foreign secretary, Viscount Palmerston, that the substantial increase in opium trading brought about by the abolition of the Company monopoly was likely to attract the attention and concern of the imperial government. His *The Chinese: A General Description* of 1836 contains an extended discussion of the trade and use of opium. He knew of the importance of the trade to the Company, but sought to blame the 'universal corruption of the government officers at Canton' for not suppressing the trade.[15] The local government, having placed itself 'in a false position' by 'its long course of secret and prohibitive practices in relation to the prohibited drug', was unable to counteract its growth after the end of the Company monopoly (1. 96–97). Despite the fact that his former employer produced and auctioned the opium in Bengal and licensed merchants to carry it to China, Davis regards the drug as a 'pernicious narcotic' used by 'all ranks and degrees in China'.

Yet in the next few sentences he can state that the value of the commodity has 'exceeded the aggregate value of every other English

---

14   *Parliamentary papers relating to the Opium Trade ... 1821–1832* (London: T Harrison, 1840), 30–31; William Storrs Fry, *Facts and Evidence relating to the Opium Trade with China* (London: Pelham Richardson, 1840), 9–10.
15   J. F. Davis, *The Chinese: a General Description of the Empire of China and Its Inhabitants*, 2 vols (London: Charles Knight, 1836), 2.130. Further references to this edition will be given in the text with short title, date and page number.

import' and stresses its crucial importance to the 'revenues of British India'. He calculates that, in 1833, opium accounts for half of the value of all British imports at Canton and Lintin, and exports of tea somewhat less. Some 23,670 chests of Bengal opium were imported annually from India into China at this time, increasing fivefold over the decade. The value of this trade is something like three to four million pounds sterling annually. Davis is aware that exports of opium have exceeded the value of all other imports combined and is intimately connected with 'the revenues of British India'. He writes that 'this pernicious narcotic has become as extensive as the increasing demand for it was rapid from the first'. The drug is 'prohibited as hurtful to the health and morals of the people'. Davis quotes at length from a state paper making it clear he fully understood the addictive nature of the drug and the effects it had, as well as the popular nature of its consumption in recent years, reaching the 'common people' of China and not being confined to any social elite:

> [T]hose who smoke opium, and eventually become its victims, have a periodical longing for it, which can only be assuaged by the application of the drug at the regular time. If they cannot obtain it when that daily period arrives, their limbs become debilitated, a discharge of rheum takes place from the eyes and nose, and they are altogether unequal to any exertion; but, with a few whiffs, their spirits and strength are immediately restored in a surprising manner ... It seems that opium is almost entirely imported from abroad; worthless subordinates in offices, and nefarious traders first introduced the abuse; young persons of family, wealthy citizens, and merchants adopted the custom; until at last it reached the common people ... opium smokers exist in all the provinces. (2. 203–4)

Davis in printing the censor's paper is thus aligning himself with those opposed to the trade. He finds that 'the pernicious drug, sold to the Chinese, has exceeded in market-value the wholesome leaf that has been purchased from them: and the balance of the trade has been paid to us in silver' (2. 208). Clearly conflicted, Davis offers no serious

7 John Francis Davis, China, the Opium Trade and First Opium War

Figure 7.1 'Mandarin with opium pipe'.

justification of the trade in 1836, except to share any blame with the Chinese, who are corrupt and complicit.

Davis, who served as the final president of the Company's Canton select committee, regarded the termination of its monopoly in 1834 as a 'most important national experiment' in answering the 'grand question' of 'the expediency of free trade against the Chinese monopoly', in which it remained to be seen how individual free traders would succeed against 'the union of mandarins and mandarin merchants' (*The Chinese* [1836] 1.100). When he wrote this, he clearly had little sympathy with the coming wave of free traders to Canton, emphasising the view that the end of the monopoly would result in an increase in smuggling and of 'all those circumstances which were calculated to embroil the English with the government of China', leading to conflict and war. Davis argued that the government should remain the conduit for both parties. This sudden 'revolution' in trading terms caught both the

Canton government and English traders by surprise and led to the debacle of Napier's period in the new role of superintendent of trade.

Davis remains sympathetic to the Chinese stance that Napier's position should have been formally approved by Beijing and announced by the Chinese government, and not de facto by Napier himself when he arrived. Davis was appointed as the second-in-command to Napier in 1834 and suggested a policy of 'remaining perfectly quiet'. He was stationed in Macao until the end of Napier's mission, taking over the role of chief superintendent on 13 October 1834, after the latter's death. Hsin-pao Chang comments that Davis' 'long association with the company and his prominent position on the select committee nurtured in him a conservative point of view that was quite out of sympathy with the new free-trade movement … his familiarity with Chinese customs and institutions prevented him from agreeing with Lord Napier's bombastic approach to handling the local government'. The free traders at Canton, such as Matheson and Jardine, who had egged on Napier, were generally hostile to his successor, the *Canton Register* sneering that someone 'brought up in the late School of monopoly can never therefore be a fit Representative and controller of free traders … who cherish high notions of their claims and privileges, and regard themselves as the depositories of the true principles of British Commerce'.[16]

In response, Davis wrote of his contempt of the 'vulgar rabble of free traders' to Palmerston and confessed that 'it is more difficult to deal with our own countrymen at Canton, than with the Chinese government'.[17] Aware of the hostility directed towards him and frustrated at not receiving any instructions from London, Davis resigned on 19 January 1835 after a mere three months and ten days in the post, to be succeeded by his deputy, George Best Robinson, claiming that 'if I find that I have nothing to do but sit still until

---

16 Quoted in Hsin-pao Chang, *Commissioner Lin and the Opium War* (New York: W. W. Norton, 1964), 62–64.
17 Davis to Palmerston, 12 November 1846 (FO 17/115). Quoted in *Great Britain and China*, 128; see Harry Gelber, *Opium, Soldiers, and Missionaries*' (Basingstoke: Palgrave, 40–41; Peyton, 'John Francis Davis'; Susanna Hoe and Derek Roebuck, *The Taking of Hong Kong: Charles and Clara Elliot in China Waters* (London and New York: Routledge, 1999), 53–55.

the Government at home have made up their minds, I shall probably accompany Mrs Davis home' (8 November 1834). He stressed that Robinson should continue his policy of quiescence until clear instructions were issued from London. Robinson's replacement, Charles Elliot (who had arrived with Napier and Davis, serving as their secretary) would have different ideas.[18] In the 1830s, at least, Davis emphasised that it was the 'subversion of the long-established system' of the Company's monopoly that led to the new and avoidable friction with the Chinese government, as it was not the existence of the opium trade per se but 'the barefaced mode of carrying it on' that now exasperated Beijing, leading to the Daoguang Emperor's prohibitionist policy implemented by viceroy Deng Tingzhen in 1836 and subsequently to the imperial appointment of the hard line Commissioner Lin Zexu in 1839 to extirpate the trade completely (*The Chinese* [1836] 1.114–15).[19]

Arriving from Bombay on the steamer *HMS Spiteful* on 7 May 1844, nine years after his last visit to China, Davis was formally appointed as the new governor and commander-in-chief of Hong Kong the next day.[20] By then the colony consisted of around twenty-four thousand people, Europeans and Chinese. Davis would be responsible not just for the colony of Hong Kong, but also for the five other new treaty ports of Canton, Amoy, Fuzhou, Ningpo and Shanghai and their respective consuls, each of which he visited on his appointment (*China During the War*, 2.41–80). He must have been aware that one of his most substantial challenges in his new role was that posed by the burgeoning and still contraband trade in opium.[21] On setting out for Hong Kong, Davis wrote somewhat optimistically that he was pleased that the government had no wish for Hong Kong to become a haven for opium trading. At that stage the British still hoped that, with increasing

---

18 Glenn Melancon, *Britain's China Policy and the Opium Crisis* (Aldershot: Ashgate, 2003), 49–51; Chang, *Commissioner Lin*, 57, 62–64.
19 For the Chinese debates about opium and the opium trade, see James Polachek, *The Inner Opium War* and David A. Bello, *Opium and the Limits of Empire: Drug Prohibition in the Chinese Interior* (Cambridge, MA: Harvard University Press, 2005), 114–76.
20 For Davis' administration, see Peyton, 'John Francis Davis'.
21 Costin, *Great Britain and China*, 115.

commerce with China, their merchants would diversify and import other British manufactures relying less heavily upon opium, which had always been their strategy. In fact, the contrary happened, as the expansion of the trade smothered other branches of commerce, as Davis remarked in *China During the War* (2.102–3).[22]

On his arrival in the colony, Davis had accepted that the opium trade was now tolerated by the Chinese government. Writing to Lord Stanley, he concluded that the only interference by the colonial government occurred to allow themselves a share of the profits and that 'any scruples on our part, within our own colony, appear to me to be more than superfluous'.[23] Almost immediately, he broached the subject of legalising the trade with Qiying. In his *China During the War* (1852), Davis recalls his first meeting with Qiying, at which the 'less welcome' subject of the 'proposed legalization of the opium trade' was first broached. He recounts how this was represented to Qiying as a 'wise and salutary measure', removing all possibilities of friction between the two governments. A measure that would provide 'ample revenue for the emperor, and check to the same extent the consumption of a commodity, which was at present absolutely untaxed'. Davis pointed out that opium was 'carried about the street in chests' and sold openly, but 'the Chinese government appeared to think it was less undignified to connive silently at a practice, than directly contradict all of its former principles by openly legalizing it'. Again, Davis accuses the Chinese of institutional hypocrisy here, but is notably silent about the contradictions of his own position and that of his government (2.22–45). In his later *Chinese Miscellanies* (1865), Davis recalled the meeting and his proposal in somewhat more detail, comparing the situation in Britain to that of China:

> Your Excellency is aware that, in the reign of the Emperor Kien-loong, opium was subject, as a medicine, to a duty. The extent of its consumption was then inconsiderable. Subsequently to that, the drug was prohibited, and penalties attached to its consumption; but this prohibition, and these penalties, instead

---

22   Munn, *Anglo-China*, 107.
23   Davis to Stanley, 28 December 1844. Quoted in Munn, *Anglo-China*, 108.

7 John Francis Davis, China, the Opium Trade and First Opium War

of preventing, appear to have increased the consumption of a noxious article in a wonderful manner, until the value in money of the prohibited opium imported has come greatly to exceed the amount of the lawful tea exported. This is the experience of China. You will therefore the more readily believe that the experience of England has been the same in reference to all commodities. Opium, having never been prohibited, is consumed in small quantities, chiefly as a medicine; and the official returns of the last year show that the whole quantity used in England was only 47,432 pounds, or 355 piculs. But, in regard to many other commodities, England formerly adopted the system of prohibitions and high duties; and these only increased the extent of smuggling, together with crimes of violence, while they diminished the revenue; until it was at length found that the fruitless expense of a large preventive force absorbed much of the amount of duty that could be collected, while prohibited articles were consumed more than ever.

The disposition of men in matters of mere sensual indulgence attaches additional value to what is difficult of attainment. If a commodity be plentiful by nature, its prohibition creates an artificial difficulty, and therefore an unnatural value. In China, since opium was prohibited, it has been greedily purchased at an enormous price; in England, where it has always been lawful, it is generally disliked, and seldom used, except as a medicine. England having for many years suffered from the evils of smuggling, as well as those of a preventive force, was at length led to annul the prohibitions against some commodities, and to lower the duties on others. The consequence has been that smuggling is no longer a gainful employment; and while the duties on useful and innoxious articles of trade have been diminished, the revenue consequent on their increased consumption has enormously increased. The total revenue of England for the last year was more than 150,000,000 taels [about £50,000,000, in 1846]. (*Chinese Miscellanies*, 5–6)

Davis is highly selective in this account, which borders on the mendacious. He says nothing about the enormous increase in the supply of opium from British Bengal (and Malwa) in the 1810s and 1820s which made the drug both cheap and plentiful. He does not allude to opium's highly addictive qualities, of which he was very well aware, but regards the matter as more one of prohibition. Qiying responded by asserting that he simply did not dare raise this subject with the emperor personally but would forward any written propositions from Davis (*China During the War*, 2.22–45).[24] Davis recalls in 1852 that both he and his predecessor, Sir Henry Pottinger, had pressured Qiying to persuade the emperor to legalise the trade and professed it as 'his own wish' to see it 'freed from the odium of illegality'. He claims that while legalisation was not possible, Qiying proposed that the 'trade should be carried on by mutual connivance'. He points out that no proclamation had been issued since the end of the war against the trade and that 'the only thing wanting was, that the emperor should publicly sanction what he had once publicly condemned, – and this was found impossible by Chinese pride or policy'. In effect he claims that the trade was now tolerated and accepted by the Chinese:

> The Chinese government was not sufficiently honest to make a public disavowal of this change in its system; but the position in which Great Britain stood became materially altered. China had distinctly declined a conventional arrangement for the remedy of the evil, and expressed a desire that we should not bring the existing abuse to its notice. The systematic manner in which the opium trade was now carried on by the officers of government, especially in the Canton river, as a sort of mandarin monopoly, led to the conclusion ... that there was at present no wish for a change. (*China During the War*, 2.202–4)

In describing legalisation as a 'conventional arrangement for the remedy of the evil', Davis effaces the violent history of the Qing's resistance to that very policy. Qiying's strategy was to appease the British, yet he rebuffed Davis' proposal as unacceptable to the emperor for moral and ethical reasons. It is clear, faced with a robust anti-opium

---

24　John King Fairbank, 'The Manchu Appeasement Policy of 1843', *Journal of the American Oriental Society* 59 (1939): 469–84.

feeling at home, that the British were unprepared to impose the 'conventional remedy' of the formal legalisation of the trade on the Chinese, however much they may have desired it. They had ostensibly fought the war not to legalise the trade but to punish the Chinese for perceived insults to British national honour and Lin's seizure of property. To insist on the legalisation of the trade, given the enormous public revulsion at its conduct, would have been politically impossible. That would have to wait until 1858 and China's second defeat at the hands of Anglo-French forces.

Davis advised that the more positive act of legalisation was politically preferable to that of the trade's exclusion, and thus British connivance with it. However, in the brave new world of laissez-faire trading relations the moral blame for the trade could be placed squarely on the Chinese:

> there is doubtless the middle term of 'laissez faire' most agreeable to English notions of freedom, and which as the subject of Chinese complaint might certainly be met with this answer: 'Look to your own custom houses and coast guards'.[25]

Davis now seems content to blame the entire trade on the Chinese, it is now a 'mandarin monopoly' rather than an East India Company monopoly (which production of the drug still was). He looks to the 'general consumption by the mandarins of that opium which they had been ordered to prohibit' as well as the 'corruption and disorganization which prevailed everywhere' and is incompatible with 'stable and effective government' (*China During the War*, 2.234). Given Davis' comments on the trade elsewhere, this is certainly hypocritical and dishonest, especially as the expedient of moving out of the trade altogether is never countenanced. It is hard to resist the conclusion that, as a government official, Davis was willing to countenance the management of a trade while, at the same time, publicly deploring it.

If the trade could not be legalised throughout China's dominions, it could still be authorised within the new colony of Hong Kong. On

---

25 Davis to Aberdeen, 26 December 1843 (BL Add. MSS. 43198, f.307). Quoted Costin, *Great Britain and China*, 110, 109–10.

13 May 1844, Davis wrote to Lord Stanley that 'almost every person possessed of capital, who is not connected with government employment is employed in the opium trade.'[26] Instructed by Stanley to raise as much revenue as possible from the sale of the drug to the Chinese within the colony, Davis was obliged to license the public sale of opium for retailing and smoking in 1845, establishing a monopoly in the drug from which the colony received income until 1941.[27] The retail sale of amounts of less than a chest of opium was now taxed. In 1847, the monopoly was replaced by a series of annual licences. This was a part of Davis' overall strategy to tax the colony to raise funds for its administration (and the establishment of a police force) and to bring the new colony towards self-sufficiency. It was, however, deeply resented by the free traders who believed such costs should be met by the home government whose will Davis too slavishly followed.[28]

Davis' legalisation of opium sales was certainly not uncontroversial, even in Hong Kong, and was vehemently opposed by one member of his own executive. Robert Montgomery Martin, the colony's treasurer and member of the legislative council from 1844–45, disagreed with Davis about the morality of raising revenue, resigning in July 1845.[29] Martin argued that 'no Government ought to make a private vice a source of public revenue.'[30] In effect Martin accused Davis of making the colony a central warehouse for the opium trade. In 1847,

---

26   Endacott, *Early Hong Kong*, 72.
27   'Regulation for the Sale of Opium by Retail made by His Excellency the Governor of Hong Kong', in Returns of the various Ports of China, for the year 1846, presented to the House of Commons by Command of Her Majesty, 1847' in Accounts and Paper. 37 vols (London: T. R. Harrison), vol. 39 relating to the Opium Trade (House of Commons, 1840), 30–31 'Copies of Ordinance No 21 of 1844, for Licensing the Sale of OPIUM within the Colony of Hong Kong dated the 28th day of February 1844', Accounts and papers of the House of Commons, vol. 40, 2–3; Munn, *Anglo-China*, 108.
28   Peyton, 'John Francis Davis, 915; Endacott, *Early Hong Kong*, 23–30.
29   Robert Montgomery Martin, *Reports, Minutes, and Dispatches on the British Position and Prospects in China*; for Martin, see Endacott, *Early Hong Kong*, 72–78.
30   No 3 – Copy of Dissent in Legislative Council of Hong Kong, by Robert Montgomery Martin on the proposition for Licensing the Retail Consumption of Opium in Hong Kong. 26 May 1844. Quoted Peyton.

7 John Francis Davis, China, the Opium Trade and First Opium War

he published his *China, Political, Commercial and Social in An Official Report to Her Majesty's Government* in which he commented that when Davis 'proposed the conversion of Hong Kong into a legalised opium shop' he advised him to follow the 'noble example of the Emperor of China', who declined to legalise the importation of the drug in 1844: 'It is true, I cannot prevent the introduction of the flowing poison; – gain-seeking and corrupt men will, for profit and sensuality, defeat my wishes; but nothing will induce me to derive a revenue from the voice and misery of my people'. Davis, the Queen's representative, had 'converted the small barren rock which we occupy on the coast of China, into a vast "opium smoking shop"' making Hong Kong 'the "Gehenna of the waters," where iniquity, which it is a pollution to name, can not only be perpetrated with impunity, but is absolutely *licensed* in the name of our gracious Sovereign, and protected by the titled representative of Her Majesty!' (2.261).

Martin devotes a full chapter to the opium trade. His views are important because they are based upon his own first-hand witnessing of the Chinese 'opium den' and are worth quoting at length:

> As a medicine, like all other poisons, it is of great value. It diminishes pain, soothes irritation, and often procures repose for the sufferers when other means have failed. In large doses it almost instantly destroys life by the destruction of the nervous energy which is indispensable to the circulation of the blood. Unless when taken for the relief of disease, and even then, administered with the greatest caution, the continued action of opium, as a sensual stimulant, *tends rapidly to the wasting of youth, health, strength, and beauty.* Those who begin its use at *twenty* may expect to die at *thirty* years of age: the countenance becomes pallid; the eye assumes a wild brightness, the memory fails, the gait totters, mental exertion and moral courage sink, and a frightful marasmus or atrophy reduces the victim to a ghastly spectacle, *who has ceased to live before he has ceased to exist.* There is no slavery so complete as that of the opium-taker; once habituated to his dose as a factious stimulant, everything will be endured rather than the privation; and the unhappy being endures all the mortification of a consciousness of his own

degraded state, while ready to sell his wife and children, body and soul, for the continuance of his wretched and transient delight ... The pleasurable sensations and imaginative ideas arising at first, soon pass away; they become fainter and fainter, and at last, entirely give place to horrid dreams and appalling pictures of death: spectres of fearful visage haunt the mind – the light which once seemed to emanate from heaven is converted into the gloom of hell – sleep balmy sleep has fled for ever – night succeeds day only to be clothed with never-ending horror ... death at length brings, with its annihilation of the corporeal structure, the sole relief to the victim of sensual and criminal indulgence. The opium shops which I visited in the East were perfect types of hell upon earth. (177–78)

Martin, who had clearly read De Quincey's *Confessions of an English Opium-Eater* (1821), was destined to become a significant anti-opium campaigner, convinced 'the devil never invented a vicious habit so plausible and pleasing in its first stages, so powerful in its hold when once established, and so pernicious in its final consequences, as is this vice of opium smoking'. He soundly praised what he saw as the courageous resistance of the Chinese government to the bribery and bullying of the British after the end of the 'unhappy war' and viewed the Second 'Opium' or 'Arrow War' simply as an attempt to attain by force what it had not been possible to obtain by intimidation. Martin added that the heroic Commissioner Lin was 'loved and honoured more than any modern statesman in China, and to this day they celebrate his praises and bless his memory'.[31] That Davis should find opposition to his policies on opium legalisation so close to home is a clear indication of how contested and controversial the subject of the opium trade and the war which it occasioned remained for many Britons. Martin left Hong Kong and took his campaign against Davis back to Britain.

---

31 R. Montgomery Martin, *The Opium Trade in China, by an Eyewitness* (London: J. Heaton, 1858), 11–17; *China, Political, Commercial and Social in An Official. A Report to Her Majesty's Government*, 2 vols (London: Madden, 1847), vol. 2, 177–78, 189, 261, 174–262.

7 John Francis Davis, China, the Opium Trade and First Opium War

Martin's accusation that Davis, in effect, was establishing Hong Kong as an opium colony was in many ways justified. Martin Booth comments that 'without opium, Hong Kong could not have evolved as it did. Not only was it originally obtained as a result of a skirmish over opium, but its initial fortunes were linked irrevocably to the trade. Within a year of it being established it had become the main opium trading centre on the China coast'.[32] Christopher Munn has shown how the viability of the colony was intimately linked to the trade, becoming the central warehouse and depot for Britain's Indian opium, with about seventy-five per cent of the crop passing through the colony by the end of the 1840s. Munn argues that 'the colony was founded because of opium; it survived its difficult early years because of opium; its principal merchants grew rich on opium; and its government subsisted in the high land rent and other revenue made possible by the opium trade'.[33] Davis, an important but comparatively minor functionary in the British colonial order, had little agency when confronted with these major economic forces.

Davis revised his study of *The Chinese* (1836) in both 1840 and 1845, bringing the volume up to date with the rapidly occurring events. In the 1840 edition he concluded his narrative of Britain's commercial relations with China just at the point of the outbreak of the war, 'the most important and momentous enterprise, next to the conquest of India, itself in which the British arms have ever been engaged to the eastward of the Cape of Good Hope'.[34] He ended this edition very pessimistically with the view that 'the smuggling of opium will continue, and that the former evils of that desperate traffic will be enhanced by an extended system of violence and bloodshed' ([1840] 3.337), a sentence that he was to remove from the 1845 edition,

---

32 Martin Booth, *Opium: A History* (New York: St Martin's, 1998), 140, 139–73. Christopher Munn, 'The Hong Kong Opium Revenues', in *Opium Regimes: China, Britain and Japan*, ed. Timothy Brook, Bob Tadashi Wakabayashi (Berkeley: University of California Press, 2000), 107, 105–26.
33 Munn, 'The Hong Kong Opium Revenues', 107.
34 J. F. Davis, *The Chinese: A General Description of China and Its Inhabitants*. 3 vols (London: C. Knight, 1840), 3. 133. Further references to this edition will be contained in the text with page numbers.

presumably as a result of his experience of legalising the trade at Hong Kong.

Throughout, Davis blames the Chinese for the opium trade, which he appears to detest. The growth in smuggling and the movement from Whampoa to Linton in the 1820s is the fault of the Chinese system of exacting substantial duties, as well as the high costs incurred in transporting Chinese produce, especially tea, all the way to Canton, instead of opening ports along the coast nearer to the areas of supply. He blames excessive duties, the 'abilities of the natives as smugglers' and the 'extreme corruption of the lowest custom-house officers' for the growth in the illicit trade that will interfere with the legitimate China trade and engulf it: 'it is the universal corruption of the government officers in Canton, in the article of opium, that makes it so difficult to stop the rest of the contraband trade near that port' ([1840] 3.200–2). The risks inherent in smuggling demand that the commodities traded are highly profitable, hence 'opium is chiefly in demand'.

> Down to the present year, 1840, the opium smuggling on the coast had gradually increased until its exclusion from Canton by Commissioner Lin has driven the whole of it eastward. At the present time it appears to be carried on with great profit in armed ships, one of which is said to carry fourteen guns; and conflicts have taken place in which lives were lost; with all this, however, European manufactures are as unsaleable as ever. ([1840]3.202–3)

In doing so, he pleads that the Company, while the monopoly was in place, had always kept the trade out of the Pearl River; with the end of the monopoly, the 'desperate traffic' increased at the expense of the legal trade, forcing the Chinese government to take notice and resulting in the implementation of prohibition policies.[35]

How then could Davis, who opposed the abolition of the Company monopoly on the China trade and characterised the opium trade as desperate and destructive, fully support the war and legalise the sale and trading of the drug in Hong Kong? How did he, against opposition,

---

35   J. F. Davis, *The Chinese: A General Description of China and its Inhabitants*. 3 vols (London: C. Knight, 1851), 3. 208.

7 John Francis Davis, China, the Opium Trade and First Opium War

reconcile all these conflicting views? Presumably, by the 1850s, Davis had at least seen a chest of East Indian opium with the Company's logo upon it? Now comfortably back in his study at his family home of Hollywood Tower, he was destined never to travel to China again. In his *China During the War and Since the Peace* (1852), his attitude to what he calls 'the Indo-Chinese nations' seems to have hardened somewhat and his conversion to global free trade been completed. Pre-empting Mr Phileas Fogg he can comment that '[w]hen the entire circumference of our planet is thus open to steam and rail, and a girdle can be put round the earth in little more than a hundred days, it will be hardly possible for such countries as Japan, Cochin-China, Corea, and Siam, notwithstanding their sullen system of seclusion, to remain long unopen to a busy, inquisitive, and progressive world' (2.260).

Now China is subsumed among the category of 'Indo-Chinese nations', just one among several and the global flow also now involves that of Chinese labourers, 'swarming from Hong Kong across the Pacific to California' (1.vi). He argues the British expedition against China was fully justified in the light of Lin's 'opium seizure, and other outrages at Canton'. No 'moderate proposals' would have had any chance of success against a Chinese government now 'bent on their annihilation'. Davis comments that the opium traffic was never mentioned in the Treaty of Nanjing and the subject has 'never once been revived since the war', rather misremembering his own interventions on behalf of its legalisation. His attitude to the opium trade changes somewhat, and he argues that it was actually undeserving of the 'full load of infamy' heaped upon it and that it only supplied 'the poison which the Chinese were not obliged to take' (1.3, 18–19). The war is to be blamed on Lin and had the counsels of Keshen, who was 'against all violent measures towards natives or foreigners', been listened to, then it might have been averted (1.26). Lin's demand for the surrender of the opium produced the war and 'not a single individual was benefitted' (1.149).

Davis still persists in his view that the piracy the trade engendered was the main cause of hostilities, not 'the honest trade' that had been carried on by the Company. The full legalisation of the trade he now judges to be a 'wide and salutary measure' for both empires. This history of the war, with its attacks on Commissioner Lin and the 'old literati of China', who instead of enlightening their country keep it in a 'Cimmerian darkness, in which the dim and dubious glimmering of the lamp of Confucius is deemed more than sufficient for all purposes' (1.33), rewrites much of Davis' earlier more positive estimations of China's peoples and its cultures. The villains of the story are the 'unprogressive literati of China' who have 'discovered that their pride had been humbled to the dust, and that the Celestial empire no longer swayed the world' (2.11) rather than the aggressive and amoral opium free traders. Modernity, represented by Britain's 'liberal enlightened' technology and free trade, now embraced the trade in opium which 'antiquated China where the mind and body are both enslaved by old custom' had so far resisted (2.101). Davis regarded the rebellions and instabilities of the 1850s in China as 'in no small degree the consequences of that disgrace and defeat which the proud and boastful government of the country sustained in the war with Great Britain' and the public humiliation of the Treaty of Nanjing (2.182, 196, 219).

While a Company employee in Canton, Davis could keep his moral distance from the opium trade, but when acting as a British colonial official he could not maintain the barrier between his self and those chests of Company opium produced in Patna. His apparent conversion to free trade and laissez-faire economics in the 1840s allowed him, like so many other Britons, to place the blame for the trade on the Chinese consumer and not the British producer and to lay the fault with an antiquated China, at odds with the modern world and its inconvenient regulations. In the last analysis, Davis was always the servant of the Company or the crown, tasked with doing a difficult job to the best of his ability, always rather disdainful of criticism from whatever quarter. After all, who was he to stand in the way of the new global commerce? If the Chinese had a problem with opium, why, they had only themselves to blame.

8
Walter Scott's Writing, Collecting and Reading China

Kang-yen Chiu

Research on Walter Scott over the past twenty years has extended beyond Scottish or British contexts. Murray Pittock's *The Reception of Sir Walter Scott in Europe* (2006), for example, focuses on the greater European context. This focus, however, has gradually been shifting to the East in recent years, with a greater number of scholars beginning to study Scott's writing and personal life in relation to the East, and particularly India.[1] To date, however, no one has investigated Scott's relationship with China, which is the primary concern of this chapter. Peter Kitson's *Forging Romantic China: Sino-British Cultural Exchange, 1760–1840* (2013) is the publication most relevant to this current investigation, but Scott himself is not mentioned in the work, as I will explore in the latter half of this chapter.

---

1   For information regarding Scott's connections with India, see Tara Ghoshal Wallace, 'The Elephant's Foot and the British Mouth: Walter Scott on Imperial Rhetoric', *European Romantic Review* 13 (2002), 311–24; Historical Note to 'The Surgeon's Daughter', in *Chronicles of Canongate*, ed. Claire Lamont (Edinburgh: Edinburgh University Press, 2000), 360; Iain Gordon Brown, 'Griffins, Nabobs and a Seasoning of Curry Powder: Walter Scott and the Indian Theme in Life and Literature', in *The Tiger and the Thistle: Tipu Sultan and Scots in India, 1760–1800*, ed. Anne Buddle, Pauline Rohtagi and Iain Gordon Brown (Edinburgh: National Gallery of Scotland, 1999), 71–79.

This chapter is divided into three sections. To begin with, I will give a brief summary of Sino–British relations during the Romantic period that Scott himself witnessed; in the second section, I will discuss Scott's writing on China in his novels, journals and letters and, lastly, I will consider several important Chinese cultural objects, most crucially the hand-painted wallpaper at Scott's home, Abbotsford, as well as the China-related books that Scott brought to his library there. This chapter will therefore illustrate and examine the relationship between China and Scott's literary creation and life.

Sino–British Relationship During the Romantic Period

The Romantic period is a critical time for those who have an interest in understanding the relationship between Britain and China since it was one of the most decisive periods in the history of modern Sino–British relations. British attitudes towards China in general had been friendly and respectful since China was regarded as both a source of ancient wisdom and the greatest power in East Asia before the Romantic period. European knowledge of China at that time derived almost exclusively from the letters and published works of French Jesuit missionaries. However, by the end of the seventeenth century, the positive image of China promoted by these Jesuits was beginning to be challenged.[2] Through the course of the eighteenth century, writings on China became increasingly critical, particularly of the country's apparent political and moral deterioration. In place of the notions of security and ancient lineage presented by the Jesuits, China began to seem to the Western trading powers as rather conservative and anti-foreign.[3] China's own corruption, as well as its supercilious attitude to other non-Chinese peoples, also provided justification for the European powers' interference in the country's territorial integrity and sovereignty.[4] For example, after learning of an imperial edict issued by the Chinese government in 1760, Lord Clive (1725–1774),

---

2   Ros Ballaster, *Fabulous Orients: Fictions of the East in England 1662–1785* (New York: Oxford University Press, 2005), 218.
3   Ballaster, 208.

8 Walter Scott's Writing, Collecting and Reading China

Commander-in-Chief of British India, proposed to his Majesty's cabinet that Britain seize China by force.[5] During the Romantic period, British diplomatic and military activity greatly intensified with, for example, Lord Macartney's and Lord Amherst's embassies to China in 1792–93 and 1816 respectively, and the First Opium War of 1839–42. The Romantic period, as a result, can be seen as a watershed in the changing relationship between Britain and China.

Despite tightly regulated conditions, there were a great number of British merchants working for the East India Company in China before the Opium War. Regardless of their quality, the first-hand experiences of these British expatriates in China became valuable sources for Romantic writers in both understanding and writing about the country. Additionally, many of the Romantic writers with whom we are familiar had family working in China and had written to some degree about the country. Jane Austen's brother, Sir Francis William Austen (1774–1865), served in the Royal Navy and acted as an agent for the East India Company in 1809–10 at Canton. The reference to Macartney's embassy to China in her novel *Mansfield Park* (1814) is clear.[6] William Wordsworth's younger brother John (1772–1805) was in the service of the East India Company and had sailed to China

---

4   'At their root was the assumption that China was the "central" kingdom and that other countries were, by definition, peripheral, removed from the cultural center of the universe.' Jonathan D. Spence, *The Search for Modern China* (New York and London: W. W. Norton, 1999), 119.
5   The Imperial Edict issued in 1760: 'Foreigners were ordered to leave Canton on the Chinese New Year, withdrawing to Macao until autumn. Chinese were ordered not to trade with or work for foreigners, under penalty of deportation. Foreigners were denied the right to learn Chinese and were permitted to have contact only with interpreters accredited by the Canton guild. Chinese officials had to be present aboard any foreign merchant ship during its stay in Chinese waters. Foreigners were forbidden to bear arms or to send couriers abroad without permission from the Chinese authorities. Finally, any foreigner involved in an incident with a Chinese would be subject to Chinese jurisdiction.' Alain Peyrefitte, *The Immobile Empire* (New York: Vintage, 1992), 53.
6   See Susan Allen Ford, 'Fanny's "great book": Macartney's Embassy to China and *Mansfield Park*', *Persuasions On-Line* 28:2 (2008), http://www.jasna.org/persuasions/on-line/vol28no2/ford.htm.

on the ship *The Earl of Abergavenny* and traded at Canton. Thomas De Quincey's son, Horace, died at the age of twenty-two of a fever contracted during the Opium Wars with China in 1842.[7] De Quincey's work, such as *The Opium Question in China in 1840*, is a clear demonstration of his anxiety about the threat from the Far East to the civilisation of the Western world.

Walter Scott, in common with the above-mentioned writers, also had family and friends working in China. For example, his cousin Hugh Scott (1777–1835), who was captain of the East Indiaman *Ceres* between 1808–16, had made several voyages to the country.[8] For this reason and also through his extensive reading, Scott's knowledge of China was, I believe, extensive. As a witness of this decisive period in the development of modern Sino–British relations, Scott's personal attitude towards China and the ways through which he comprehended the country are the main concerns of this chapter.

Scott's Writings on China

Scott produced a total of twenty-seven novels, eleven narrative poems and a number of prose works during his lifetime. Although none of his writings has its sole focus on the depiction of China, many of them mention things pertaining to China. In *Waverley* (1814), Fergus, the clan chief, compares himself to the emperor of China.[9] In *Rob Roy* (1817), Martha, the old housekeeper, is confident that her wine is better than all the tea in China.[10] In the same novel, the hospitable host Bailie Nicol Jarvie entertains his guests by offering his precious

---

7   Peter J. Kitson, *Forging Romantic China: Sino-British Cultural Exchange 1760–1840* (Cambridge: Cambridge University Press, 2013), 11.
8   Helen Clifford, 'Chinese Wallpaper Case Study: The Importance of Gifts', *East India Company at Home* (February 2013), http://blogs.ucl.ac.uk/eicah/chinese-wallpaper-case-study/chinese-wallpaper-case-study-the-importance-of-gifts/.
9   Walter Scott, *Waverley* (1814), ed. P. D. Garside (Edinburgh: Edinburgh University Press, 2007), 269.
10 Walter Scott, *Rob Roy* (1818), ed. David Hewitt (Edinburgh: Edinburgh University Press, 2008), 122.

tea from the Far East.[11] *The Pirate* (1821) mentions the East India Company's vessels which are homeward bound from China.[12] *The Fortunes of Nigel* (1822) touches upon fashionable Chinese dishes and ornaments.[13] *Saint Ronan's Well* (1823) speaks of the mysteries of the Chinese herb, tea.[14] In *The Talisman* (1825), the hero lies beneath 'a silken pavilion, which blazed with the richest colours of the Chinese loom'.[15] These six novels all briefly allude to things related to China, but none includes detailed descriptions. With regard to Scott's letters and journal, he does mention 'Chinese pagodas' and 'the Wall of China' in two of his letters, although still without any description of the country.[16] The reason that in *Waverley* Scott mentioned China was likely because he intended to show that both the Highlands and China were not under the rule of law. They were countries governed by rulers whose personal will was more powerful than laws. Concerning the rest of the five novels mentioning China, they all emphasise Britain's obsession with Chinese objects, a proper reflection of eighteenth-century chinoiserie.

This scant trawl of references can hardly give us a satisfactory picture of Scott's view about China. However, as Hugh Cheape and others have argued, 'As material culture offers a context of the past and one which Scott himself could describe with such relish, objects also bring us closer to our subject and the circumstances of his own

---

11   Scott, *Rob Roy*, 194.
12   Walter Scott, *The Pirate* (1821), ed. Mark Weinstein and Alison Lumsden (Edinburgh: Edinburgh University Press, 2001), 127.
13   Walter Scott, *The Fortunes of Nigel* (1822), ed. Frank Jordan (Edinburgh: Edinburgh University Press, 2004), 94.
14   Walter Scott, *Saint Ronan's Well* (1823), ed. Mark Weinstein (Edinburgh: Edinburgh University Press, 1995), 126.
15   Walter Scott, *The Talisman* (1825), ed. J. B. Ellis with J. H. Alexander, P. D. Garside and David Hewitt (Edinburgh: Edinburgh University Press, 2009), 210.
16   Scott to Sophia Baillie, 13 March 1810, in Sir Herbert Grierson's edition of *The Letters of Sir Walter Scott* (1932–37), vol. 2, 310, http://www.walterscott.lib.ed.ac.uk/etexts/etexts/letters2.PDF; Scott to Miss Smith, 11 December 1812, in Sir Herbert Grierson's edition of *The Letters of Sir Walter Scott* (1932–37), vol. 3, 207, http://www.walterscott.lib.ed.ac.uk/etexts /etexts/letters3.PDF.

life'.[17] We may therefore infer that the underlying meaning of China to Scott might be found in a material, instead of historical, philosophical or even political, existence. Consequently, in order to understand the novelist's connection with the country I will now focus on Chinese objects at Abbotsford, including the wallpaper, porcelain and books Scott collected during his lifetime.

Scott's Collection of Chinese Objects

In 1812, Scott moved from Ashestiel to Abbotsford, and planned the rebuilding of the small farmhouse there. The building of Abbotsford was undertaken in two phases: the first from 1817 to 1819, and the second from 1822 to 1825. Scott lived there with his family from 1812 to his death in 1832. When he was furnishing the house, Scott received generous gifts from both family and friends. Some of these gifts were particularly important to the interior decoration of Abbotsford, as I shall explore.

Abbotsford has around seventy Chinese items in total, and most of them (such as the Chinese silk-embroidered panels, snuff bottle and summer robe) were most likely collected by Scott's descendants. Of the twenty or so pieces of Chinese porcelain (including vases, tea bowls and boxes), only a small number can be confirmed as of true Chinese manufacture during the contemporary Qianlong period. Since we lack any written record, their origins cannot be verified. In addition to this Chinese porcelain, the collection also holds ivory chopsticks, a pole arm, a short sword, and an impressive black and gilt lacquer coffer-on-stand that were most likely collected by Scott himself. However, since again there are no written records relating to these objects, their significance for Scott cannot be gauged in quite the manner of other items in the collection, such as the wallpaper.

---

17   Hugh Cheape, Trevor Cowie and Colin Wallace, 'Sir Walter Scott, the Abbotsford Collection and the National Museums of Scotland', in Iain G. Brown, ed., *Abbotsford and Sir Walter Scott: the Image and the Influence* (Edinburgh: Society of Antiquaries of Scotland, 2003), 49–89 (52).

Scott says nothing with regard to his collection of Chinese objects, except for his Chinese wallpaper. It is mostly likely that such reticence was due to the fact that these objects, like the habit of drinking tea,[18] had already been domesticated and had entered widely into ordinary British households. Expensive hand-painted Chinese wallpaper like that owned by Scott, however, had never been easily available to ordinary people during the Romantic period. In a letter to his cousin Hugh Scott on 6 October 1822, Scott wrote:

> Nothing can be more grateful and acceptable to my wife and me than the kind token which assures us that you have remembered us in China. The paper will arrive in excellent time as we shall be fitting up our new drawing room next summer and I will take care that it is hung up by someone who perfectly understands it.[19]

The paper, as Scott revealed in a letter to his friend Daniel Terry (1780–1829, the actor, theatre impresario and Scott's instructor in decorating Abbotsford), was actually twenty-four pieces of hand-painted Chinese wallpaper given as a special gift from the aforementioned Hugh Scott, who was then working for the East India Company in Canton, to decorate the drawing room and two upstairs bedrooms (Lady Scott's bedroom above the entrance hall and another bedroom above the dining room) at Abbotsford.[20] This Chinese wallpaper was most likely hung by David Ramsay Hay (1798–1866), a Scottish interior decorator who was actively involved in the interior design of Abbotsford.[21] This wallpaper illustrates ordinary Chinese

---

18   Alan and Iris Macfarlane, *Green Gold: The Empire of Tea* (London: Ebury Press, 2004), 66–71.
19   Scott to Hugh Scott, 6 October 1822, in Sir Herbert Grierson's edition of *The Letters of Sir Walter Scott* (1932–37), vol. 7, 261–62, http://www.walterscott.lib.ed.ac.uk/etexts/etexts/letters7.PDF.
20   'Hawl the second is twenty-four pieces of the most splendid Chinese paper, twelve feet high by four wide, a present from my cousin Hugh Scott, enough to finish the drawing-room and two bed-rooms.' Scott to Daniel Terry, 10 November 1822, in *Letters* , vol. 7, 272.
21   See Clive Wainright, *The Romantic Interior: the British Collector at Home 1750–1850* (New Haven and London: Yale University Press, 1989), 167.

figures (both young and old), flowering trees, a variety of vividly depicted birds, as well as a traditional Chinese pavilion. This depiction of idyllic scenes of everyday Chinese life was meant to represent a harmonious universe, according to Confucian, Taoist and Buddhist philosophies.[22]

Patrick Conner has shown that Chinese wallpaper is almost entirely a European phenomenon, Chinese interiors being devoid of decoratively painted paper. Such wallpaper was specifically prepared for a European market. In Britain, it continued to be imported throughout the eighteenth century, with a peak in popularity in the 1750s and 1760s, and it was one of the most highly fashionable Chinese decorative adornments at the time.[23] Apart from their intrinsic beauty and their suitability for use in the spacious Georgian mansions of the period, E. A. Entwisle argues that these Chinese wallpapers had additional appeal because all the work was done by hand, no two sheets being exactly alike. Being hand-crafted, each sheet was subtly different. The appeal of the authentic touch was in contrast to those produced by means of more industrialised methods.[24] The following description by David Beevers of the Chinese interior decoration of a British household closely corresponds to the drawing room at Abbotsford:

> Women's bedrooms, dressing rooms and, later, drawing rooms were frequently hung with expensive hand-painted Chinese wallpaper and furnished with oriental porcelain and, occasionally, chinoiserie furniture ... the fantastic birds and figures on Chinese export wallpaper seemed particularly appropriate to *the land of dreams*.[25] [emphasis added]

---

22 The information comes from an unpublished article, 'The Chinese Wallpaper at Abbotsford', written by Abbotsford staff for their visitors to read. This article was kindly given by the Heritage & Engagement Assistant Miss Velvet Colton of the Abbotsford Trust.

23 Patrick Conner, *The China Trade 1600–1860* (Brighton: The Royal Pavilion, Art Gallery & Museums, 1986), 138; Maxine Berg, *Luxury and Pleasure in Eighteenth-Century Britain* (Oxford: Oxford University Press, 2005), 115.

24 E. A. Entwisle, 'Wallpaper and Its History', *Journal of the Royal Society of Arts*, 109 (1961), 450–67 (457).

8 Walter Scott's Writing, Collecting and Reading China

The reason why Beevers described the images illustrated on the Chinese wallpaper as from 'the land of dreams' could be because they were so culturally remote from Europe, but they were at present so vividly displayed right before their eyes. Scott explicitly noted how much he liked the wallpaper in two of his letters, such as on 13 March 1824 when he wrote 'The Chinese paper in the drawing-room is most beautiful'.[26] Such wallpaper serves as evidence of the penetrative force of Chinese culture in Europe. While the seventeenth- and eighteenth-century taste for chinoiserie had greatly declined in the early nineteenth century, Scott's evident enthusiasm for the wallpaper strongly suggests that he had fully embraced that earlier Sinomania. Equally his emphasis on the authentic article may have drawn him to these genuine articles. To visitors, the wallpaper remains one of the most striking of Abbotsford's interiors. Recently, the Abbotsford Trust has been moved to select a part of this wallpaper as the cover of its guidebook to Scott's home and as the base for designing its merchandise.[27]

Although this Chinese wallpaper is only one among the many objects of Scott's important collection, the significance of the wallpaper is worthy of detailed investigation. As Ann Rigney has argued, 'The house itself, [in] both its architecture and its furnishings, can be "read" as another one of his creations and a tissue of reference to his own work'.[28] As with Keats' musing on a Grecian urn or Chapman's Homer, the two-dimensional representation of a work-a-day domestic scene

---

25   David Beevers, '"Mand'rin only is the man of Taste": 17th and 18th Century Chinoiserie in Britain' in *Chinese Whispers: Chinoiserie in Britain, 1650–1930*, ed. David Beevers (East Sussex: The Royal Pavilion & Museums, Brighton & Hove, 2008), 13–25 (22).
26   Scott to Daniel Terry, 13 March 1824, in Sir Herbert Grierson's edition of *The Letters of Sir Walter Scott* (1932–37), vol. 8, 213–14, http://www.walterscott.lib.ed.ac.uk/etexts/etexts/letters8.PDF. In another letter, Scott also described it to Terry as 'the most splendid Chinese paper' on 10 November 1822, in Sir Herbert Grierson's edition of *The Letters of Sir Walter Scott* (1932–37), vol. 7, 278–80, http://www.walterscott.lib.ed.ac.uk/etexts/etexts/letters8.PDF.
27   *The Place I Have Created: A Short Guide to Sir Walter Scott's Home at Abbotsford* (Melrose: The Abbotsford Trust, 2013). This tourist guide was produced by the staff of the Abbotsford Trust, and the author's name is not printed on the guide.

provides a portal for Scott's imaginings of a spatially close but culturally distant and exotic site. In this understanding of the presence of the wallpaper, China no longer remains a geographical 'other' far away in the East; it instead forms an important part of 'us' in the West. The palpable and immediate presence of China in an artistic piece has closed the distance between the East and West since the wallpaper is deeply embedded in the everyday life of Scott's home.

It might also be inferred that Scott's intention was to integrate Chinese culture into his own material life. The message the wallpaper carries, particularly through its visual narration of Chinese stories of everyday life, is very different from the Oriental characters Scott himself produced in both *The Talisman* (1825) and 'The Surgeon's Daughter' (1827) – characters who could be read as the embodiment of the anxieties of the empire, to use Nigel Leask's expression.[29] The Orient illustrated on the Chinese wallpaper is seen as the manifestation of prosperity, happiness, tranquillity and love. It has nothing to do with power and politics; the illustration on the Chinese wallpaper is purely about the everyday life of people in China. Scott places the wallpaper so centrally within the imaginative schema of his home that this act cannot be regarded as an unconscious imperial activity of aggrandising acquisition. Despite the fact that the Chinese wallpaper was not Scott's own design, his incorporation of the wallpaper into the greater design of Abbotsford was itself a creation since the paper was given new life and meaning in the new cultural context.

As Scott's own words tell of his appreciation and fondness for the popular culture of China that is illustrated on the wallpaper, they could, to some extent, be seen as an expression or creation of his 'Romantic Orientalism' in life.[30] This wallpaper is related to other exotic items in Abbotsford, such as the South African horns, Malaysian Krises, Indian armour and Inca relics, and can be interpreted as an important collection

---

28 Ann Rigney, *The Afterlives of Walter Scott: Memory on the Move* (New York: Oxford University Press, 2012), 141.
29 Nigel Leask, *British Romantic Writers and the East: Anxieties of Empire* (Cambridge: Cambridge University Press, 1992).
30 See the definition of 'Romantic Orientalism' in http://www.wwnorton.com/college/english/nael/romantic/topic_4/welcome.htm.

of Scott's 'repository of empire' (using Katie Trumpener's phrase).[31] While this interpretation may be valid, and despite the fact that Scott was known as active in an imperial network of patronage, power and influence, I believe the Abbotsford collection reveals more about Scott's personal interest in historically and culturally significant objects than in any manifestation of the sense of belonging to an empire.[32]

Besides, as we may further infer, the placing of the wallpaper in such a prominent public room was a major statement about what Scott expected others to think of him since he never did anything without a great deal of careful thought. Abbotsford, the 'romance of a house I am making',[33] was one of the most consciously constructed houses by a British author (together with Horace Walpole's Strawberry Hill and William Beckford's Fonthill Abbey). As well as demonstrating his aesthetic posture, with his Chinese wallpaper Scott consciously sought to show visitors that he had a worldview that was cosmopolitan, as Abbotsford, using Rigney's words, 'was a materialized form of self-fashioning'.[34]

Scott's act of integrating Chineseness into the foundation of his personal identity has also reflected what Eugenia Zuroski Jenkins has argued: 'By the nineteenth century, it was impossible to conceive of English identity without attendant notions of Chineseness', and also that 'Writing China into English selfhood was one way of asserting England's global relevance as a cosmopolitan nation'.[35] Further, as Jean Baudrillard has also maintained in *The System of Objects*, 'what you really collect is always yourself'.[36] Abbotsford's collection of Chinese

---

31 Katie Trumpener, *Bardic Nationalism: The Romantic Novel and the British Empire* (Princeton: Princeton University Press, 1997), 243.
32 As Rigney argues, Trumpener's notion of 'repository of empire' seems 'exaggerated'. Rigney, 273.
33 Scott to Lord Montagu, 14–15 March 1822 and 14 November 1822, in *Letters*, vol. 7, 100, 111; Scott to Mrs Hughes in *Letters*, vol. 8, 282 ; quoted in Brown (ed.), *Abbotsford and Sir Walter Scott*, 18.
34 Rigney, 145.
35 Eugenia Zuroski Jenkins, *A Taste for China: English Subjectivity and the Prehistory of Orientalism* (New York: Oxford University Press, 2013), 1, 4.
36 Jean Baudrillard, *The System of Objects*, trans. James Benedict (London: Verso, 1996), 97.

objects also reveals the collector's strong desire to be associated with Chinese metropolitan culture.

In addition to the above-mentioned wallpaper, Scott had collected some fine pieces of Chinese porcelain featuring images of Chinese daily life. They may not be as eye-catching as the wallpaper, but they, too, conveyed something of Chinese life and culture to those who saw them in Scotland. However, it seems more likely that most of Scott's collection of Chinese porcelain may not have been of Chinese origin. Chinese porcelain was introduced to Europe in the sixteenth century and was much sought after by the nobility. Many of these families even placed orders with Chinese factories directly for table services with their own heraldic crests.[37] However, partly due to the enforcement of a maritime embargo in China in 1656, European countries began to attempt their own porcelain production. By the end of the eighteenth century, the technical standards of European porcelain were almost as good as those in China.[38] From that time, European-made Chinese-style porcelains entered widely into ordinary European families. In his essay 'Old China', collected in *Elia and The Last Essays of Elia*, Charles Lamb (1775–1834) notes that 'I am not conscious of a time when china jars and saucers were introduced to my imagination'.[39] At the time Scott was furnishing Abbotsford, therefore, British taste for porcelain was considerable.

Scott's Collection of China-related Books and His Reading of Periodicals

In addition to the wallpaper and porcelain, Scott had a collection of nine China-related books at Abbotsford.[40] When this number is

---

37 Robert Finlay, *The Pilgrim Art: Cultures of Porcelain in World History* (Berkeley and Los Angeles: University of California Press, 2010), 27.
38 Susan Leiper, *Precious Cargo: Scots and the China Trade* (Edinburgh: National Museums of Scotland, 1997), 33.
39 Charles Lamb, *Elia and The Last Essays of Elia*, ed. And with an introduction by Jonathan Bate (Oxford: Oxford University Press, 1987), 281.
40 These books were sourced through the searchable catalogue for the Library of the Faculty of Advocates, Edinburgh.

compared with Scott's collection of over nine thousand books, they occupy only a very tiny space on his Abbotsford bookshelves. However, based on my research and information gleaned from Kitson's *Forging Romantic China*, these nine books emerge as highly valuable. Each of them has its own special meaning in the construction of what Kitson has called 'Romantic Sinology'.[41] More importantly, each of these books provides a specific contribution to Scott's understanding of China. The list commences with:

Thomas Percy, Hao Kiou Choaan, or The Pleasing History (1761)

Thomas Percy (1729–1811), bishop of Dromore, is mostly known in British Romantic-period literature as the editor of *Reliques of Ancient English Poetry* (1765). Among the first of the great collections, the *Reliques* contributed to the ballad revival, itself a significant part of the Romantic movement. However, before the publication of this collection of ballads, Percy had already produced a Chinese work, *Hao Kiou Choaan, or The Pleasing History* in 1761. In a letter to John Murray (1778–1843) in 1808, Scott asked his publisher to get him this book since 'it is a work of equal rarity and curiosity' as *Old Manor House* (1793) by the English novelist Charlotte Smith (1749–1806).[42] This is the first full publication in English of a Chinese novel, and, as Kitson argues, 'Percy's text … is not simply an imaginative recreation of China, a work of fashionable literary chinoiserie … but rather a serious, if flawed, attempt to translate and understand China, the pioneering project of a nascent British Romantic Sinology'.[43] Scott's awareness of the publication of *Hao Kiou Choaan* reveals his keen interest in the cultural interactions between the countries.

---

41 Kitson, 2.
42 Scott to John Murray, 2 November 1808, in *Letters*, vol. 2, 120. The most likely reason that Scott compared *Hao Kiou Choaan, or The Pleasing History* to *Old Manner House* was because that Chinese novel was, like the latter one, also a famous work of romance.
43 Kitson, 27.

Joshua Marshman, The Works of Confucius; Containing the Original Text, With a Translation (1809); Dissertation on the Characters and Sounds of the Chinese Language (1809)

Joshua Marshman (1768–1837), a Baptist missionary, arrived at Serampore in 1799 to support the first Baptist missionary to India, William Carey.[44] In 1809, some twelve years before his main task, the first full translation into Chinese of the Bible, Marshman published *The Works of Confucius; Containing the Original Text, with a Translation*. Kitson claims that this volume contained the first published translation into English of the *Lunyu*. As far as is known, the *Lunyu* and Percy's *Hau Kiou Choann* were the first two direct translations of a Chinese text published in English.[45] It is worth noting that the very first European translation of *Lunyu*, in Latin, appeared in 1687; the English version arrived more than a hundred years later. *Lunyu*, generally known in the West as the *Analects of Confucius*, has been one of the most influential books in the history of China, and remains to this day an enormous influence on Chinese and East Asian thought and values. Scott also collected Marshman's other work, *Dissertation on the Characters and Sounds of the Chinese Language* (1809), a work which is yet to be the subject of scholarship.

John Leyden, Dissertation on the Language and Literature of the Indo-Chinese Nations (1808)

John Leyden (1775–1811), the linguist, poet and Orientalist, had an important role in assisting Scott in his collection of materials for the *Minstrelsy of the Scottish Border* (1812). His post as assistant surgeon at Madras was partly secured by Scott. It is widely believed that Scott's character Adam Hartley in 'The Surgeon's Daughter' is based on Leyden.[46] Leyden's *Dissertation on the Language and Literature of the*

---

44   Kitson, 60.
45   Kitson, 64.
46   Brown, 'Griffins, Nabobs and a Seasoning of Curry Powder', 75. See also Graham Tulloch, 'Scott, India and Australia: Personal and Literary Connections', presented at Global Romanticism, the 2nd Biennial Conference of the Romantic Studies Association of Australasia. University of Sydney, Australia, 2013.

Indo-Chinese Nations (1808) was sent to Scott by the author himself. This work contains a detailed survey of fourteen different languages and literatures sited geographically between India and China.[47]

Basil Hall, Voyage to Loo-Choo, and Other Places in the Eastern Seas, in the Year 1816 (1826)

Captain Basil Hall (1788–1844) was a close friend and admirer of Scott. In 1826, when Scott had suffered a series of strokes and was in poor mental and physical health, it was Hall who organised a trip to Naples for Scott and his daughter, managing to persuade the government to place a ship at his disposal. His *Voyage to Loo-Choo, and Other Places in the Eastern Seas, in the Year 1816* (1826) is one of the first descriptions of Korea by a European, and he shared with Scott stories of his voyage to the Loo-Choo Islands and of a visit to Napoleon at St Helena.[48] In *The Life of Napoleon Buonaparte* (1827–28), Scott mentions the several interviews Lord Amherst had with the emperor Napoleon at St Helena. It is likely that his information came from the writings of Hall and that of Ellis, who follows.

Henry Ellis, Journal of the Proceedings of the Late Embassy to China (1817)

In 1816, Sir Henry Ellis (1788–1855) accompanied Lord Amherst on his mission to China. The mission, to negotiate a new trade agreement, was unsuccessful. Ellis was not impressed by the Chinese, whom he considered xenophobic, ultra-traditional and uninteresting.[49] Ellis recorded his experiences in the *Journal of the Proceedings of the Late Embassy to China* (1817). Scott's copy of the *Journal* was given by John Murray.

---

47 T. W. Bayne, *rev.* Richard Maxwell, 'Leyden, John', *Oxford Dictionary of National Biography*, http://www.oxforddnb.com.
48 Edgar Johnson, *Sir Walter Scott: The Great Unknown*, 2 vols (London: Hamish Hamilton, 1970), 1190–91, 618.
49 R. M. Healey, 'Ellis, Sir Henry', *Oxford Dictionary of National Biography* http://www.oxforddnb.com.

John Francis Davis, Lau-Seng-Urh, or An Heir in His Old Age: A Chinese Drama *(1817);* Chinese Novels *(1822);* The Fortunate Union *(1829)*

In 1813, John Francis Davis (1795–1890), a pupil of Percy, was appointed as a writer to the factory at Canton. Davis, as Kitson argues, was 'a key instrument in carrying out British policy in China ... Davis considered that the translation of Chinese literature was closely related to British interests in the region'.[50] Davis once served as an interpreter on Lord Amherst's embassy to China. Scott collected three of Davis' translations. The first of these was *Lau-Seng-Urh, or An Heir in His Old Age: A Chinese Drama*, originally the work of Wu Han Chin of the fifteenth-century Yuan Dynasty. The translated work was published in Britain by John Murray in 1817. Another translated work by Davis was a collection of short stories called *Chinese Novels* (1822) written by Li Yu (1611–1680). Li's original work contained twelve stories, although Davis' edition contained only three, 'The Shadow in the Water', 'The Twin Sisters' and 'Three Dedicated Rooms'. However, as Kitson argues, Davis' most important contribution to Romantic sinology was to follow in his teacher's footsteps with a popular new translation of the *Haoqiu zhuan* as *The Fortunate Union* in 1829. Scott also had a copy of this translation. Together with Percy and Goethe, Davis, as Kitson argues, was one of the pioneers of China's profile in world literature.[51]

Each of Scott's nine China-related books is a significant production of Sino–British relations, and a result of cross-cultural exchange. Scott would have gone to some lengths to possess them since they were not readily available. But there remains a question as to whether or not Scott had actually read them. The only way of confirming that Scott had read any individual item in the library was whether he had annotated it, or if no pages remain uncut. Lindsay Levy, the former librarian of the Library of the Faculty of Advocates and an expert on Scott's collection of books, has revealed that none of the Chinese books is annotated, although none has uncut leaves. While not in itself definitive evidence, Levy has argued that it is most likely that Scott had read most of his China-related items simply because

---

50   Kitson, 106–7.
51   Kitson, 106.

there were very few books in the library that he had not read. However, one has no way of proving this conclusively.

In her doctoral thesis, 'A Life in Books: Walter Scott's Library at Abbotsford' (2014), Levy has also cogently argued that 'the Library at Abbotsford can be used as a biographical source to cast light on certain aspects of Scott that have been overlooked or distorted by his earlier biographers'.[52] Thus my current study of the above-mentioned books, the wallpaper and other objects can also be seen as useful reference points for us in understanding Scott's close connection with the empire's enterprise in China. Even if we are now denied access to his personal opinion about the country, there is no denying that Scott 'materially' benefited from his connections with those active participants in the development of the empire since his books, the wallpaper and other objects came from or were produced by these people (including missionaries, government officers, merchants, soldiers, explorers and Orientalists). Moreover, from his collection of China-related items, we can also argue that Scott was well informed about the development of Sino–British relations in politics, culture and literature during his own lifetime. Furthermore, his insight into the value of the above-mentioned books has particularly revealed a characteristic trait of a world writer.

Scott's interest in China can possibly be traced back to his early reading of *The Arabian Nights*. John Gibson Lockhart's *Life of Sir Walter Scott* describes Scott's reading of the work:

> Notwithstanding the rigidly Presbyterian habits which this chronicle describes with so much more satisfaction than the corresponding page in the Ashestiel Memoir, I am reminded, by a communication already quoted from a lady of the Ravelstone family, that Mrs. Scott, who had, she says, 'a turn for literature quite uncommon among the ladies of the time,' encouraged her son in his passion for Shakespeare; that his plays, and the Arabian Nights, were often read aloud in the family circle by Walter, 'and served to spend many a happy evening hour.'[53]

---

52 Lindsay Levy, 'A Life in Books: Walter Scott's library at Abbotsford' (unpublished doctoral dissertation, University of Glasgow, 2014), 225.
53 J. G. Lockhart, *Memoirs of the Life of Sir Walter Scott* (Edinburgh: Robert Cadell, 1842), 31–32.

Several of the stories in *The Arabian Nights* mention China and, although they hardly provide an accurate picture of the country, they may well have whetted Scott's appetite, just as his childhood reading about India influenced his later fascination with that country.

In addition to books, periodicals were an indispensable element of Scott's everyday reading. The periodical was a special product of the Romantic period. It was one of the major media for the dissemination of information in the public sphere; it was also a key means for intellectuals to voice their opinions. Moreover, as Mark Schoenfield argues, periodicals were highly pertinent to the formation of British identity during that period of time.[54] Scott was not only a regular contributor to a number of major British periodicals, he was also a principal promoter of the establishment of the *Quarterly Review*, the idea of which was first put forward by John Murray. Although Scott declined Murray's invitation to be the editor, he remained active in helping Murray to select the editor, contributors and books for review.[55] In addition, Scott contributed twenty-four articles to the *Quarterly Review*, including topics relating to Scottish history, literature and culture during the time when William Gifford (1756–1826) served as the first editor (1809–24).[56] Between 1826 and 1853, Scott's son-in-law, John Gibson Lockhart, also served as the editor of the *Quarterly*. These facts are a clear indication of Scott's close relationship with the *Quarterly*. His active involvement during the early days of the *Quarterly* had directly decided the political and cultural stance of this review.[57] Although Scott never made comments on Britain's imperial enterprise in the Far East, the relatively high percentage of articles in the *Quarterly Review* about the development of the British Empire in Asia could be a result of Scott's devoted participation. At the same time, Scott's knowledge about this imperial enterprise in the East most likely came from his reading of the *Quarterly*.

---

54 Mark Schoenfield, *British Periodicals and Romantic Identity: The 'Literary Lower Empire'* (New York: Palgrave Macmillan, 2009).
55 Sharon Ragaz, 'Walter Scott and the *Quarterly Review*' in Jonathan Cutmore, ed., *Conservatism and the Quarterly Review: A Critical Analysis* (London: Pickering & Chatto, 2007), 107–32 (118).
56 Ragaz, 119.
57 Ragaz, 110.

John Barrow (1764–1848), one of the most active writers among the regular contributors to the *Quarterly*, was a 'traveller, author, colonial administrator, influential member of the Royal Society, co-founder of the Royal Geographical Society and Second Secretary to the Admiralty for forty years'.[58] In the space of thirty years, he contributed over two hundred articles to the *Quarterly*.[59] Barrow mainly used the review to promote the nation's business in Asia. He once worked as Lord Macartney's secretary on the latter's historic embassy to China.[60] Barrow's *Travels in China* (1804) was praised by Francis Jeffrey (1773–1850), editor of the *Edinburgh Review*, as the 'most sound, judicious and candid' account of the country.[61] Barrow's account of his experiences, as Michael Adas concludes, 'formed the nucleus of a cluster of ideas about China that informed virtually all nineteenth-century accounts of the Qing empire'.[62] Scott, both a regular contributor and reader of the *Quarterly*, had very likely read Barrow's articles in that periodical and it is reasonable to infer that Barrow's writings had a direct influence on Scott's understanding of China.

Conclusion

Cheape's theorising on the insights of material culture enables us to argue that through the systematic fashion in which Scott gathered materials about him in Abbotsford we have a clear insight into the man's preoccupations. This is clearly borne out by the survey of Chinese and Chinese-related objects within Abbotsford. These materials, coupled with his energetic engagement in the periodical review activity of his day, demonstrates that while Scott was not a sinologist per se, his

---

58 J. M. R. Cameron, 'John Barrow, the *Quarterly*'s Imperial Reviewer' in Jonathan Cutmore, ed., *Conservatism and the Quarterly Review: A Critical Analysis* (London: Pickering & Chatto, 2007), 133–50 (133).
59 Cameron, 133.
60 Cameron, 144.
61 Cited in Cameron, 144. [Francis Jeffrey, 'Barrow's Travels in China', *Edinburgh Review* 5 (January 1805), 259–88].
62 Michael Adas, *Machines as the Measure of Men: Science, Technology, and Ideologies of Western Dominance* (Ithaca, NY: Cornell University Press, 1989), 183.

lively interest in China supplements and contextualises the substantial corpus of material outlined above. It reflects not simply a pedestrian accumulation of quaint material culture but rather a nuanced appreciation of the nation and culture these objects represented.

Acknowledgements

This essay was originally published in Chinese by *The Wenshan Review of Literature and Culture*, 11–1 (2017), 89–113, and was slightly revised. Special thanks to Dr Coinneach Maclean who helped and contributed a lot to the writing of this work. During the editing stage, Prof. Will Christie's and Dr Angela Dunstan's patient involvement was also of great help. This is deeply appreciated. However, if there are still errors, they all remain mine.

9

'Sheer Memory': The Victorian Idea of Confucian Education

Dongqing Wang

In his public lecture series on hero-worship, delivered in May 1840, Thomas Carlyle celebrated Chinese literati as a fine example of the 'hero as man of letters', a modern form of philosopher-king:

> By far the most interesting thing I hear about the Chinese is … that they do attempt to make their Men of Letters their Governors! … The man of intellect at the top of the affairs: this is the aim of all constitutions and revolutions, if they have any aim … Get *him* for Governor, all is got; fail to get him, though you had constitutions plentiful as blackberries, and a Parliament in every village, there is nothing yet got![1]

If Carlyle seriously considered Confucian meritocracy as a 'precious' political experiment and a promising alternative to English parliamentary democracy, he would be shocked to find that, in the same year, the First Opium War shook Qing China's confidence in the Confucian world order. Within one month of Carlyle's statements, the British expeditionary forces, with steam-powered gunboats carrying over four thousand soldiers, approached Canton from Bombay and

---

1   Thomas Carlyle, *On Heroes, Hero-worship, and the Heroic in History* (London: Chapman and Hall Ltd., 1840), 199–200.

Singapore.² Confronted with the seemingly invincible British gunboats, the Chinese literati were anxious and helpless, since most of them remained largely ignorant of the military and technical power of industrial civilisation. The classically educated mandarins still recognised Britain as a 'barbarian' and 'tributary' nation, failing to understand why a few steamboats could force their empire's door open.

The Opium Wars marked an early moment when the admiration of Confucian meritocracy began to be questioned and the limits of classical Chinese learning came into discussion among the Westerners. William A. P. Martin, a Yale-educated Presbyterian missionary and leading educational reformer in late Qing China, attributed China's failure to the narrow-mindedness of Confucian education. When a limited number of ancient classics were taught by rote, education was a matter of 'sheer memory', only to repress the nation's potential for creativity:

> Instead of requiring a lad, dictionary in hand, to quarry out the meaning of his author, the teacher reads the lesson for him, and demands of him nothing more than a faithful reproduction of that which he has received; memory again, sheer memory! Desirable as this method might be for beginners, when continued, as the Chinese do, through the whole course, it has the inevitable effect of impairing independence of judgment and fertility of invention, ... for the deficiency of which they are, no doubt, indebted to this error of schoolroom discipline.³

As this essay intends to show, the significant rupture between Carlyle's early celebration of Chinese literati and Martin's stern critique of Confucian pedagogy allows us to recognise an epistemological change in the social imaginary of how to educate modern human subjects. Tracing the changing ideas of Confucian education in the Victorian period, this

---

2 See Edgar Holt, *The Opium Wars in China* (London: Putnam, 1964), 96–97. See also Peter Ward Fay, *The Opium War, 1840–1842: Barbarians in the Celestial Empire in the Early Part of the Nineteenth Century and the War by Which They Forced Her Gates Ajar* (Chapel Hill: University of North Carolina Press, 1975), 213–15.
3 William A. P. Martin, *The Lore of Cathay: or the Intellect of China* (Edinburgh; London: Oliphant, Anderson & Ferrier, 1901), 292.

9 'Sheer Memory': The Victorian Idea of Confucian Education

essay seeks to understand the rise of liberal education as a product of cross-cultural social debates on industry, culture and democracy in the context of global modernity. It further explores how the Orientalist critique of Confucian pedagogy played a revolutionary role in making the modern mind and shaping social democracy in China.

Beyond Memory: A Liberal Education

In 1596, Matteo Ricci presented Lu Wan'gai, the consul of Jiangxi, with his own work, *Treatises on Mnemonic Arts*, in the hope of introducing the European art of memory to the Chinese literati. The 'memory palace', borrowed from the Renaissance tradition, served to map loosely connected impressions and concepts in a fixed spatial system, consisting of imaginary 'rooms' filled with various objects in assigned positions, each representing an idea to be remembered.[4] For Ricci, memory was both a classical art and a scholastic tradition, a God-given power for collecting and organising knowledge.[5] Curiously, Ricci expected the mnemonic method to grow popular as it would enable Chinese scholars to memorise Confucian classics required for imperial civil service examinations. The art of memory, employed by Ricci to establish a sphere of influence for the Jesuits, acted as a shared tradition between Catholicism and Confucianism.

There's a certain irony in the sharp contrast between Ricci's early obsession with improving mnemonic methods and the missionary educators' idea of the Confucian practice of memorising classics. Having gained wider access to inland China after the Second Opium War, the Euro-American missionaries commonly considered the lecturing in local schools as offering a smattering of classical texts through repetitive cramming. Arthur Evans Moule, working in China

---

4 See Matteo Ricci, *Treatises on Mnemonic Arts* [Xiguo jifa], in Zhu Weizheng ed., *Works of Matteo Ricci in Chinese* [Limadou zhongwen zhuyiji] (Shanghai: Fudan University Press, 2001), 143, 168. See also Jonathan Spence, *The Memory Palace of Matteo Ricci* (New York: Viking, 1984), 1–23.
5 For the European tradition of mnemonic practice, see F. A. Yates, *The Art of Memory*, F. A. Yates: *Selected Works*, vol. 3 (London and New York: Routledge, 2001).

for thirty years as a member of the Church Missionary Society, recalled how the trimetrical primer was taught to local schoolboys:

> This book is learnt by rote. The master shouts out the first sentence, each word being carefully enunciated, intonated, and explained. The boys, standing in front of the master, in chorus repeat the same sentence, and after a while they return to their seats, and swaying their bodies to and fro, declaiming their passage as loud as they can.[6]

This is a Chinese teacher *par excellence*, since, as William Martin noted, 'Severity is accounted the first virtue in a pedagogue; and its opposite is not kindness, but negligence'.[7] The worse examples soon reminded Martin of a Dickensian case of educational tyranny:

> In charity-schools, the portrait of Squeers in *Nicholas Nickleby* would be no caricature. With modifications and improvements in the curriculum, a teacher has nothing to do. His business is to keep the mill going, and the time-honored argument a posteriori is the only persuasion he cares to appeal to.[8]

In Dickens' early novel *Nicholas Nickleby*, Wackford Squeers is headmaster of Dotheboys Hall, a Yorkshire private boarding school where schoolboys are not only ill-educated but abused and tortured. Squeers remains a notorious representative of the greedy, cruel and ignorant educator. To meet the growing demands from the rising middle class for a proper education, the business of private schools boomed. Many of them, in the name of educating 'little gentlemen', were run as asylums, mainly open to disabled or illegitimate children. Teaching became a boring ritual:

---

6   Arthur Evans Moule, *New China and Old: Personal Recollections and Observations of Thirty Years* (London: Seeley and Co. Ltd., 1891), 244.
7   Martin, *The Lore of Cathay*, 291.
8   Martin, *The Lore of Cathay*, 291.

9 'Sheer Memory': The Victorian Idea of Confucian Education

> The children were arranged in a semicircle round the new master, and he was soon listening to their dull, drawling, hesitating recital of those stories of engrossing interest which are to be found in the more antiquated spelling books.

Martin's allusion to Dickens is not simply anecdotal digression. As Dickens' assault on private schools articulates the Victorian anxiety about the quality of middle-class education, it points to a Victorian self lurking in Martin's critique of the Chinese Other. There is a striking similarity of grind and repetition between the 'drawling' recital of spelling books and the declaiming 'chorus' in a Chinese class. This veiled connection has come to the surface in the way missionary reformers imagined a dystopia of classical philology that stretched across Europe and China.

In Martin's critique of the fossilised style of the classical Chinese essay (*wenzhang*), an analogy that immediately came to his mind was the composition of Latin verse. Martin wrote: 'A juster parallel for the intense and fruitless concentration of energy on this species of composition is the passion for Latin verse which was dominant in our halls of learning until dethroned by the rise of modern science.'[9] Whereas Ricci saw the art of memory as the fruit of a classical tradition formed globally, Martin recognised the preoccupation with memory training as a general problem of classical education that troubled both Confucian China and Victorian Britain. Here, the battle between classical literature and modern science displaced the assumed opposition between China and the West. John Barrow, third commissioner of Lord Macartney's embassy to China, noted the similarities between the 'mode of Chinese education' and the 'plan of educating youths in the public grammar schools of our own country':

> Some of the most precious years of their lives, when the faculties were in growing vigour, and the plastic mind most susceptible of receiving and retaining impressions, are wasted in poring over the metaphysics of a Latin Grammar, which they cannot possibly comprehend; and in learning by heart a number of declinations,

---

9   Martin, *The Lore of Cathay*, 296.

conjugations, and syntax rules, which serve only to puzzle and disgust, instead of affording instruction or amusement.[10]

The habitual cross-reference between the Chinese Other and the Victorian Self may allow us to situate the idea of Confucian education in a global context, and trace a critical tradition that many Protestant missionary educators had been following and developing in examining Confucian learning. For Martin and Barrow, the eight-legged essay and Latin verse expressed the common defect of classical philology.

With state supervision and the liberal educators' organised resistance, the authority of classics had received a range of serious social challenges in mid-Victorian England. Classical learning, now regarded as strongly exclusive in terms of both knowledge scope and social class, had begun to lose its monopoly over the educational market and to give way to curricular pluralism. Following the broadened franchise of the 1867 Reform Act, the prospect of an industrialised democracy urged a group of academic liberals and social reformers to establish a curricular scheme more inclusive and practical for 'our future masters'. Unlike classical learning that encouraged intellectual detachment from professional pursuits, a modern liberal education intended to arm the rising middle class with sciences and modern languages in an age of mechanical reproduction, market competition and mass culture.[11]

In 1867, a group of Oxbridge reformers and liberal schoolmasters contributed to a major critique of classical education in a collection of essays entitled *Essays on a Liberal Education*.[12] F. W. Farrar, chief editor of this volume, held China as a warning example of how a blind imitation of the ancients impeded intellectual progress and encouraged social stagnation:

---

10   John Barrow, *Travels in China*, 260–61.
11   For how state intervention and social campaigns challenged the authority of classical education, see Christopher Stray, *Classics Transformed: Scholars, Universities, and Society in England* (Oxford: Clarendon Press, 1998), 83–113.
12   *Essays on a Liberal Education*, ed. F. W. Farrar (London: Macmillan & Co., 1867). The original title of this collection was *Essays on a Classical Education*. See Stray, *Classics Transformed*, 95.

9 'Sheer Memory': The Victorian Idea of Confucian Education

Are we, in the nineteenth century, to learn no more and to teach no more ... than was learnt by young Romans in the school of Quintilian, or at best by Gregory and Basil in the retirement of Athens? ... Are we alone to follow the example of the Chinese in a changeless imitation of our ancestors, and to confine our eager boys for ever between the blank walls of an ancient cemetery, which contains only the sepulchres of two dead tongues?[13]

This evolutionary idea of modern education was deeply rooted in the structure of industrial modernity. In a world transformed by mass production and the global market, the liberal minds questioned the necessity of classical scholarship that served primarily as a symbol of social privilege and ignored 'the actual world and living men'.[14] Whereas a courtier might calculate intricate social networks according to the subtle responses of his peers, a merchant's choices entirely followed the iron law of supply and demand. Since personal virtues and manners helped little in calculating market prices and making legal contracts, modern education required not so much a pure soul as an analytical mind. As a result, T. H. Huxley defined liberal education as learning the rules of a mighty game:

The chess-board is the world, the pieces are the phenomena of the universe, the rules of the game are what we call the laws of Nature. The player on the other side is hidden from us. We know that his play is always fair, just and patient. But also we know, to our cost, that he never overlooks a mistake, or makes the smallest allowance for ignorance. To the man who plays well, the highest stakes are paid ... And one who plays ill is checkmated – without haste, but without remorse.[15]

---

13 F. W. Farrar (ed.), *On Some Defects on Public School Education: A Lecture Delivered at the Royal Institution* (London: Macmillan & Co., 1867), 23.
14 Lord Houghton, 'On the Present Social Results of Classical Education', in Farrar, ed., *Essays on a Liberal Education* (London: Macmillan & Co., 1868), 368.
15 T. H. Huxley, 'A Liberal Education; and Where to Find It', in *T. H. Huxley on Education* (Cambridge: Cambridge University Press, 1971), 78.

In spite of the social Darwinist thinking involved, the significance of Huxley's metaphor lies in the epistemological foundation it seeks to establish for what Carlyle calls an 'age of Mechanism'. Since the laws of nature apply to 'men and their ways' as well as 'things and their forces', society runs as an abstract, autonomous system of individual competition,[16] in which human players calculate their next moves according to the given rule. Huxley's chessboard exemplified a social imaginary modelled on industrial production and market competition.

To produce competitive players in this market of intelligence, liberal educators modelled the human mind on an industrial division of labour and thus recognised it as a *system* of intellectual faculties, managing various spheres of human experience including perception, memory, understanding, reasoning, judgement and imagination. Accordingly, any subject of teaching had to justify its value by being capable of developing a certain aspect of mental power. Even those 'old humanists' had to defend classical education in this way: classical languages helped to stimulate memory, classical poetry refined imagination, and so on.[17] This battle marked a revolution in the English understanding of human subjectivity: insofar as the human mind was conceived as a machine with all its intellectual cogs in place, the classical cultivation of morality and tastes would necessarily be marginalised. Those virtues that formerly made a gentleman ended up in an isolated mental faculty – moral judgement. The ideal state of the human intellect, according to Huxley, was a 'clear, cold logic engine, ... ready ... to be turned into any kind of work'.[18]

Reading Dickensian satire on the smattering of classical learning, missionary reformers had launched the project of liberal education at the imperial periphery. In 1869, two years after *Essays on a Liberal Education* had been published in London, William Martin was appointed chancellor of the Foreign Language Academy (*Tongwen*

---

16 As to how industrialism altered the English notion of 'society' and 'individual', see Raymond Williams, *Keywords: A Vocabulary of Culture and Society* (New York: Oxford University Press, 1983), 291–95.
17 For the Victorian theory of cognitive faculties, see Sheldon Rothblatt, *Tradition and Change in English Liberal Education: An Essay in History and Culture* (London: Faber and Faber, 1976), 126–32.
18 Huxley, 'A Liberal Education', 81.

9 'Sheer Memory': The Victorian Idea of Confucian Education

Guan), the first state-run modern college in Beijing. The college developed an eight-year program of general education, covering a wide range of subjects from astronomy and anatomy to world history and international law.[19] The unprecedentedly broad scope of the college curriculum served China's urgent need to build its industrial and military power, and produced an early generation of translators, diplomats and liberal-minded reformers.[20] No less significantly, it began to transform the mode of knowledge production formerly dominated by Confucian pedagogy. Thus, Martin's critique of the Dickensian schoolmaster was more than the dissemination of an idea from the centre of empire to its Asian periphery; it demonstrated how a social imaginary could be institutionalised so as to reproduce and circulate knowledge as such.

However, as many missionary educators in China became aware, it would be difficult to promote scientific knowledge before they could reshape the Chinese conception of knowledge in the first place. As Martin recalled, his Chinese assistants remained indifferent to the telegraph performance, 'without showing any sign of intelligence or interest'. Ironically, they enjoyed catching magnetic fish and chasing magnetic geese, 'chuckling all the while over the novelty of the sport'.[21] Science, as a system of knowledge and a mode of social understanding,

---

19   For the college syllabus, see *Zhongguo jindai jiaoyushi ziliao huibian: yangwu yundong shiqi jiaoyu* (Primary sources for education in modern China: education in the self-strengthening movement), eds. Gao Shiliang and Huang Renxian (Shanghai: Shanghai jiaoyu chubanshe, 2007), 92–99. Hereafter, the volume is cited as *YW*. For the history and organisation of the college and a brief account of its teaching faculty and students, see Su Jing, *Qingji Tongwen Guan jiqi shisheng* (*Tongwen Guan* in the Qing Dynasty: its faculty and students) (Taibei: Sujing, 1985); Sun Zihe, *Qingdai Tongwen Guan zhi yanjiu* (A study of *Tongwen Guan* in the Qing Dynasty) (Taipei: Jiaxin shuini gongsi wenhua jijinhui, 1977).
20   In addition, technical and industrial schools were established to train engineers for shipbuilding, mining, the telegraph, and railways, and soldiers for using modern arms. Important institutes of this kind included Fujian Naval Academy (*Fujian chuanzheng xuetang*, 1866) and Tianjin Telegraph School (*Tianjin dianbao xuetang*, 1867).
21   William A. P. Martin, *A Cycle of Cathay* (New York: Fleming H. Revell, 1900), 299–300.

remained alien to classically trained mandarins. Therefore, the key to a modern liberal education would be the development of a liberal understanding of education. Methodist A. P. Parker, president of the Educational Association of China, came to define the human mind as a system of mental powers in an 1890 conference speech:

> The Chinese need improved educational methods. Their system, while it develops the memory in a wonderful manner ..., dwarfs the other powers of the mind, ruins the reasoning faculty, destroys the imagination, prevents independence of thought, checks original investigation, and is altogether vicious and totally inadequate to develop the God-given powers of the human mind.[22]

Following Victorian liberal educators in promoting the cultivation of the cognitive faculties, Parker and his fellow reformers felt it necessary to abolish the monopoly of memory and reassert a balance of mental powers so as to create liberal minds that could function in a globalised China. In Parker's view, the system of mental faculties provided an epistemological basis for the new taxonomy of knowledge, curriculum, and academic disciplines, and marked a significant change in the nature of education. Liberal education shifted its goal from social character formation to intellectual training: the will to know and understand the world took priority over the demand for giving a moral order to it. Among the educational association members, the Prussian missionary and sinologist Ernst Faber's radical reassessment of Confucian learning exemplified such a social imaginary in the wake of industrial modernity. For him, the moral universe that inhabited the Confucian classics had collapsed, and therefore the texts should be read as documents of 'national history'. Faber stated:

---

22 A. P. Parker, 'Our Opportunity', in *Records of the Triennial Meeting of the Educational Association of China* (Taipei: Reprinted by Ch'eng Wen, 1971), 50. This reprint collects the records of three triennial meetings, held at Shanghai successively in 1893, 1896 and 1899. The pages of each meeting's record are separately numbered. The quotation comes from Parker's speech given at the first meeting, 2–4 May 1893.

9 'Sheer Memory': The Victorian Idea of Confucian Education

The Chinese classics have their proper place in our educational work in connection with Chinese literature. Literature, however, can only be taught intelligently as an important part of the national history. The time has gone by when it was possible to regard history as consisting principally in the stories of kings and their wars and literature in dry particulars about books and authors. We see now in history the development of human life in all its manifestations, evil as well as good. We trace events to their causes and follow out the consequences of particular acts, whether virtuous or vicious. The literature of a nation is one manifestation of its life, and it affords a deeper insight into the national *heart*, into its feelings and aspirations, than do actions and external circumstances. We should teach Chinese history from this high standpoint.[23]

As Faber argued, Chinese classics ought to be read and taught as literary representations of Chinese society and history. These representations were essentially amoral, covering figures and events and actions, 'virtuous or vicious', although they could be taught as moral exemplars or religious lessons at a later point.[24] Such was his attempt to dethrone the universal authority of classical Chinese learning and reduce it to a record of national psychology and action. Though it was partly a Christian response to heathen thoughts, the attempt to provincialise Confucian universalism equally marked a radical form of historicism and empiricism in the sweeping advance of industrial modernity.

The Protestant missionaries' promotion of liberal education provided a critique of and an alternative to Confucian pedagogy in late Qing China, but their ambition was beyond training schoolboys. Teaching knowledge marked the beginning of social reform, as such knowledge had to be circulated, accepted and authorised before it could create a sphere of influence. When Martin was complaining about the prospect of the Foreign Language Academy and seeking to 'open a field

---

23 Ernst Faber, 'What Shall We Do with the Chinese Classics and the Wen-chang in Our Educational Work', the second triennial meeting, 6–9 May 1896, in *Records of the Triennial Meeting*, 75.
24 Faber, 75.

of influence wider than ... the wayside chapels of Peking',[25] his attention was directed to the last barrier against the sprouting of liberal education in China: the imperial civil service examinations.

Expanding Democracy: A Public Examination System

As early as the sixteenth century, a bureaucracy produced through competitive examinations had captured the European imagination on issues of justice, democracy and social mobility. John Francis Davis, who later became the second British governor of Hong Kong, admired the examination system for creating a 'road open to talents':

> The impartial distribution (with few exceptions) of state offices and magistracies to *all* who give evidence of superior learning or talent, without regard to birth or possessions, lies probably at the bottom of the greatness and prosperity of the empire.[26]

Before the First Opium War, Davis and Carlyle were not alone in considering Chinese literary examinations as a cure for the corrupt patronage system in English official appointments. Though it would be difficult to specify the Chinese influence on particular operations in English civil service reform, the China model played a significant role in the social debates on the adoption of the civil service examination system in the 1850s.[27]

Ironically, as the Opium Wars exposed the incompatibility between classical learning and modern governance, it soon allowed the education reformers to see the historical limits of an examination-based meritocracy. The civil service examinations, as a competitive system

---

25 As Martin told the Qing mandarins, 'The care of only ten boys who learn nothing but English is for me too small a business'. Martin, *Cycle*, 298.
26 John Francis Davis, *The Chinese: A General Description of the Empire of China and its Inhabitants*, Vol.1 (London: Charles Knight & Co., 1836), 259.
27 For the European admiration of the imperial examination system since the sixteenth century, see Ssu-yü Teng, 'Chinese Influence on the Western Examination System', in *Harvard Journal of Asiatic Studies* (September 1934), 276–92.

9 'Sheer Memory': The Victorian Idea of Confucian Education

that awarded candidates academic titles, dominated the distribution of literary reputation, official position and social privilege. In setting up a scheme of subjects, questions and procedures, the imperial examination shaped the intellectual formation of the ruling elites through the inclusion of 'proper' knowledge and the assertion of an authorised epistemology. The slow progress of a liberal education in China was believed to result primarily from the exclusion of Western learning in the examination system, whose syllabus remained dominantly classical, largely confined to a list of pre-Han Dynasty Confucian classics, aided with poetry composition and policy questions.[28]

For Martin and many other educational reformers, the incompetence of Chinese mandarins resulted from the limits of knowledge production: 'If these men [the Qing officials] are not highly educated, it is the fault not of the competitive system ... but of the false standard of intellectual merit established in China'. Martin believed that the knowledge that the examination system encouraged candidates to produce was defective because in the imperial examinations, 'letters [were] everything and science nothing'. The solution was to introduce Western scientific subjects into the examination so that such knowledge could be authorised and promoted: 'Millions of aspiring students ... soon become as earnest in the pursuit of modern science as they now are in the study of their ancient classics'.[29] Furthermore, it could assert Western knowledge as a sphere of political influence in an imperial bureaucracy.

Martin believed that the door of the imperial examinations stayed 'sufficiently ajar' to practical learning by including statecraft issues in the policy questions.[30] However, the epistemological pattern involved in the questions was different from that of 'scientific understanding'. A case in point was a question about weaponry:

---

28 The format of the provincial and metropolitan civil examinations before the 1898 reforms was basically as follows: session one's questions were based on quotations from the Four Books, with a poetry question; in session two, questions referred to the Five Classics; the final session covered policy questions. See Benjamin Elman, *A Cultural History of Civil Examinations* (Berkeley: University of California Press, 2000), 737.
29 Martin, *The Lore of Cathay*, 323.
30 Martin, *The Lore of Cathay*, 323.

Fire-arms began with the use of rockets in the Chou Dynasty (B.C. 1122–256); in what book do we first meet with the word for cannon? What is the difference in the two classes of engines to which it is applied (applied also to the catapult)? Is the defense of K'ai Feng Fu its first recorded use? Kublai Khan, it is said, obtained cannon of a new kind; from whom did he obtain them? The Sungs had several varieties of small cannon, what were their advantages? When the Mings, in the reign of Yung Lo, invaded Cochin-China, they obtained a kind of cannon called the 'weapons of the gods'; can you give an account of their origin?[31]

As Martin noted, this question signalled a primary divergence between modern science and classical philology.[32] The question does not take the cannon as a *thing* of use; instead, it requires a full knowledge of 'allusions' to the cannon, totally confined to the 'circle of classical literature'. Thus, the cannon is considered less a lethal weapon than an object of philological inquiry. This philological approach aims to unveil the classical *representations* of things, rather than the things themselves. Such knowledge is essentially textual, not practical. Therefore, Martin argued that knowledge was not treated 'in a scientific manner' in Chinese learning as in the West, because words were favoured over things.[33]

From the 1880s, as the Qing court created special subjects and degrees for modern sciences, candidates specialising in non-classical learning could pass the provincial examination and acquire academic titles under a special quota.[34] The missionary educators saw it as a

---

31 Martin, *The Lore of Cathay*, 323 fn.
32 Elman, *From Philosophy to Philology: Intellectual and Social Aspects of Change in Late Imperial China* (Cambridge, MA: Council on East Asian Studies, Harvard University, 1984), 83–85.
33 Martin, *The Lore of Cathay*, 322.
34 In 1887, to abolish the monopoly of moral philosophy and classical philology over the civil service examination system, the Ministry of Foreign Affairs introduced natural and social sciences into the examination subjects, especially those closely relevant to modern statecraft such as physics, mechanics, international law and world history. See the memorial by the Ministry of Foreign Affairs, *WX*, 670–72. For the creation of the statecraft degree in 1898, see Yan Xiu, Education Commissioner of Guizhou, 'Zouqing she jingji zhuanke zhe' (A proposal for creating a special degree of statecraft,

9 'Sheer Memory': The Victorian Idea of Confucian Education

perfect moment to establish a privileged status for Western learning in the imperial bureaucracy. Presbyterian missionary Gilbert Reid expressed his hearty praise: 'New life is to be breathed into the system, and new lines to be marked out for the youthful ambitions of the literati of China'.[35] In his 1895 essay published in *The Globe Magazine* (*Wanguo gongbao*), a popular reading among the imperial reformers, Reid affirmed the urgency of civil service examination reform:

> Since the Confucian classics are concerned with morality alone, and the civil service examination assigns priority to written compositions, how could we fully fulfill the potential of education? The solution is to include a variety of learning [science, engineering, navigation, economy, law, philosophy, etc.] in the civil service examinations, ... and then the government may endorse special admission of those candidates of different majors so that the talents won't fall into oblivion.[36]

Finally, the expansion of Western schools in China allowed them to develop an alternative to the examination system. In 1890, British missionary W. T. A. Barber, president of a church school in Wuchang, proposed creating a public examination system for the modern schools in China, for which a board of examiners would codify subjects,

---

16 December 1897. *WX*, 53–56; the Ministry of Foreign affairs and Board of Rites, 'Zunyi kaishe jingji teke zhe' (A scheme of the special degree of statecraft), 27 January 1898. *WX*, 56–58.

35 Gilbert Reid, *Peeps into China* (London: Religious Tract Society, 1892), 159.

36 Reid, 'Chuangshe xuexiao yi' (On the founding of schools), *The Globe Magazine*, Vol. 84, 1895, 580. The essay was published under his Chinese name, Li Jiabai. In late Qing terminology, the term *wenxue* in this essay was rendered as 'education'. This seems to go against our modern notion of *wenxue* as 'literature', but it was among the late Qing terminology of translation, modelled on the Japanese expression for education. The Chinese translation of *Education in Japan*, for instance, was entitled *Wenxue xingguo ce*. The translator was Young John Allen, an American Methodist missionary who founded and edited *The Globe Magazine*. See *Education in Japan: A Series of Letters Addressed by Prominent Americans to Arinori Mori* (New York: D. Appleton, 1873) and its Chinese translation *Wenxue xingguo ce* (Shanghai: Shanghai shudian chubanshe, 2002).

syllabuses and academic certification.³⁷ As he envisioned, this system would consist of a list of set subjects, a syllabus of textbooks, and a procedure for granting certificates. The public examination system would encourage local schools to adopt a codified course of study and to self-regulate their teaching programs.

In 1891, the Educational Association of China set up a committee on the scheme of public examinations, chaired by Barber and attended by D. Z. Sheffield and A. P. Parker. In 1899, in collaboration with the Society for the Diffusion of Christianity and General Knowledge among the Chinese (*Guangxue hui*) headed by Timothy Richard, the Educational Association of China published the public examination scheme in *The Globe Magazine*.³⁸ Notably, Barber borrowed the idea of a public examination from the Oxbridge scheme of the Middle-class Local Examinations. Barber saw the public examination as a form of educational democracy that provided the poor broader access to higher education. Barber wrote:

> A Board of Examiners was appointed, a syllabus of study, with set subjects, issued; and all the schools in the country were invited to send their pupils in for competition … .[C]lever boys of the middle-class, who formerly were utterly and hopelessly outside the chance of the expensive English university life, gained courage by early successes; the avenues to Cambridge and Oxford were thrown open … [and] the general educational standard of the whole nation has been sensibly raised.³⁹

In E. F. Gedye's view, this democratic system not only was 'thoroughly feasible' in China; it would also establish the authority of Western learning. In his 1899 speech at the Triennial Meeting of the Educational

---

37 W. T. A. Barber, 'A Public Examination for Western Schools in China', *The Chinese Recorder*, March 1890, 129–31.
38 The Society for the Diffusion of Christianity and General Knowledge among the Chinese, 'Tuiguang shixue tiaoli' (A scheme of promoting practical learning), December 1899, in *Wanguo gongbao wenxuan* (Selections from *The Globe Magazine*), ed. Zhu Weizheng (Hong Kong: Sanlian shudian, 1998), 662–65.
39 Barber, 'A Public Examination', 130.

9 'Sheer Memory': The Victorian Idea of Confucian Education

Association of China, Gedye believed the examination scheme would fulfil the goal of the failed reforms in 1898:

> We all hope and expect that the reform movement in China is not dead. ... If we can now found an examination board, in a few years it ought to become a power in China. Those who have passed the examinations will obtain posts as teachers in government schools.[40]

Gedye expected this examination system to mobilise educational reform, and to create and distribute Western learning as a form of cultural capital. In addition, China needed to extend mass schooling with a standard in-class teaching system. Both served to restore the autonomy of the schooling program by freeing it from the market of civil service.

As mass schooling replaced examination-oriented elite education, the official literati, who were formerly the nexus of knowledge, morality, and state power, gave way to professional intellectuals. The system of modern schools, advocated by the missionary educators and Qing reformers, aimed at producing a strong and civilised nation.

In contrast to the marginalisation of Confucian learning in the search for a modern China, the revival of Confucianism occupies the central ideological concern of the postcolonial and postrevolutionary present.[41] The political call for a Confucian state, along with the global sprouting of state-sponsored 'Confucius Institutes' and the popular representation of Confucian doctrines as 'ancient wisdom', exemplifies China's attempt to claim an alternative modernity on the basis of the nation's cultural past. Both the May-Fourth era repression of and the postrevolutionary revival of Confucian values, ironically, have been built on an essentialist, ahistorical understanding of national culture. In this context, Orientalism played a central role in shaping revolutionary

---

40   E. F. Gedye, 'An Examination Board for China', 17–20 May 1899, in *Records of the Triennial Meeting*, 55.
41   For a critique of the Confucian revival's ideological complicity with global capitalism, see Arif Dirlik, 'Confucius in the Borderlands', in *Culture & History in Postrevolutionary China* (Hong Kong: The Chinese University of Hong Kong, 2011), 97–156.

criticism and cultural conservatism alike. To fully understand the paradox of Third-World criticism in the age of global modernity, we must examine its (semi)colonial origins in terms of how Orientalist discourse undermined the authority of subaltern culture and at the same time preserved it as a provincialised tradition.

10
The Life and Death and Life of Augustus Raymond Margary

Elizabeth Hope Chang

Writing to his mother in July of 1874, the young British vice-consul Augustus Raymond Margary described with excitement his latest assignment – an expedition up the Yangtze River and across western China aiming to chart a new overland passage through Burma to British India. 'It is a long, and, to a certain extent, a perilous journey', he acknowledges, continuing: 'I can't disguise that fact, and that for three months I shall be beyond the reach of all news of the outer world. You must picture me trudging on through strange cities, stared at by pig-tailed mobs ... you may look at the map and fancy you see a solitary European standing above the last pass on the borders of China, and anxiously gazing through his binoculars for the advent of Indian helmets from the West'.[1] Margary's imagined vision was realised – 'I am the first European who has traversed the trade-route of the future', he wrote after successfully connecting with British agents travelling to meet him from India – but his mission ended in tragedy only a month after that reunion.[2] On 21 February 1875, Margary, along with a few of his Chinese servants, was ambushed and speared to death outside Manwyne, a walled city in Shan tribal territory at the western borders of Yunnan Province.

---

1   Augustus Margary, *Notes of a Journey from Hankow to Ta-li Fu* (Shanghai: F. & C. Walsh, 1875), 102.
2   Margary, *Journey*, 307.

The ensuing controversy sparked a brief but intense crisis in Sino–British relations as Thomas Wade, then minister plenipotentiary to Beijing, took sharp and independent action to address other unrelated diplomatic concessions as a part of the indemnity package resolving Margary's death. The resolutions offered by the Chefoo convention – monetary compensation to Margary's family as well as a relaxing of Chinese control on British activity in the interior of the country and a slackening of tariff controls on various import goods – neither entirely satisfied British interests nor resolved Qing resistance to foreign presence along the frontier. As the 'Margary Affair' (as it came to be called) has faded from the forefront of historical consciousness, so too have the questions that Margary's journey, murder and posthumous literary reputation raised about the relationship between this frontier territory and the metropoles of the Chinese and British imperiums. Yet these questions are closely connected to newly re-energised debates over sovereignty, ethnicity and border thinking at the height of nineteenth-century empire.

Reading official correspondence negotiating the right to travel alongside popular travel narratives claiming those rights lets us recognise how these different sources used shared rhetoric to establish British presence in a contested geography. Further, the specificity with which Margary's particular name and character were invoked throughout this 'affair' lets us connect the narrative strategies used to delineate individual mobility with the trans-subjective semiotic of international law. To approach how the everyday Victorian reader might have understood British claims to this border territory, we must recognise that debates over extraterritoriality can be and are framed for readers using strategies drawn from a range of literary genres. Patrick Brantlinger has influentially described Victorian travel narratives as 'nonfictional quest romances in which the hero-authors struggle through enchanted, bedeviled lands toward an ostensible goal',[3] and indeed many accounts of the young and charismatic Margary's life fit this heroic template. Yet as much as the texts of the Margary Affair are rewritings of fiction as nonfiction, they are also the opposite, at least as

---

3 Patrick Brantlinger, *Rule of Darkness: British Literature and Imperialism, 1830–1914* (Ithaca, NY: Cornell University Press, 1988), 180.

10 The Life and Death and Life of Augustus Raymond Margary

much as we can understand the constitution of the individual traveller to be beholden to developing fictional techniques.

Claiming this Sino–South-East Asian borderland territory as the 'trade-route of the future' of course involves rhetorical strategies closely studied in recent decades by literary critics, historians and geographers alike. As recent scholarship on travel writing in Asia has pointed out, however, the postcolonial turn cannot direct literary criticism of writings from China uniformly.[4] Nor, as recent shifts in Chinese historiography have shown, can we take for granted the official Qing claims to its empire's fixed and expansive borders or accept the formulations of radiating control that assumed unquestioned dominance of Yunnan by Beijing. Writing about the Margary Affair instead must be understood to hinge on a calculated and geographically specific British engagement with the complex network of local agents with more than a passing interest in Margary's actions and demise. This network includes not only the familiar antagonisms of the Great Game, but also the Qing empire's own historically shifting claims to its border provinces and populations, where ethnicity and imperial affiliation stand as practically and locally expressed conditions.

Pamela Crossley's call to include consideration of forms of ethnic identity in the study of modern Chinese history has been a major factor in the direction of more recent studies. Crossley, in her seminal 'Thinking about Ethnicity in Early Modern China', teases out the multiply inflected implications and purposes of the definition of an 'ethnic group', as expressed either by nineteenth-century Qing elites or by twentieth-century scholars of Chinese history. As she points out: 'The legitimation of the concept of ethnic identity, its imposition upon select groups, and its internalization by individuals are products of an imperial culture'.[5] Both in the case of 'imperialist incursion by Westerners', as well as in the 'refinement of the imperial tradition within

---

4   See, for example, S. H. Clark and Paul Smethurst, eds., *Asian Crossings: Travel Writing on China, Japan and Southeast Asia* (Hong Kong: Hong Kong University Press, 2008); Douglas Kerr and Julia Kuehn, eds., *A Century of Travels in China: Critical Essays on Travel Writing from the 1840s to the 1940s* (Hong Kong: Hong Kong University Press, 2007).
5   Pamela Kyle Crossley, 'Thinking About Ethnicity in Early Modern China', *Late Imperial China* 11:1 (2011), 1–35 (27).

China itself', that is, codification of ethnic difference and a correspondent attention to geographies that produce this difference shaped the purpose of empire. Despite other theoretical conflicts, practitioners of what has been termed the 'New Qing History' all productively draw from these historical tensions surrounding real and imagined boundaries of Qing rule; as Joanna Waley-Cohen explains in her review essay of the same name, '[c]entral ... is the new Qing history's revelation that at the height of their power, the Qing regarded China not so much as the centre of their empire, as only a part, albeit a very important part, of a much wider dominion'.[6]

Margary's case casts light on this wider dominion from the British perspective, drawing our attention to this territory as a site for the conception of the travelling individual as an imagined textual object developed within the archives of informal empire. The invention of the individual for the purposes of exploiting pre-existing networks in a multiply colonised territory misleadingly claimed as a 'frontier' by several different empires was an important rhetorical conceit that enacted very real geographical and historical change. In bringing together a range of activities connected to larger social and political organisations under the name of a single individual, British writers

---

6   Joanna Waley-Cohen, 'The New Qing History', *Radical History Review* 88 (2004), 193–206 (194–95). Other examples of this attention to borders and frontiers in 19th century Chinese historiography include Laura Hostetler, *Qing Colonial Enterprise: Ethnography and Cartography in Early Modern China* (Chicago: University of Chicago Press, 2001); Peter C. Perdue, *China Marches West: The Qing Conquest of Central Eurasia* (Cambridge, MA: Belknap Press of Harvard University Press, 2005); Stevan Harrell, ed., *Perspectives on the Yi of Southwest China* (Berkeley: University of California Press, 2001); Pamela Crossley, Helen F. Siu and Donald S. Sutton, eds, *Empire at the Margins: Culture, Ethnicity, and Frontier in Early Modern China* (Berkeley: University of California Press, 2006); Nicola Di Cosmo and Don J. Wyatt, eds., *Political Frontiers, Ethnic Boundaries, and Human Geographies in Chinese History* (London: Routledge, 2003); James Leibold, *Reconfiguring Chinese Nationalism: How the Qing Frontier and Its Indigenes Became Chinese* (New York: Palgrave Macmillan, 2007); and James Millward, 'New Perspectives on the Qing Frontier', in Gail Hershatter et al., eds, *Remapping China: Fissures in Historical Terrain* (Stanford, CA: Stanford University Press, 1996).

gave false personal shape to the ongoing battles for self-determination engaged in by groups not in fact so singularly defined. By doing that, British writers made the individual – both on China's south-western frontier and elsewhere in the empire – the structurally integral lynchpin of imperial progress, and, further, established the standards of imperial advance and definition to be standards arranged around the logic of the individual, on both popular and policy levels. 'Margary's personal experiences have so wide a significance from political and commercial points of view, it becomes necessary to state … what they were', as the *Examiner* claims in 1876.[7]

Postcolonial scholarship has critically interrogated the figure of the hero-explorer for his supposed moral and physical superiority as manifested by his claimed literal and figurative command of the landscape in European travel literature of the nineteenth century. Margary's case redirects that interrogation to a related question: of what value is the continued delineation of the body of an individual explorer in demarcating a territory of multilateral and multi-ethnic character? Laura Franey's suggestion that, in Victorian writing on Africa, '[t]ravelers' rhetorical assumption of personal sovereign authority in areas not yet under European control was an important prefiguration of the sovereignty that European nations would eventually arrogate to themselves' conforms with postcolonial readings of the succession.[8] We have more to do, however, to accurately account for the extent to which the body of the individual became a rhetorical tool of both the individual and the state, and thereby empowered nationalist claims and formations in importantly accommodating ways even after these broader arrogations were underway.

Both the terms of Margary's travel and the terms of restitution for his death depended for their foundation on the abstract notion of the individual travelling body. This explains how British officials and the British public came to accept an expanded range of free European movement as just retribution for Margary's murder – as John Anderson put it in one Victorian history of the affair, '[Margary] may be said to

---

7 'Southwestern China', *The Examiner* (29 July, 1876): 857–9 (859).
8 Laura Franey, *Victorian Travel Writing and Imperial Violence: British Writing of Africa 1855–1902* (London: Palgrave Macmillan, 2004), 45–46.

have bequeathed it as a public duty – made more imperative by its being the most fitting tribute to his worth – to establish in those border lands the right of Englishmen to travel unmolested'.[9] The identity of Margary's particular killers quickly was assumed by many British observers to be both impossible to determine and ultimately inconsequential, as any individuals were surely being manipulated by larger imperial forces – thus, a punishment that targeted only those individual Chinese or tribal agents could not carry real meaning. Yet even as the native individual faded as a subject of consequence, the European individual, both abstract and real, gained further status as a register of satisfaction achieved on behalf of the martyr Margary, himself a thoroughly textual and abstracted production.

Examining the processes which posthumously construct this sentimental figure can lead us to a renewed discussion of the rhetoric of the imperial frontier, one in which we perceive the biographical tradition to both authorise British travel through these frontier spaces and to reframe imperial encounter as a story of mobile individual experience by ignoring other, more culturally entangled kinds of sovereign subject-making. Studies of the bounds of nineteenth-century empire have multiplied in the past decade, with James Hevia's *English Lessons* and Lydia Liu's *Clash of Empires* both masterfully describing the history of British claims to China in the nineteenth century.[10] But they have also left open several significant areas. Among these is a more thorough consideration of the way that imperial travellers interact with foreign geographies in global boundary spaces. While we know (or think we know) what empire looks like from the perspective of London, Bombay or Shanghai, we know much less about what the empire looks like from the perspective of the borderlands – those places where the frontier arrives from multiple directions and where conventional formulations of coloniser and colonised prove inadequate.

---

9   John Anderson, *Mandalay to Momien: A Narrative of the Two Expeditions to Western China of 1868 and 1875, Under Colonel Edward B. Sladen and Colonel H. Browne* (London: Macmillan, 1876), 451.

10 See James L. Hevia, *English Lessons: The Pedagogy of Imperialism in Nineteenth-Century China* (Durham, NC: Duke University Press, 2003); Lydia H. Liu, *The Clash of Empires: The Invention of China in Modern World Making* (Cambridge, MA: Harvard University Press, 2004).

10 The Life and Death and Life of Augustus Raymond Margary

Part One: Life

'Here I am at the very end of China, and at the goal I sought; but I am going farther.' — Augustus Margary to his parents, 5 January 1875[11]

Augustus Raymond Margary (1846–1875), a young and relatively inconsequential diplomat (who failed the foreign service entrance exam three times due to poor spelling) in life, became after his death an emblematic hero of the Victorian imperial age. It was in fact his relative, the well-known archaeologist Austen Henry Layard, who had initially obtained Margary's entry to consular service in 1867. After a period of service as a student interpreter in Beijing, however, Margary proceeded to the consulate in Taiwan where he gained recognition and the silver medal of the Royal Humane Society on his own merit by rescuing forty-two from drowning during a typhoon.[12] His promotions through the ranks of service in China were steady, and he was serving as interpreter at Yantai (then Chefoo) in April 1874 when he was called to join Colonel Horace Browne's ill-fated second mission from Mandalay to Momien. This journey followed many previous in an effort to claim a land passage between British holdings in India and the trading routes of Western China.

Browne, who, in the company of Colonel Sladen, had attempted this passage first in 1868, was widely deprecated for his repeated attempts to establish this mercantile connection over such forbidding and complex terrain. John Anderson, the expedition's medical officer and naturalist, defended Browne and Sladen's decisions in the popular travel narrative *Mandalay to Momien: A Narrative of Two Expeditions to Western China* (1876). Published shortly after Margary's death, Anderson's narrative tacks on a hasty account of the failed 1875 mission to a full accounting of the equally unsuccessful 1868 mission, with the reasoning that public interest in the 'tragedy' of Margary's death would compel readership of

---

11   Letter from Augustus Margary to his parents, 5 January 1875, quoted in *Journey*, 296.
12   G. C. Boase, 'Margary, Augustus Raymond (1846–1875)', rev. K. D. Reynolds, *Oxford Dictionary of National Biography* (Oxford: Oxford University Press, 2004), http://www.oxforddnb.com/view/article/18053.

his 'compendious and popular account' of the earlier journey. Anderson, like others to follow, firmly connects the passage that Margary described as the 'trade route of the future' to the native past:

> an unbroken chain of tradition and history indicated the natural entrepot of the commerce between Burma and China to be at or near Bhamô, on the left bank of the upper Irawady, and close to the frontier of Yunnan ... The Burmese annals testified that during several centuries this had been the passage from China to Burma either for invading armies or for peaceful caravans.[13]

Browne and Sladen did succeed in travelling from the court of Burmese kings at Ava to Bhamô, but in the end, this first expedition ended up mostly serving to establish that the territory along the border was indeed unsettled following the decades of Muslim revolt in the area; as Anderson put it:

> Where Burma ended, and China commenced, was a problem, for the ancient frontier lines had been temporarily obliterated, the authority of the mandarins had receded into the interior of Yunnan, and that of the usurping Mahommedan rulers was only partially felt to the westward of Momien.[14]

Sladen's report is indeed even more blunt. He writes that:

> [t]he country beyond the Kakhyen hills, as well as the whole Chinese frontier in the direction we proposed travelling, had lapsed into a state of dangerous disorganization, and was preyed upon by large bodies of marauders ... The head Chinaman asked repeatedly with bitter significance, 'How do you expect to succeed when Kings even have tried and failed?'.[15]

---

13 Anderson, *Mandalay to Momien*, 3.
14 Anderson, *Mandalay to Momien*, 331.
15 Edward Bosc Sladen, 'Official Narrative of the Expedition to Explore the Trade Routes to China via Bhamo, under the guidance of Major E. B. Sladen', *Accounts and Papers of the House of Commons* 15 (1871), 1–166 (16).

Sladen's reasoning for pursuing the mission despite these obstacles is equally blunt: simply that:

> It is now a significant and important truth, that 130 miles of road or railway on the most practicable line between Bhamo and Momien would effectually tap the resources of Yunnan and put us into direct communication with the wealth and resources of South-Western China.[16]

Thus for the second expedition of 1874, organised to capitalise on the relative calm in the area after the pacification of the Muslim rebellions, it was then decided that a British agent should travel westward from Shanghai simultaneously with Colonel Browne's party moving east from Mandalay; the officer selected for this solo west-bound mission was Margary. His consciousness of the mission as one of unusual danger is highlighted by his posthumous biographers; the Preface to the *Journal of Augustus Raymond Margary* remarks that 'No one knew better the intense dislike of the Chinese to any such extension of the rights of foreigners in the interior and western provinces as the mission foreshadowed'.[17] But Margary did manage to succeed in fulfilling his half of the mission, and, as he assures his parents in a republished letter, this success is buoying:

> The enormous difficulties which stood in the way of the last expedition in 1867 have been guarded against on the present occasion, and Colonel Browne seems to do just what he likes with Burmans and Kakhyens. My arrival from the China side created a wonderful sensation among the Bhamô population, and has done wonders in smoothing matters on this side. They would not believe that we had any officials in China, and my arrival from that side considerably surprised them. I am called the 'Pekin man,' i.e. the Pekin mandarin.[18]

---

16 Sladen, 'Official Narrative', 123.
17 Margary, *Journal*, xix.
18 Margary, *Journey*, 309.

In a notable slippage, Margary the British agent and Margary the traveller licensed by the Qing imperium based in Beijing join as one. Here the line of power from metropole to frontier is understood as the defining category of control for British writers and readers. In framing their perception of the land through the language of state control, of course, they echo long-established Qing claims to the same territory charted along the same radius. As Margary's account and afterlife make clear, however, such claims did not translate to practical command of these border regions, even if his narrative was held to show with 'perfect truth ... the relations maintained between the provincial authorities and the population, at a distance from Pekin, and away from the coast, together with the amount of obedience rendered by both to the decrees of the Sovereign power at Pekin'.[19]

Popular British periodical writing, cognisant of this discrepancy, had throughout the later nineteenth century urged greater attention to this geography. Noting that Yunnan is a region of 'more than usual interest', the *Cornhill Magazine* explains the border's fluidity as a reflection of its ethnic mixture in 1876:

> The western frontier of Yun-nan has never been very clearly laid down. The hill ranges which separate it from Burmah, and the unruly inhabitants which dwell among them, are not possessions of sufficient value to make either the potentate at Peking or his ally at Mandalay anxious to claim them; besides, the Chinese power has never been so firmly established in the province as to make the exploration of the mountains which skirt its frontier advisable. And the result has been that the hill tribes have been left in undisturbed possession of their mountain fastnesses. In some parts the only intimations their Chinese neighbours have of their existence are when they swoop down to carry off the salt or other coveted property of the celestials; but, in others, Chinese civilisation has drawn those most accessible to it within its influence, and these show a ready appreciation of its advantages.[20]

---

19   Margary, *Journey*, 347.
20   [R.K.D.], 'Yun-nan', *Cornhill Magazine* 34:200 (August 1876), 193–205 (200).

10 The Life and Death and Life of Augustus Raymond Margary

As David Atwill demonstrates in his scholarship on the so-called Panthay rebellion, Yunnan society of this era was in fact 'multilateral and transnational', a 'world that heeded the Qing presence but often circumvented its centralized bureaucracy'.[21] Both topographical and ethnic conditions made Yunnan multiply-connected within and without the borders of China proper. The *Cornhill*, like so many others, relies on a geography made manifest by the co-ordinated actions of groups, whose swoopings out and drawings in define the territorial boundaries.

Indeed, the territory that Margary was sent to 'open' encompassed not only the Qing province of Yunnan, but also parts of the latter-day kingdoms of Burma and Siam, as well as a number of indigenous territories. The history of the Chinese frontier lacks any clearly defined point of first contact between settlers and nomadic indigenes and also lacks a clear moment of termination when the frontier transformed into irrevocably settled land. Rather, the constant advances and retreats by various Chinese regimes make the frontier fluid and ongoing; scholars have adopted the term 'persistent frontier' to describe this constant and far from static effect. In another departure from our modern understandings of territorial sovereignty, we cannot construe this space as a place where nation-states exercised control over proximate but separate regions. Instead, the political entities involved in this region, which included the courts of Siam and Burma as well as the Qing emperors and some fifty-six local rulers, operated under a complex system of interpenetrating influence; natives paid tribute to one or more ruling courts while also asserting a measure of autonomous control.[22]

The British were relatively late comers to this web of influence, arriving after the Qing Empire had annexed a wide realm of western territory in the eighteenth century as part of a historical cycle of broad expansion. But once British territory expanded north from India into southern Burma after wars in the 1820s and 1850s, the idea of controlling the region's long-established trading routes in order to

---

21 David G. Atwill, *The Chinese Sultanate: Islam, Ethnicity, and the Panthay Rebellion in Southwest China, 1856–1873* (Stanford, CA: Stanford University Press, 2006).
22 Charles P. Giersch, *Asian Borderlands: The Transformation of Qing China's Yunnan Frontier* (Cambridge, MA: Harvard University Press, 2006), 12.

connect British colonial territory in India to British concessions in Shanghai began to seem possible, and the continued lack of boundaries grew more troubling. The vast western interior of China was a space of great symbolic interest to the British; it was this terrain that best produced and represented the British fantasy of free movement in China beyond Qing constraints, not to mention ample commercial promise. Yet it was a promise that would remain perpetually unfulfilled; as late as 1890, British writers were still noting that to the north of Bhamô, 'there is no frontier. In fact this is at this moment a *terra incognita*, inhabited by Singphos, Kachyens, and other cognate tribes. It must eventually be annexed to Burma and Assam, and then a frontier with China will be demarcated'.[23]

In neither the British nor the Qing case did occupation of the border lands exclusively involve the two-step process of confrontation and assimilation, as much as linear models of history might wish to impose such a narrative. Rather, it is as Leo K. Shin has recently explained, as much a story of 'demarcation and differentiation' as of 'colonization and acculturation';[24] causing the formation of the state itself to emerge from the process of forming group boundaries. Legal claims, most notably the much-debated condition of extraterritoriality, which made the parameters of unrestricted mobility not just the plot of the travel narrative but the substance of the legal and diplomatic recognition of the land in particular. As translated to the popular context, the legality of relations between crown subjects and all others was especially understood through terms of physical movement within the popular press; claims the *Saturday Review*: 'It is no longer considered expedient or lawful to open markets by force against the will of the parties immediately interested; but it may be perfectly justifiable to assert, even at the cost of war, a right of way which already legally exists. It is not to be endured that a potentate occupying a strip of territory between India and China should, in disregard of his own

---

23 ['A.C.Y.'], 'The Frontiers of India', *Calcutta Review* 90:180 (1890), 297–302 (300–1).
24 Leo Kwok-yueh Shin, *The Making of the Chinese State: Ethnicity and Expansion on the Ming Borderlands* (Cambridge: Cambridge University Press, 2006), 4–5.

engagements, permanently stop the road'.²⁵ Turan Kayaoğlu has argued that 'the story of the rise and decline of extraterritoriality is also a story about the origins and nature of sovereignty',²⁶ persuasively making the case for considering extraterritoriality in the imperial arena not as separate to, but constitutive of, the development of European sovereignty in the nineteenth century.

Geographers and other scholars of border studies have noted that political delineation of borders along strict lines was a phenomenon brought to Asia by Europeans in the early part of the twentieth century. Charles Maier has argued in his account of modern world history's periodisation that we must think of history in units of developments of what he calls 'territoriality' – that is, the framework of bordered political space that defines a nation.²⁷ The Margary Affair's emphasis on heroic movement suggests the ways that a person can signify an area bounded (temporally or geographically) that operates under a different set of principles than political distinctions. Literary studies can complement geographical studies here by analysing the heroic rhetoric that informs and creates these individual boundary-makers, who operate in conjunction with, but not necessarily identically to, traditional modes of political boundary-making. By tracing the operations of the individual actors, we can follow the nascent establishment of the parameters of international law and its correspondent ceding of sovereignty via the peripatetic travel narrative.

Margary's writings reflect his unquestioned faith in the force of the individual to make these delineations; as he writes to his parents, 'I am proud to think that I have drawn a successful trail across a large extent of country'.²⁸ Similarly, and perhaps not surprisingly, he also frames his arrival and the zenith of his mission in the particularly individual terms of a handshake: 'Now I am over the savage hills and have wrung the

---

25 'Burmah and Western China', *Saturday Review* 39:1021 (22 May 1875), 644–5 (644).
26 Turan Kayaoğlu, *Legal Imperialism: Sovereignty and Extraterritoriality in Japan, the Ottoman Empire, and China* (Cambridge: Cambridge University Press, 2010), 3–4.
27 Charles S. Maier, 'Empire's Past … Empire's Future', *South Central Review* 26:3 (2009), 2–19.
28 Margary, *Journey*, 280–81.

hands of fellow countrymen again ... It was one of the most delightful periods of my life to come in sight of the British flag again, and to be congratulated on my splendid journey by the Indian officers. I look forward with intense pleasure to spending hours in such intelligent company'.[29] Despite his awareness of 'intrigues going on which require my most careful watchfulness',[30] Margary remained confident in the textual protection afforded to him by the Chinese government; as he explains to his mother: 'The letters and passes furnished me by the Imperial Cabinet will command respect from all the officials, high and low, throughout my route; so that, though no doubt innumerable schemes may be devised to hinder my progress, I shall be hedged around with protection. Is it not a splendid mission?'[31]

Part Two: Death

The protection that Margary relied on and the delight that Margary anticipated were, of course, both short-lived, and the narrative control that Margary exerted over his own story equally quickly terminated. After arriving at Bhamô on 17 January 1875, he spent some days reporting on his route and recording ethnographic details of the indigenous population. It was only on his return back into Chinese territory that the party began to be particularly cautious of hostile intentions by members of what Margary and others called 'wild hill tribes'. Nevertheless, Margary separated from the larger party to explore a side route later that month, accompanied only by his Chinese writer and a few other servants. Later testimony by a Chinese observer would claim that, on 21 February, 'Mr. Margary and Chow the cook, jumped over the wall at Man-ying, which were not very high, to get a cold bath. The Pan-yi people opened the gates and pursued them, and murdered them under a tree bearing a yellow fruit, not more than a hundred yards from the walls. Their ears were cut off and the bodies thrown in the water'.[32] His recorded life may be said to have ended even earlier, as the

---

29   Margary, *Journey*, 307–8.
30   Margary, *Journey*, 304.
31   Margary, *Journey*, 106.

10 The Life and Death and Life of Augustus Raymond Margary

entire last third of his diary was also lost, presumably because he had it with him during the attack.

News of Margary's death soon made its way to minister plenipotentiary Wade, along with an account of the concurrent, unsuccessful attack on Browne's much larger party of men. His initial telegram of 12 March to Prince Kung did not hesitate to assign responsibility, insisting that the expedition was attacked 'by a large body of Chinese and hill men, the advanced guard of a force of 3,000 men, sent forward by a high authority of Momien to annihilate the British party'.[33] In this first discussion of the events, Wade already confidently asserts that 'the attacking party was commanded by a nephew of Li-ssü-ta-ye, Chief Authority of Nan-tien'.

Wade's subsequent telegrams to the Prince continue to work to broaden the consequences of the attack, as he reminds Kung that Margary's 'murder and mutilation' will remind England of 'sundry acts of violence and treachery which have ... endangered relations between China and foreign powers'.[34] These negotiations, heated enough to bring the two countries to the brink of armed conflict, continued for nearly a year after the deaths, with Chinese officials assigning responsibility to local tribesmen and Wade continually insisting on 'a very different version of the story'.[35] Immediate popular response, particularly from interested parties like the businessman Archibald Little, who hoped to claim further rights in China's interior, supported Wade's aggressive negotiations, labelling the Chinese version of events a 'tale' to be 'palm[ed] upon the British minister'.[36] Notably, the territory in question was by this point held to be fully controlled by the Qing, despite evidence to the contrary; as Wade reports to the Foreign Office,

---

32   *Correspondence Respecting the Attack on the Indian Expedition to Western China, and the Murder of Mr Margary: Presented to Both Houses of Parliament by Command of Her Majesty, 1876* (London: Harrison, 1876), 37.
33   *Correspondence*, 2.
34   *Correspondence*, 5.
35   *Correspondence*, 53.
36   Archibald Little, 'Retrospect of Events in China for the Year 1875', *Journal of the North China Branch of the Royal Asiatic Society* 10 (1876), 310–24 (313).

the Government of China claims full power over these tribes, whether in respect of control or protection. Its relation to them is precisely the same as that entertained by it to many wild highland races in the heart of the Empire ... the Prince of Kung in his late correspondence with me has nowhere attempted to deny the ability of the Chinese Government to do its duty as a Government in the country in question.[37]

As part of his campaign to disprove the Chinese version of the story as well as to assert the continued right to British travel in these western territories, Wade dispatched the British chargé d'affaires in Beijing, T. G. Grosvenor, accompanied by the explorer E. Colborne Baber, to investigate the incident – an occasion which for Baber offered equal opportunity to substantiate the reports of Margary and Marco Polo alike.[38] The mission was consumed with frustration, as Grosvenor notes the 'numerous irregularities and impossibilities' of the Qing report in his official correspondence. For one, he writes that the Chinese map of the territory of Margary's murder 'interposes a range of hills' which is 'absolutely nonexistent'; further, the Chinese report implies that these hills 'are [on paper] provided with a population of no less than three savage tribes, with their designations carefully appended', while British experience shows that '[t]his tract consists, as a fact, of a few rice fields, bordered by the sandy river shore, and uninhabited. It was our usual bathing place while at Manwyne'.[39] Likewise, at the trial itself, Grosvenor reports that 'It was evident that the wild people did not

---

37 *Correspondence*, 22–3. It is notable, however, that Wade himself could not be sure immediately of this claim. Further correspondence shows that Wade himself used the Chinese Repository's reprinted (from the *Journal of the Asiatic Society of Bengal*'s) version of Colonel Burney's translation of an account of a 1787 embassy from the Burmese court of Ava to Peking to confirm the location and allegiance of the town: 'it appears that Man-wyne, there spelt Mó-wún, is the Chinese city of Lung-chuen-fu, a prefecture, or department, of the Province of Yünan. In the language of the Shan tribes it is called Mung-wan' (*Correspondence* 25, see *Chinese Repository* 9 [1840], 473).
38 See Edward Colborne Baber, *Report of Mr. E. C. Baber's Journey Through the Province of Yunnan with Mr. Grosvenor* (Calcutta: Foreign Department Press, 1877).'

realize their situation, and understood the linguist with difficulty',[40] making their confession, the foregone conclusion of the assembly, worthless in British eyes. Grosvenor concludes that, in the Chinese report, 'It is a weary task to indicate the numerous contradictions and impossibilities which comprise the Chinese official case. It would almost seem as if they have not even taken the trouble to make their story consistent. The requirements of time and place are alike outraged'.[41] In these official documents, as in the later popular descriptions of Margary's death, the investigation is as much an inquiry into proper representations of these border zones and the individuals that populate them as it is into those responsible for Margary's murder.

From our vantage point, it remains impossible to determine exactly what factors combined to doom Margary and his servants in 1875. The most sustained treatment of the affair to date, S. T. Wang's 1938 *The Margary Affair and the Chefoo Agreement*, methodically lays out the possibilities for blame: 'The outrage might be attributed to a strong band of local robbers, to the local Chinese officials instigated by the King of Burma, to the local Chinese officials acting on their own initiative and actuated by an anti-foreign spirit, or to a deliberate plot of the Yunnan provincial authorities or of the central government of Peking'.[42] Whether Victorian readers anticipated Wang's conclusion that it was likely the third option, or chose another interpretation, they uniformly found in Margary's death a suitable martyr to unite the land of China with a British character. As a later history recorded:

> The mission had failed on the very threshold of its enterprise, and one more youngster of high promise had fallen, as so many Englishmen have fallen, in the foremost skirmishing-line of the Empire. The man who had crossed China from the sea to Burma without any armed escort, and had thus accomplished something

---

39 *Further Correspondence Respecting the Attack on the Indian Expedition to Western China and the Murder of Mr. Margary: In Continuation of Correspondence Presented to Parliament Aug. 1876* (London: Harrison, 1877), 49.
40 *Further Correspondence*, 26.
41 *Further Correspondence*, 49.
42 Shên-tsu Wang, *The Margary Affair and the Chefoo Agreement* (London: Oxford University Press, 1940), 54.

the memory of which will never be forgotten, was not quite nine and twenty years old at the time of his premature death.[43]

Part Three: (After) Life

At this point, Margary's story takes two different paths; ones which, I would argue, are not as separate as they may seem. On the diplomatic path, Wade seized the opportunity to demand large concessions from the Qing for several longstanding complaints – the system of taxation known as 'likin' and the adherence to previous treaty stipulations that British governmental agents be given appropriate ministerial privileges. Many of Wade's colleagues did not support this bold attempt to stretch the boundaries of the indemnity for Margary's death; but Wade continued to insist on the necessity of resolving all these separate crisis points together, even taking it upon himself to act in advance of telegraphed orders from England upon occasion. He was at last able, however, to ensure most of the demands sought – first, cash reparations on behalf of the murdered Britons; second, establishment of enhanced equality between British and Chinese officials in China; and third, broadened designation of zones where taxes on British goods could not be collected.

The final text of the Chefoo agreement, signed on 13 September 1876, establishes all these and also contains a significant clause insisting that a proclamation consisting of the text of the treaty as well as the Qing imperial decree accepting the treaty's terms be distributed throughout the country, and that for 'two years to come officers will be sent, by the British minister, to different places in the provinces, to see that the proclamation, is posted'.[44] The effective result, as one of the most widely read Victorian histories of China explained, was that

---

43 Hugh C. Clifford, *Further India. Being the Story of Exploration from the Earliest Times in Burma, Malaya, Siam, and Indo-China* (London: Lawrence & Bullen, 1904), 292–93.
44 William Frederick Mayers, ed., *Treaties Between the Empire of China and Foreign Powers: Together with Regulations for the Conduct of Foreign Trade*, 2nd ed. (Shanghai: 'North-China Herald' Office, 1897), 44.

'[t]he proclamation was posted very widely (three thousand copies in Kiangsu province alone), and through it the people learned that the safety of all foreigners travelling through their country was guaranteed by the Emperor'.[45] James Hevia notes that this treaty established the profound discrepancies in the 'equality' of Sino–British relations, as these relations did not only 'undermine Qing sovereignty', but 'constitut[ed] the Qing in colonial terms. The emperor of China had become much like "native" princes under British "indirect" rule'.[46] Through the circulation of the proclamation, Margary's name was placed in Victorian parallel with the longstanding custom of Qing emperors of recording their claim to a frontier space via inscriptions upon stelae erected throughout the territory. Peter Perdue has argued that these proclamations were charged with a more complicated task, as they both 'evoked multiple moral traditions ... but ... could never entirely suppress latent contradictions between the generalized invocation of moral norms and the realities of sovereignty on the ground ... This tension between universal moral claims and bounded territorial sovereignty is characteristic of all imperial spatial claims, British or Chinese'.[47]

Thus the diplomatic conclusion to the Margary Affair rests heavily on the circulation of a narrative, just as, in a parallel development, the popular rhetorical enshrinements of Margary, a 'whole-hearted, vigorous, and observant man', themselves multiply and circulate throughout England and China.[48] The simultaneous publication of letters and diaries revealing his life along with reports from the official investigation into his death emphasised his production as a literary character. Periodical responses capitalised on this feeling; as the American periodical the *Galaxy* concludes in one of the many

---

45 Samuel Wells Williams, *The Middle Kingdom: A Survey of the Geography, Government, Literature, Social Life, Arts, and History of the Chinese Empire and Its Inhabitants* (New York: C. Scribner's Sons, 1882), 725.
46 James Louis Hevia, *English Lessons: The Pedagogy of Imperialism in Nineteenth-Century China* (Durham, NC: Duke University Press, 2003), 151.
47 Peter C. Perdue, *China Marches West: The Qing Conquest of Central Eurasia* (Cambridge, MA: Belknap Press of Harvard University Press, 2005), 436.
48 'Politics, Sociology, Voyages and Travels', *Westminster Review* N.S. 50 (October 1876), 525–40 (535).

contemporary reviews of his journal: 'Reading these pages, it is impossible to realize that he who wrote them is dead. It is with a mournful feeling of utter and fatalistic helplessness that we follow this young and generous hero while he travels, all unconsciously, down to his death.'[49]

Margary, a man 'to whose name a melancholy interest attaches',[50] was in fact the posthumous author of two volumes: *Notes of a Journey from Hankow to Tali-Fu* (1875) and *The Journey of Augustus Raymond Margary* (1876). *Notes of a Journey*, a reproduction of Margary's official diary, was immediately published upon his death by a Shanghai-based English publishing house with the official sanction of British ministers in China as an 'acceptable souvenir' of Margary's life. *The Journey*, on the other hand, carried the full title *The Journey of Augustus Raymond Margary: From Shanghai to Bhamo, and Back to Manwyne*, and thus immediately emphasised that his murder took place on the return leg of his journey, after his charge to meet the Indian helmets had been heroically fulfilled. In *The Journey*, the anonymous editor interweaves Margary's official journal with his personal letters and biographical anecdotes in order to 'set before his countrymen, in his own words, the story of [Margary's] crowning work.'[51] The wider range of sources serves to establish more precisely Margary as a single textual character, one whose final actions and range of possible futures must ultimately be decided by the reader himself. Margary, like a character in a novel, entered the Victorian reading imagination both fully formed and inextricable from the setting that produced his words.

Margary could maintain an especially close connection to the territory as the Sino-South-East Asian borderlands lacked the charismatic popular exploration accounts that had shaped public knowledge of the interiors of Africa and South America. Of the Victorian travellers to Western China, none had achieved literary distinction nor travelled as far as Margary.[52] At the time of Margary's death, the explorations of the upper Yangtze by the French explorer

---

49 Walter Burlingame, 'The Murder of Margary', *The Galaxy* 23:2 (February 1877), 175–82 (178).
50 Margary, *Journey*, 68.
51 Margary, *Journey*, viii.

10 The Life and Death and Life of Augustus Raymond Margary

Francis Garnier, recorded in his *Voyage d'Explorations en Indo-Chine* (1873), were the most recent and best-known descriptions of this area for many readers.⁵³ Indeed, no one knew better than Margary himself how inextricably cntexted his every experience must be. As he writes near the end of his journey to his parents: 'There are rumours among the Chinese of the approach of foreigners from Burmah and I trust it is a true bill. I have so much to do and so much to write that I cannot give you much more. You can review each step of my way when my journal is printed'.⁵⁴

Thus, Margary's name and character exerted powerful influence as textual effects warranting free British movement in a wide range of travel narratives that followed, and his death came to establish the right to travel in Western China as a paradoxically durable monument. The introduction to the *Journey of Augustus Raymond Margary*, not surprisingly, most stridently insisted on this need for such textual perpetuation:

> [H]is short story, if read aright, and in spite of its violent ending, adds yet another testimony that a little genuine liking and sympathy for them, combined with firmness, will go further and do more with races of a different civilization from our own than treaties, gunboats, and grape-shot, without it. If the route is ever to be a durable and worthy monument of the man, it must be opened and used in his spirit, by fair means, and for beneficent ends. If a reluctant consent is only forced from the Chinese by threats of war, and the route becomes the highway for the opium

---

52 See also Thomas Blakiston, *Five Months on the Yang-Tsze: And Notices of the Present Rebellions in China* (London: J. Murray, 1862) and T. T. Cooper, *Travels of a Pioneer of Commerce in Pigtail and Petticoats: Or, an Overland Journey from China Towards India* (London: J. Murray, 1871).
53 See Marie Joseph Francis Garnier, *Voyage D'exploration En Indo-Chine, Effectué Pendant Les Années 1866–1868 Par Une Commission Française, Présidée Par Le Capitaine De Frégate Doudart De Lagrée, Et Publié Par Les Ordres Du Ministre De La Marine, Sous La Direction Du Lieutenant De Vaisseau François Garnier, Avec Le Concours De M. Delaporte, Lieutenant De Vaisseau, Et De Mm. Joubert Et Thorel, Médecins De La Marine* (Paris: Hachette, 1873).
54 Margary, *Journey*, 279.

traffic, it may enrich the spinners of Lancashire, and the planters of Bengal, but it will never be a true or satisfactory memorial of Augustus Raymond Margary.[55]

What I take to be of particular interest here is the complicated result of this charge 'to maintain' the 'right to traverse' a 'route' as a 'durable monument' that transcends economic profit to prioritise simply movement itself. This is in keeping with the effects of the Margary proclamation. Travel narratives and other writings on Western China published after his death, then, had at least two circulating versions of Margary to engage with; not only the history of his travels as described in his own journal and in the narratives of his fellow travellers, but also the movements (or lack of movement) of the proclamation bearing his name. In bringing these two versions together, writers also made the borderlands narratively coherent along the lines of singular identity, rather than ethnic distribution or political boundary.

Thus in William Gill's *The River of Golden Sand*, a travel narrative of Western China published five years after Margary's death, he addresses the former version of Margary by titling one chapter 'In the Footsteps of Marco Polo and of Augustus Margary'. In this chapter he visits the site of Margary's murder and writes:

> It was our fortune to be the humble instruments of … honouring his name, but any feeling of gratification was lost in the thoughts of that rueful scene that had been enacted on that fatal shore. We had claimed the legacy bequeathed by him, but it was in sorrow that I felt we had redeemed the right his life had purchased. For a moment I thought of sketching a spot which will ever be a hallowed one to Englishmen; but it might have raised suspicions in the superstitious minds of our companions; and long after such a paltry record would have perished his name will stand bright and clear in the recollection of his regretful countrymen.[56]

---

55 Margary, *Journey*, 326–27.
56 William Gill, *The River of Golden Sand: The Narrative of a Journey Through China and Eastern Tibet to Burmah* (London: Murray, 1880), 389.

10 The Life and Death and Life of Augustus Raymond Margary

Gill, a member of the Royal Corps of Engineers possessed of a large personal fortune who himself met an untimely death on an expedition in Egypt, gained particular sanction for his account; the posthumous second edition of his narrative was condensed by Edward Baber and edited by Sir Henry Yule, both noted Victorian sinologists. *The River of Golden Sand* absorbs and continues the after-effects of Margary's story through the broadening body of travel accounts in the western frontier.

Yet while Gill is insistent in making the literal site of Margary's death serve a transcendent purpose, he is surprisingly literal in understanding the abstract claims to freedom of circulation ensured by the legal concessions marked by the Chefoo convention. For Gill, the Margary proclamation is most significant as a tangible object centring and locating Chinese official presence in the multi-ethnic space of the Asian borderlands through which his journey takes him. Thus, his description of his entry into Chinese civilisation (as opposed to Tibetan or other indigene settlement) is invariably marked by a description of the exact location of the posting of the Margary proclamation. Two examples from the many in his text: 'But here [in Tibet] there is scarcely ever such a thing as a village, and the few that there are, are generally occupied by the Chinese, as was the case at Ngoloh, or Tung-Golo, as the Chinese call it … where we halted, and where the Margary proclamation was posted in the portico of the Chinese hotel, in which we found chairs and a table';[57] and later, 'There was nothing to vary the monotony of the march down the mountain; seven miles in driving wind and rain brought us to the Chinese village of Ho-chu-ka, consisting of two or three miserable tenements, of which the house we stopped in was the best. This was the governmental building, or Kung-Kuan, for the use of travelling officials, and as such was of course out of repair, though the Margary proclamation had been posted for our edification.'[58] Following in the footsteps of Margary through a terrain organised around ever-multiplying displays of Margary's name, then, draws together two ways of making the Chinese borderlands both bounded and comprehensible under a single British surname.

---

57 Gill, *The River of Golden Sand*, 129.
58 Gill, *The River of Golden Sand*, 154.

So closely are Gill and Margary linked that the *Saturday Review*'s treatment of *The River of Golden Sand* opens with an assessment of Gill as '[t]he first Englishman who took full advantage of the Chefoo convention; the first – save officials – to visit the scene of Margary's murder, and by following in his steps from China to Burmah to pay the best tribute to his memory, may be said, without any hesitation, to have fairly earned the right to publish his travels'.[59] Later narratives, including Edward Colborne Baber's own *Travels and Researches in Western China* (1882), Archibald Colquhoun's *Across Chryse* (1883), and the inimitable Isabella Bird's *The Yangtze Valley and Beyond* (1899), to name only a few, occasioned the general consensus that such books were now 'far from rare' since Margary's death 'opened up the way'.[60] Even the early narratives by George Bogle and Thomas Manning of journeys to Tibet in 1774 and 1811, collected and published together for the first time in 1876, became enmeshed with Margary's legacy through the associative work of periodical reviews.[61]

Missionaries, particularly quick to take advantage of the expanded access the Chefoo agreement offered, also represented the most challenging test case of the post-Margary rhetoric because the

---

59 Gill, *The River of Golden Sand*, 340.
60 'Across Chryse', *Saturday Review of Politics, Literature, Science and Art* 55 (1883), 601–3 (601). See Edward C. Baber, *Travels and Researches in Western China* (London: J. Murray, 1882); Archibald R. Colquhoun, *Across Chryse: Being a Narrative of a Journey of Exploration Through the South China Border Lands from Canton to Mandalay* (London: Sampson Low, Marston, Searle, and Rivington, 1883); Isabella L. Bird, *The Yangtse River and Beyond: An Account of Journeys in China, Chiefly in the Province of Sze Chuan and Among to Man-Tze of the Some Territory* (London: J. Murray, 1899). Others include: Alexander Hosie's *Three Years in Western China: A Narrative of Three Journeys in Ssu-chuan, Kuei-chow, and Yun-nan* (London: George Philips, 1890); R. Logan Jack's *The Back Blocks of China: A Narrative of Experiences among the Chinese, Sipans, Lolos, Tibetans, Shans and Kachins, Between Shanghai and the Irrawadi* (London: Edward Arnold, 1904), and R. F. Johnston's *From Peking to Mandalay: A Journey from North China to Burma Through Tibetan Ssuch'uan and Yunnan* (1908).
61 See Thomas Manning, George Bogle and Clements R. Markham, *Narratives of the Mission of George Bogle to Tibet and of the Journey of Thomas Manning to Lhasa*. Edited, with Notes, an Introduction, and Lives of Mr Bogle and Mr Manning, by Clements R. Markham (London: Trübner, 1876).

10 The Life and Death and Life of Augustus Raymond Margary

unlimited mobility their narratives sought to claim expands beyond categories of national sovereignty into a universal human nature predicated on Christian salvation. Such was the debt that the work of the China Inland Mission (CIM) society, led by Hudson Taylor, owed to Margary in particular that his death became a part of the missionary's basic understanding of the territory. The CIM's standard-issue map of the area, meant to 'illustrate the relations of British India, Burmah, Assam, and S.W. China', also makes a point of highlighting the site of Margary's murder as a place to 'be noticed with interest'.[62] One of the first to test the limits of the new relations post-1876 was CIM missionary John McCarthy, who proceeded on foot from Shanghai to Bhamô from December 1876 to August 1877, a distance of about three thousand miles, making him 'the first non-official traveller who has thus traversed the entire width of the empire'.[63] McCarthy's account 'Across China from Chin-kiang to Bhamo, 1877', read before the Royal Geographical Society in 1879 and subsequently reprinted in the proceedings of that society, reports that a fellow-traveller 'bought some eggs from the mother of the man who is said to have killed poor Mr. Margary. Some of the people seemed desirous to refer to Mr. Margary's murder; I did not deem it wise to do so, but always spoke of it as a thing that was long passed, and said that a better understanding now existed between England and China, so that nothing of the kind could occur again'.[64]

Even as missionaries proleptically charted a territory receptive to their proselytising, however, liberal Victorian periodicals remained suspicious of the charge to advance commercial and legal claims in Margary's name. J. H. Bridges, writing in the *Fortnightly*, asks:

> Shall an English subject be assassinated? has been the cry of late; and who is there to inquire into the antecedents of Mr. Margary's mission? Bewail the fate of a brave man; assuredly. But none the

---

62 'A Map of Burmah', *China's Millions* 1:1 (August 1875), 14.
63 'Geographical Notes', *Proceedings of the Royal Geographical Society*, New Monthly Series 1:2 (1879), 123–32 (127).
64 John McCarthy, 'Across China from Chin-Kiang to Bhamo, 1877', *Proceedings of the Royal Geographical Society*, New Series, 1:8 (1879), 489–508 (505–6).

less let us ask, not merely whether the scene of his death was a wild far-off highland region filled with half-savage hill tribes, over whom a government more powerful than that of China would find it hard to exercise responsible control; but also whether the business on which he was sent was such as to the Chinese people and their governors must seem a formidable source of new dangers to their internal peace: a wanton aggravation of evils already inflicted.[65]

A suspicion of British success in claiming the Chinese 'land-frontier' was advanced even more strongly by the *Spectator*, which concluded: 'Into the Chinese provinces no Englishman has found his way, except he came from the sea-coast of China itself; and until this charm is broken – and it will not be broken by the daring of any single individual – it is impossible to attach much political weight to the recent explorations in Western China'.[66] Repudiation of the dominant language of heroic individualism, notably, must be heavily emphasised in this rebuttal, so pervasive was Margary's influence.

Sir Rutherford Alcock, the then just-retired minister plenipotenary to Beijing, acknowledged these barriers even as he reiterated attempts to give Margary's death meaning and beneficial consequence, writing in the Afterword to the *Journey of Augustus Raymond Margary* that '[t]here is a Nemesis attaching to failure in the East, which no Asiatic power can afford to disregard. However questionable might have been our right, in an international point of view, to insist on the concession of a free passage and trade with Yunnan from Burmah originally, we could have very little choice left afterwards'.[67] In a causal reversal, it is not Margary's successful movement but rather the permanent failure of his movements that becomes the signal instance instituting free circulation. That is to say, it is the fact of Margary's death itself that demands the legal regulation of the right of transit. Here we see most clearly British conflation of individual movement and the general ability to move as

---

65   J. H. Bridges, 'Is Our Cause in China Just?', *Fortnightly Review* 18:107 (1875), 642–63 (644).
66   'The Future Relations between England and China', *The Spectator* 51 (8 June 1878) 725.
67   Margary, *Journey*, 359.

granted by international law and further the necessity of the rhetorical figuration of the individual in the codifications of international relations.

It was not enough for Victorian travellers to understand mobility as a right granted to an abstract notion of an individual, of course, even if local residents adopted this broader formulation. Edward Baber writes in *Travels and Researches in Western China*:

> It must not for a moment be supposed that the natives of Western China draw any distinction between one foreign nation and another; so far from that, they are apt to include Japanese and Nipalese, and even Manchus and Mongols, in the same category with Europeans. One very soon discovers that any discrimination of so minute a character is far beyond the range of native intellect. I was therefore obliged to accept the position of a *foreigner in general*, without distinction of race or religion, nationality, language or business. The authorities believed that my errand was to verify the publicity of the Margary proclamation, and accordingly it was generally posted in some situation conspicuous to our view whenever we entered a city. I took every occasion to explain that such was only a part, though a very important part, of my duty. I wished also to see how officials and people were disposed towards foreigners. I hoped that the civility which I had received would not prove exceptional. I had been sent to the province to inquire about its commerce, its routes, its produce, and its geography generally. It is needless to say that nobody believed me.[68]

This hollow category of the 'foreigner in general', a kind of randomly drifting body bereft of direction or intention, is particularly offensive to Baber because it evacuates his encounters with local authorities of both respect and recognition. The ethical attention due to the unjustly slaughtered Margary, or to his surrogate traversing his established route in proxy, was not so clearly due to a singular traveller who represented nothing but the fact of difference. As negotiations over

---

68   Emphasis added. Edward C. Baber, *Travels and Researches in Western China* (London: J. Murray, 1882), 85.

extraterritoriality and sovereignty under international law continued, mostly to Qing detriment, the biographical and character-based shape given to the operations of empire in these writings becomes increasingly clear. Travel narratives and novels have long since been understood to share ideas about the constitution and distribution of their heroes and villains; but codes of law and fictional narratives equally develop joint understandings of the relations between place and person. The legal right of extraterritoriality depends on the ability to imaginatively transcend physical setting as much as does any novel.

What is important to us here, then, is not ultimately the continued distribution of Margary's life, death and afterlife through later travel narratives. After all, we know that the claim to permanence ultimately faded. Rather, the benefit that a careful attention to the rhetoric of post-Margary writings can give us is rather an idea about the ways that popular travel narratives helped produce the space of these borderlands that has remained dominant. The paradoxical impulse to attach a name and sentimental history to a broader phenomenon of extra-national mobility allows us to trace the evolution of this boundary space across the span of many different journeys to the west. That is to say, Margary's personal narrative gives a false but instructive individual biographical outline to the in fact transpersonal function of place-making in the Victorian understanding of China – the understanding of Western China as a whole came via human-shaped and sized stories.

The biographical form must ultimately occlude the drive towards broad perception implicit in the British accounts, however, because it reframes questions of travel as encounters between the centralised bureaucratic apparatus of the Qing imperium and the individual mobility of the British traveller. The individuation of international law through the 'Margary proclamation' is one of the clearest – though certainly not the only – example of this occlusion. In understanding how Margary evolves from a person who writes his own experience to a name by which experience can be written, that is, we learn something about how the concept of individualism (as opposed to the acts of the individual) controls the writing of places throughout the course of empire. Thus, if the fiction of free individual movement throughout the ambiguous frontier space of Western China represents a powerful structuring model for these late nineteenth-century travel narratives, it also operates as a wedge admitting further British claims and conditions of subjecthood upon the land and the people of China.

11
Linguistic Nationalism and Its Discontents: Chinese Latinisation and Its Practice of Equality

Lorraine Wong

In *Addresses to the German Nation* (1807), Johann Gottlieb Fichte suggested that the German people had an 'original language' that could articulate the cultural distinctiveness and native superiority of this people.[1] 'To begin with, and above all else', Fichte maintained, 'the first, original and truly natural frontiers of states are undoubtedly their inner frontiers. Those who speak the same language are already, before all human art, joined together by mere nature with a multitude of invisible ties'.[2] Amidst the crisis of Napoleon's conquest, Fichte celebrated the German language as an inner frontier more original and fundamental than territorial frontiers sanctioned by a sovereign state. Language was singled out among other criteria, such as race and territory, as the embodiment of the German nation, when 'Germany' was nothing more than an ambivalent geographical idea, or a non-state being made into the satellite of Napoleonic imperialism. Fichte believed that the German people, in the absence of sovereign power and territorial statehood, could gather their own continuous history in their living national language and in so doing they could practise a form of freedom more original than those made possible through *Realpolitik*.

---

1 Johann Gottlieb Fichte, *Addresses to the German Nation*, ed. Gregory Moore (Cambridge: Cambridge University Press, 2008), 60.
2 Fichte, *Addresses to the German Nation*, 166–67.

The perceived inherent tie between language and nation constitutes the ideological backbone of modern nationalism, which began to appear in Europe during the nineteenth century and came to define the norm of political, economic and cultural life around the world in the twentieth century and beyond. Critiques of linguistic nationalism suggest that national language does not embody individual and collective freedom from statehood, as imagined by Romantic nationalists such as Fichte. According to historian Hugh Seton-Watson, language is central to what he calls 'official nationalism' in the Austro-Hungarian empire and the Russian empire in the nineteenth century. The liberal-minded nobility and educated philologists acted as a nationally conscious elite and imposed a sense of nationality on all imperial subjects, regardless of their religion, language or culture. In doing so, the nationalist elite would strengthen the state under the authority of which they launched their nationalist-linguistic projects.[3] Eric J. Hobsbawm, another historian of nationalism, points out that nation-states in the nineteenth and twentieth centuries claimed to be the guarantor of the equality and freedom of all citizens. Citizens were equal since they were given the same chance of receiving national education, which was conducted in a living national language accessible to everyone. The greatest patron of linguistic nationalism was historically the lower middle class, or what Hobsbawm calls the 'vernacular middle strata'.[4] They learned enough of the official national language to get by and function in modern nation-states. Hobsbawm considers national language to be a means through which the lower middle class, or 'the petty bourgeoisie', functioned as a cog in the state machine.

While the state has a stake in linguistic nationalism, the market also capitalises on the existence of a national language. Benedict Anderson reminds us that nation as political collectivity was historically embedded in the rise of print capitalism in the late eighteenth century and throughout the nineteenth century. People recognised their shared identity as co-nationals through their consumption of newspapers and

---

[3] Hugh Seton-Watson, *Nations and States: An Enquiry into the Origins of Nations and the Politics of Nationalism* (Boulder, CO: Westview Press, 1977), 148.

[4] Eric J. Hobsbawm, *Nations and Nationalism since 1780* (Cambridge: Cambridge University Press, 1990), 118.

novels in urban centres. Individuals were bound together as an imagined community, even though they came from diverse regional and social backgrounds and were never in face-to-face communication. A standardised national language created a sense of national cohesion; it was also required by the reproductive logic of capitalism.[5]

This essay picks up where these critiques of linguistic nationalism leave off, namely at the point of the simultaneous rise of linguistic nationalism and communism in the non-Western world, as is found in China. In such a situation, linguistic nationalism was complicated by the struggle for social equality and the communist revolution against capitalism. The problematic relation between linguistic nationalism and communism is articulated into the Chinese Latinisation movement in the 1930s and 1940s. As a mass literacy campaign, Chinese Latinisation sought to create a Latin-alphabet-based phonetic writing system, known as 'New Writing' (新文字 *xin wenzi*), in China. It was expected that previously unrecognised linguistic demands of the commoners, who had little right to literacy and literature under the pre-modern imperial system and contemporary statehood, could be articulated into the Chinese national language (國語 *guoyu*), if this national language was to be written by an alternative script unburdened by the graphic baggage of Chinese characters and accessible to both the cultural elite and the commoners. The Latin alphabet was held to be this ideal script, one that was able to facilitate national awakening and social equality simultaneously.

According to Qu Qiubai (1899–1935), a founding member of the Chinese Communist Party (CCP), creator of New Writing and translator of Marxist philosophy into Chinese, Chinese characters traditionally brought out the 'effects of assimilation' (同化作用 *tonghua zuoyong*) in the Far East. In the past, foreign races such as the Jurchen, the Tangut, the Mongol and the Manchurian had to live with Chinese characters and the feudal economic order of the Han. Reflecting on the contemporary condition of Euro-American imperialism, Qu suggested that China was reduced to the position of an oppressed people comparable to the former tributaries under the Chinese territorial empire. For Qu, China

---

5   Benedict Anderson, *Imagined Communities: Reflections on the Origins and Spread of Nationalism* (London, New York: Verso, 2006), 24, 46.

was left with no choice but to give up on the policy of common writing (同文政策 *tongwen zhengce*) and of assimilation (同化政策 *tonghua zhengce*). This would allow Chinese people to realign themselves with other oppressed peoples around the world, in their common resistance against European, American and Japanese imperialisms and in their shared struggle for national independence.[6]

Upon its arrival in 1930s China, the Latinisation movement quickly won the support of left-wing intellectuals, within and outside the CCP, who agitated for the right to literacy and literature of those they considered to be the toiling masses. What distinguished the Latinisation movement from other proposals for script reforms in late Qing and early Republican China is not its reduction of writing to the propaganda of an international communist revolution but this movement's augmentation of the power of writing in reconfiguring the existing discursive order. This movement certainly had its practical goals, like the political mobilisation of ordinary folk into the communist cause, and the smooth communication of new information to the ordinary folk who were expected to understand this information through a writing system that represented their speech. However, merely focusing on these speech-centred practical goals would make us believe that Latinisation subscribed to a phonocentric and logocentric view of writing, which considers speech to be closer than writing to the referent, and that it is no different from other nationalist projects that sought to alphabetise and vernacularise writing in the nineteenth and twentieth centuries. This essay explores the primacy of *writing* and *grammar* in the Latinisation movement, questioning the ideology of orality that seems to define this movement's goal of representing *speech* directly. It probes linguistic nationalism by dislodging the idea of national language from an abstract imaginary realm to the discordant material realm of the social.

Along with the idea of national language, the concept of class and its differentiation of the intellectuals and the masses are also

---

6   Qu Qiubai 瞿秋白, 'Luomazi de zhongguo wen haishi roumazi de zhongguowen?' 羅馬字的中國文還是肉麻字的中國文 [The Roman Chinese or the creepy Chinese?], in *Zhongguo yuwen de xinsheng* 中國語文的新生 [A new life of the Chinese language] (Shanghai: Shidai chubanshe, 1949), 30.

problematised in this movement. Qu Qiubai sought to elevate the political consciousness of his fellow countrymen by articulating what they wanted to say but could not, due to their exclusion from literacy, education and culture. What distinguishes Qu from other nationalist intellectuals of his time is his insistence on integrating with the masses and reconstituting China as a nation on this basis. In the early 1930s, Qu was estranged from the leadership of the CCP and the Comintern, at which point he began to take up leadership in the leftist literary scene and contributed a series of important essays on the problem of national language and mass literacy in China. Born into a falling scholar-gentry family, Qu was hurried on by the currents of history and attracted to the politics of revolutionary renovation in China. His life ended in his arrest and execution by the ruling Nationalist party in 1935. He could have remained a traditional man of letters, yet he chose to become a communist revolutionary at the threshold of history. Such a decision has often been understood as the split personality of a freedom-loving gentry-aristocrat, who was accidentally entangled with dehumanising communist politics, or as the tragic failure of a revolutionary who could never weed out his old thoughts and accommodate himself to the needs of the masses.[7]

As this essay is going to show, the questions addressed by the Chinese Latinisation movement, namely mass literacy and writing as a medium of revolutionising society, were not the outcomes of Qu's inert revolutionary whimsy. They were responses to actual and material changes of China in the real world of anti-colonial nationalist struggles. Inasmuch as writing has a differential and material existence (for instance between the Chinese script and the Latin alphabet), adopting a different script or mode of writing can turn the consciousness of an

---

[7] See Tsi-an Hsia, *The Gate of Darkness: Studies on the Leftist Literary Movement in China* (Seattle and London: University of Washington Press, 1968), 8, 52; see also Paul G. Pickowicz, *Marxist Literary Thought in China: The Influence of Ch'ü Ch'iu-pai* (Berkeley: University of California Press, 1981), 218. This understanding of Qu is based on 'Superfluous Words', an essay penned by Qu at the time of his execution. Read like Qu's final confession of his regret about committing himself to communism and Marxism, this essay remains disputable as to whether it had been tampered with before it passed for Qu's work in the press.

intellectual inside out and expose it to the wilderness of history. Just as Qu and his fellow Latinists learned to understand the behaviours and thoughts of those whom they considered to be the masses, they recognised writing as a differential aspect of language, because of which it figures in the actual contexts of social conflicts, and because of which it contributes to the dynamic process of becoming, just like other happenings in history. After examining Latinisation's linguistic forms, this essay turns to the Latinised translation of Lu Xun's 'Diary of a Madman' (1918), exploring how Lu Xun's 'madman' can be a means into the forces of writing, forces that were newly recognised by the intellectuals standing at the crossroads of history.

Latinisation and Its Communisation of Writing

Published in the Soviet Union in 1930, 'The Latinised Alphabet of China' (中國拉丁化的字母 *Zhongguo ladinghua de zimu*) was created by Qu Qiubai in collaboration with Soviet sinologists. It included twenty-eight letters, a set of orthographic principles (拼音規則 *pinyin guize*), an outline for drawing word boundary (書法大綱 *shufa dagang*), as well as a simple set of morphological and syntactic principles (文法規則 *wenfa guize*).[8] New Writing was intended to be more than a notation scheme for representing and standardising speech sounds. Enabling the commoners, in Qu's vocabulary 'the masses' (大眾 *dazhong*), to write as they come to hear and speak is the point of departure and not the ultimate purpose of this movement. In fact, Qu dissociated the masses from mere orality and aimed to derive a written grammar embedded in their daily life. For Qu, the masses suffered from an inarticulate presence, which can be attributed to 'a mule language' being circulated in society at that time.[9] In Qu's depiction, this sterile linguistic offspring, 'neither horse nor donkey', is a mongrelisation of three incongruous forms of written Chinese: first, Classical Chinese

---

8   Qu, 'Xin zhongguo wen cao'an' 新中國文草案 [Draft of new Chinese writing], in *Qu Qiubai wenji: wenxue bian* 瞿秋白文學編 [Qu Qiubai's literary works], vol. 3 (Beijing: Renmin daxue chubanshe, 1998), 432–56.

11 Linguistic Nationalism and Its Discontents: Chinese Latinisation

still in use in official and intellectual writing; second, the new written vernacular that was partially Europeanised in style but out of touch with the average readership; and third, the old written vernacular that was popular in the marketplace for middlebrow fictions.[10] Through developing a Latinised written grammar, Qu expected to achieve a written Chinese language that could even out these incongruities. 'With the onslaught of imperialism and capitalism', Qu argues,

> new relationships, new things, new ideas and new phenomena have transformed the spoken language at such an irreversible scale and to such an extent that the Chinese characters of the classical literary language can no longer act against the tide and rein it back. Chinese characters are just the ghostly undead. For the better and full development of the spoken Chinese language and its suitability to the new cultural life of the masses, Chinese characters have to be abolished. Why? It is not simply because they keep the majority from easy access to literacy and education, but more importantly, Chinese characters hinder the progress appearing in the grammar of the emerging new language and hamper the acceptance of new words and new concepts of science and arts that are in use among advanced countries in Europe and America.[11]

According to Qu, the meanings conveyed by Chinese characters are out of touch with the rapidly changing world. For example, the new coinage

---

9   Qu, 'Xuefa wansui!' 學閥萬歲 [Long live the literary caste], in *Qu Qiubai sanwen* 瞿秋白散文 [Prose of Qu Qiubai] (Beijing: Zhongguo guangbo dianshi chubanshe, 1997), 48.

10 Qu, 'Guimenguan yiwai de zhanzheng' 鬼門關以外的戰爭 [Battling outside the gate of hell], in *Qu Qiubai sanwen* 瞿秋白散文 [Prose of Qu Qiubai] (Beijing: Zhongguo guangbo dianshi chubanshe, 1997), 29–30.

11 Qu, 'Putong zhongguohua de ziyan de yanjiu' 普通中國話的字眼的研究 [An analysis of word in the Chinese common language] in *Zhongguo yuwen de xinsheng* 中國語文的新生 [A new life of the Chinese language] (Shanghai: Shidai chubanshe, 1949), 48–49. Unless stated, all translations are the author's own.

of the time, 國家(nation) consists of two characters, namely 國 and 家. Qu thinks that the specific meaning of 國家 has nothing to do with the respective meaning attached to 國 (state) and 家(family), when these two characters function on their own.[12] In other words, the specific meaning of 國家 is not a combination of the meaning of 國 and the meaning of 家; the combined meaning of these two characters suggests something like 'a state as a family' or 'a family as a state'. This, for Qu, is a distortion of what 國家 (nation) means. Another example is 帝國主義者 (imperialist). In Qu's view, the combined meaning of these five Chinese characters does not articulate the specific meaning of 'a person in support of Western imperialism'. 帝 carries the meaning of 'emperor' or 'king' whereas 國 carries the meaning of 'country', 'nation' or 'state'. These five Chinese characters fail to introduce the contemporary condition of Western imperialism; they also mislead people with an absurd meaning like 'a supporter of an ideology that endorses having an emperor to run the country'.[13] Thus, in Qu's understanding, the meanings conveyed by Chinese characters are burdened by the graphic baggage from the past and out of touch with the epistemological horizon of the contemporary world.

Chinese script is monosyllabic, each character constituting one syllable. For Qu, the monosyllabism of Chinese characters is at odds with the many polysyllabic expressions that make up the spoken Chinese language and its rapidly changing lexicon. To Latinise is to combat Classical Chinese, which is an essentially written, formulaic and inherited form of language, as well as registering the changes in contemporary linguistic and social environments. Monosyllabic Chinese characters afford vibrant semiotic flows, as they can potentially move from one morphological context to another and thus create protean combinations of meanings. For Qu, this 'mobility' of Chinese characters would lead to chaos in coining new words, especially when there was as yet no rule regulating how Chinese characters should be

---

12 Qu, 'Putong zhongguohua de ziyan de yanjiu' [An analysis of word in the Chinese common language], 50.
13 Qu, 'Putong zhongguohua de ziyan de yanjiu' [An analysis of word in the Chinese common language], 50.

combined to represent polysyllabic neologisms such as 國家 (nation) and 帝國主義者 (imperialist), whose meanings, according to Qu, can easily be distorted and misunderstood.[14] Inasmuch as Chinese characters are circulating 'flexibly' without also referring to specific referents, they are, according to Qu, haunting readers like the 'ghostly undead (僵屍 *jiangshi*)', functioning like corpses without a soul, or signifiers without a signified.[15]

In Tani Barlow's analysis, Qu was obsessed with establishing 'what amounts to a Chinese habitat for logos'.[16] His drive to exorcise the haunted house of Chinese characters and to standardise a Chinese written language (through Latinisation) was driven by his embrace of sociological reasoning, the reasoning that put trust in the signified of society, the 'logos of the social'.[17] Given the continuous practices of Chinese script in today's Chinese-speaking world, Qu's depiction of the graphic burden of Chinese characters is far-fetched. As Barlow points out, Qu broached in a confused and fuzzy way a problem that bordered on a 'logocentric puzzle': Why did Chinese characters exercise overwhelming power over the masses in such a way that they deprived the masses of equal access to a rational epistemology?[18] As Qu aspired to enable each and everyone to grasp the meaning of social life accurately, he also raised the problem of whether he created a transcendental truth in the midst of society, a truth independent of linguistic and script-related determinations. Inasmuch as Qu sought to standardise a Chinese written language so that it could present the logos of the social truthfully, had not literary writings, fictional or otherwise, become redundant and unnecessary? Would Qu also want to eliminate the polysemous meanings articulated in literary writings?

---

14   Qu, 'Putong zhongguohua de ziyan de yanjiu' [An analysis of word in the Chinese common language], 50–51.
15   Qu, 'Putong zhongguohua de ziyan de yanjiu' [An analysis of word in the Chinese common language], 48–49.
16   Tani Barlow, 'History's coffin can never be closed: Qu Qiubai translates Social Science', *Boundary 2* 43:3 (August 2016), 274.
17   Barlow, 'History's coffin can never be closed: Qu Qiubai translates Social Science', 274.
18   Barlow, 'History's coffin can never be closed: Qu Qiubai translates Social Science', 266.

If so, did it compromise Qu's role as a literary critic and also as a prolific translator of Russian and Soviet literature into Chinese? If Qu is a logocentric thinker, why didn't he deny the priority of writing? All these questions make for the logocentric puzzle that Barlow suggests.

Instead of debating whether Qu subscribed to logocentrism or the Western metaphysics of presence, a more important question is why Qu addressed grammar, written and literary language in conjunction with his Marxist attempt to popularise or communise social knowledge. As Barlow points out, Qu sought to disaggregate knowledge, or 智識 (zhishi) in Chinese, from the moralist value attached to it in the traditional structure of society. For Qu, the notion of 'knowledge' conveyed by the Chinese characters 智識 discriminated against the illiterate and attached morality to the proportion of people who knew how to read and write, namely the men of letters (文人 wenren) in Chinese culture. Qu thought that written Chinese language in his time obscured the notion of truthful and scientific knowledge that he would like to translate from Western Marxist methodology into the Chinese epistemological horizon. The absence of a proper Chinese term to refer to Qu's Marxist notion of truthful and scientific knowledge also prompted him to examine why differences in knowledge existed in China. Insofar as knowledge is truthful and scientific, knowledge should not be an individual possession but a communal experience. Whereas wealth and property can improve life, they should not be exclusive to the masses; this Marxist notion of equality also applies to knowledge: Everyone is free to use knowledge to mould his or her life for the sake of a better livelihood.[19]

We can break away from the 'logocentric puzzle' by asking why it is that Qu focused on the writing system and grammar of written and literary language, not on the institution of school, in his attempt to contest the monopolisation of knowledge by those who knew how to read and write in Chinese characters. It is noteworthy that when Qu sought to liberate and communise knowledge, he did not prioritise redistributing the right to knowledge by transforming the school

---

19 Barlow, 'History's coffin can never be closed: Qu Qiubai translates Social Science', 265.

system and making it more accessible to the masses. Instead, he tackled the Chinese literary heritage and its moralisation of knowledge and combated what he called the 'Chinese pictographic system' (象形制度 *xiangxing zhidu*).[20] This depicted primitivism of Chinese characters is mistaken since the very identification of Chinese characters with pictographs – the written marks that depict things or actions naturally and carry meanings directly without recourse to any unit of speech – turns a blind eye to the dominant existence of ideo-phonetic characters (形聲 *xingsheng zi*) in the Chinese writing system. Whether Chinese characters represent speech sound effectively is derived from the question of how the historicity and retentiveness of Chinese characters, or their graphic burden from the past, led to inequality in knowledge acquisition and production.

Qu's politicised statement about Chinese characters can be understood by his determination to draw on contemporary content to overthrow the spectral presence of ancient content. Emphasising contemporary content also created an equal footing for both the masses and the elite to locate social truth and produce accurate knowledge, since neither the masses nor the elite seem to enjoy an advantage in understanding a world that was disorientating. New Writing was as much an estrangement to the unschooled commoners as it was to the elite men of letters, who had to renounce their vested interest in Chinese characters if they were to commit themselves to the Latinisation movement. The Latinised orthography was intended to achieve the common property of which Chinese society at that time was deprived, namely a written Chinese language that was understandable to both the masses and the elite when it was read aloud. In this sense, writing or written language is part of the material reality in which it is embedded, similar to wealth, property, school and means of production. Writing or written language can play a semi-autonomous role in changing the world of which it is at one and the same time a representation.

---

20 Qu, 'Guimenguan yiwai de zhanzheng' [Battling outside the gate of hell], 30, 32.

Here Qu's departure from logocentrism is striking. While Plato, in his *Phaedrus*, is concerned with how each and everyone has a role to play so that he or she can speak properly in an order of discourse,[21] for Jacques Rancière the circulation of written words creates an excess of meanings that disrupt the order of discourse, as well as calling into question a mode of communication that legitimates 'proper' speech. For Rancière, written language has the power to put into circulation more words in relation to the things named, exceeding the function of rigid designation. Power holders, who claim to speak 'properly', unceasingly seek to maintain the designation and to deny the ability of 'illegitimate' people to speak. When those who are 'illegitimate' can proliferate words, they are empowered to reconfigure the relation between words and bodies, the sayable meanings and the visible subject-persons.[22]

Even though Qu intended to standardise a Chinese written language, it does not necessarily mean that he sought to arrest the excess of words in order to create a rigid designation between words and things, written language and social reality. New Writing designates the masses, or in Rancière's vocabulary those who are 'illegitimate', as a new subject (in language and history) who would put into circulation new words and excessive meanings. Latinisation switches the question of *what* the logos or truth is to *how* logos or truth is articulated through multiple socio-discursive practices. The logos of the social is thus not independent of linguistic and script-related determinations; rather it has an immanent (or historical) relation to the material forms of language, be it the Chinese script or the Latin alphabet, Classical Chinese or vernacular Chinese, standard and non-standard written forms (and such material forms can be extended to other sonic or gestural realisations of language). Articulated through a series of discursive acts, the logos of the social registers a *universalisable* that is not actually *universalised*. These discursive acts reconfigure the field of

---

21 Plato, *Phaedrus*, trans. Stephen Scully (Newburyport, MA: Focus Publishing, 2003), 64–65.
22 Jacques Rancière and Davide Panagia, 'Dissenting Words: A Conversation with Jacques Rancière', *Diacritics* 30:2 (Summer, 2000), 115.

11 Linguistic Nationalism and Its Discontents: Chinese Latinisation

perception and societal power, enabling the logos to take leave of itself and become an other in the contested ground of history.[23]

If we follow through Rancière's critique of Western logocentrism to his critique of the modern school system, we can better understand the priority of written language in the Latinisation movement and its target of the unschooled adults who were marginalised by the contemporary school system. In his answer to the question 'What is Enlightenment?' published in *Berlinische Monatsschrift* in 1784, Immanuel Kant suggests that Enlightenment is 'man's emergence from his self-incurred immaturity'.[24] Rancière pushes the limit of Enlightenment reason and questions the sense of 'progress' hidden in the notion of men's advancement from a reluctance to use one's reasoning power to the confident exercise of reason. Kant believes that man's ignorance is self-incurred because it has to do with a lack of resolution to use reason without the guidance of another. However, Enlightenment reason can also be appropriated by a modern school system that entrusts to teachers the gradual growth of individuals from ignorance to reason.[25] In *The Ignorant Schoolmaster*, Rancière recounts the story of how Joseph Jacotot, while being in exile during the Restoration, taught students whose language he did not speak.[26] This unusual pedagogical condition made Jacotot aware of the hierarchical power structure ingrained in the modern school system, which regards speech-based

---

23 The distinction between 'universalisable' and 'universalised' is made by Nergis Ertürk and Özge Serin in their analysis, via Gayatri Spivak, of the crucial role of translation and translatability in Marxism. See 'Marxism, Communism, and Translation: An Introduction', *boundary 2* 43:3 (2016), 6.

24 Immanuel Kant, 'An Answer to the Question: "What is Enlightenment?"' in *Kant's Political Writings*, ed. Hans Reiss, trans. H. B. Nisbet (Cambridge: Cambridge University Press, 1970), 54.

25 Jacques Rancière and Davide Panagia, 'Dissenting Words: A Conversation with Jacques Rancière', 122.

26 In March 1815, Jacotot was forced into exile by the restoration of the Bourbons. He obtained a professorship by the generosity of the King of the Netherlands. Since Jacotot did not speak Flemish and his students did not speak French, he relied on a bilingual edition of *Télémaque* and asked his students, through an interpreter, to learn the French text with the help of the translation. Jacques Rancière, *The Ignorant Schoolmaster: Five Lessons in Intellectual Emancipation* (Stanford, CA: Stanford University Press, 1991), 1–2.

explication as necessary in order for students to learn. 'In an explicative order', Rancière argues,

> an oral explication is usually necessary to explicate the written explication. This presupposes that reasonings are clearer, are better imprinted on the mind of the student, when they are conveyed by the speech of the master, which dissipates in an instant, than when conveyed by the book, where they are inscribed forever in indelible characters.[27]

For Rancière, since written words circulate and become equally available to those entitled to use them and those who are not, writing can verify equality as the point of departure, not as the ultimate goal of education. That equality is verified by letting each and everyone acquire knowledge through writing does not mean that everyone has the same level of intelligence.

Instead, the verification of equality gives rise to multiple acts of reasoning. This comes down to a redistribution of the demarcations between those who have speech, reason and logos and those who do not. The old epistemology of the power holders is interrupted when those, originally considered only to be able to produce 'noise', are empowered to cut into the field of perception and to become speaking subjects. For Rancière, the 'speaking' subject does not reaffirm the primacy of speech; instead, he reveals the centrality of writing to the equalitarian practice of knowledge, which entails reshaping the discursive and political order, as well as unsettling the logos that separates those who have speech and those who only produce noise.[28]

Rancière's theory of writing illuminates what Qu was trying to do in the Latinisation movement. Latinisation was expected to generate a new discursive energy outside the school system and unsettle existing class differentiation by redistributing literacy and cultural capital across the elite and the masses. New Writing could potentially disrupt the instituted discursive order so that what was previously excluded from

---

27 Rancière, *The Ignorant Schoolmaster*, 5.
28 Jacques Rancière, *Dis-agreement: Politics and Philosophy*, trans. Julie Rose (Minneapolis: University of Minnesota Press, 1999), 2, 23.

the horizon of perceptible knowledge – the commoners' perception – could appear. New Writing could also potentially carve out a place in the community of speaking subjects for the unschooled commoners. In its short span of experiment in the 1930s and 1940s, New Writing was driving both unschooled commoners and the cultural elite sympathetic to leftwing politics to the unfamiliar frontiers of meaning making. Interruption of the discursive order was countered by what Qu considered to be the need for communicating truthful and scientific knowledge. One does not have truthful and scientific knowledge to communicate unless such knowledge has become a real thing. Had not Qu endorsed, to borrow Walter Benjamin's words, the 'bourgeois conception of language', which regards language primarily as a means of communicating an abstract content always identical to itself?[29] How did Qu contest the ideological rigidity of this semanticist approach to language, which lurks behind Latinisation's otherwise radical move to break through immanence and recognise the materiality of language?

Latinisation and its Living Written Grammar

In his introduction to 'The Latinised alphabet of China', Qu explains that New Writing has to be grounded in a rigorous grammar. As with any phonetic writing system in the world, New Writing needs to have a 'physiognomy' (形體 *xingti*), a regulated way of writing that is derived from the rules of orthography, word-boundary demarcation, and grammar.[30] What Qu refers to as 'grammar' has less to do with the underlying structural features of the Chinese language (as a closed system) than with Latinised word formation (as an open process of generation). V. N. Vološinov, a Marxist thinker contemporary with Qu, suggested that a 'word is the most sensitive *index of social changes*, … of changes still in the process of growth, still without definitive shape and not as yet accommodated into already regularized and fully

---

29   Walter Benjamin, 'On Language as Such and on the Language of Man', in *Reflections: Essays, Aphorisms, Autobiographical Writings*, ed. Peter Demetz, trans. Edmund Jephcott. (New York: Schocken Books, 1986), 318.
30   Qu, 'Xin zhongguo wen cao'an' [Draft of new Chinese writing], 444.

defined ideological systems'.³¹ Vološinov's observation illuminates how Qu sought to adapt to the grammatical structure of the Chinese language verbal practices that are socially vital and constant, and that are embedded in the material life of the toiling masses as a particular community of speakers.

Qu negotiated between the Latinisation of Chinese characters (漢字拉丁化 *hanzi ladinghua*) and the Latinisation of Chinese speech (中國話寫法拉丁化 *Zhongguohua xiefa ladinghua*) in making a Latinised orthography. The semantic and grammatical units in New Writing are located in the alphabetised 'word', or what Qu called 字眼 (*ziyan*), and not in the Chinese character per se. Qu suggested some semantic and grammatical criteria in stabilising the spelling of Latinised words. These criteria were simple and sketchy. However, as more and more people were expected to adopt New Writing and perfect this writing system through constant usage and regular practice, New Writing could hopefully achieve an equilibrium between conciseness and verbosity, or a balance between economy and intelligibility. Tuo Mu, who systematised in *The Full Journey of Chinese Latinization* (1939) many of the grammatical rules Qu suggested in the first version of the 'Latinized alphabet of China', explained the way in which the long-term practices of the masses could improve this writing system: 'Not only are the masses the users of writing, they are also the improvers of writing. Only the improvements made by the masses are reasonable, scientific and consequential. It is because they bring about the improvements through practical uses; these improvements are also subtle and imperceptible'.³²

Each Chinese character in current use acquires a spelling in the Latinised orthography, which includes an index of character–Latinisation conversion.³³ Some Latinised words contain only one Chinese character and are monosyllabic, others are polysyllabic words having more than one Chinese character. For

---

31 V. N. Vološinov, *Marxism and the Philosophy of Language*, trans. Ladislav Matejka and I. R. Titunik (Cambridge, MA: Harvard University Press, 1986), 19.

32 Tuo Mu 拓牧, *Zhongguo wenzi ladinghua quancheng* 中國文字拉丁化全程 [The full journey of Chinese Latinisation] (Shanghai: Shenghuo Shudian, 1939), 165.

33 Qu, 'Xin zhongguo wen cao'an' [Draft of new Chinese writing], 492–586.

11 Linguistic Nationalism and Its Discontents: Chinese Latinisation

instance, the word *cinjy* (青魚 / Black carp) is a combination of an adjectival-character 青 (green) and a noun-character 魚 (fish).[34] Other such adjectival-nouns include *damen* (大門 / big door) and *siaohaez* (小孩子 / small kid). If the adjectival-noun combination does not refer to a specific entity, this rule of word formation does not apply. For example, the expression *da dao* (大刀 / big knife) functions like a short phrase, 'a knife that is big', instead of functioning as a bi-syllabic, adjectival-noun. Characters are joined together whenever they can produce a new word referring to a specific entity or having a stable meaning. This semantic criterion of word-boundary reveals the mimetic use of language in Latinisation; yet this semantic criterion can also be arbitrary. Why is 'black carp' associated with 'greenness' and referred to as *cinjy* (青魚)? What is it that differentiates *damen* from *da dao*? Latinised orthography registered the speculative, the metaphorical and representational use of language.

Qu's goal was not to dress existing Chinese characters in an alphabetic garb, but to draw word-boundaries semantically and parse a sentence into its component parts of speech with some explanation of the morphological rules.[35] For example, the letter *h* has a specific function in Latinisation. Interestingly, it works ideographically rather than phonetically in Qu's orthography. The *h* in *hueh* (會 / meeting) does not stand for any speech sound, and is not supposed to be pronounced. It signifies the semantic and grammatical status of a set of words functioning as a new technical term, a new conceptual noun or as a new name for a new thing in society, such as *fah* (閥 / powerful and

---

34 Ou, 'Xin zhongguo wen cao'an' [Draft of new Chinese writing], 438. The spellings of Latinised words in this essay follow the version of Latinised orthography first created by Qu Qiubai. This version of spelling resembles *Hanyu Pinyin*, the official notation scheme of the PRC but they are not exactly alike.

35 This explains why tonal spelling is applied to only 227 homophonous characters in order to disambiguate their meanings. See Qu, 'Xin zhongguo wen cao'an' [Draft of new Chinese writing], 453. *Gwoyeu Romatzyh* (G.R.), an official notation scheme under the Nationalist government, adopted a more vigorous set of phonetic principles to indicate the tones of Chinese characters.

influential group like 'warlords'), *feih* (費 / fee), *sueh* (稅 /tax), *buh* (部 / department), *koh* (科 / bureau), *cuh* (處 / office), *gyh* (局 / ministry), *seih* (社 / association or community centre) and *hueh* (會 / union or meeting). In the Latinised orthography, the character 會 in *gonhueh* (工會 / labour union) and *kaehueh* (開會 / hold a meeting) refers to a specific social group and institution. Thus, this character needs to be differentiated from the 會 in a question like *hue-buhue?* (會不會? / Can you or can you not?), as well as from the 會 in the conceptual term *seihue* (社會 / society).[36] Morphological distinctions concealed in Chinese characters are articulated in the Latinised orthography.

Expressions from classical Chinese are Latinised if they are already part of daily oral usage with a commonly accessible meaning; the characters concerned should come together as a polysyllabic expression, such as *cijuceli* (豈有此理 / unreasonable or unjustifiable) and *wuyenwugud(t)* (無緣無故(的)(地) / without a reason).[37] The deposited meanings from the past might continue to hover around, but at the revolutionary moment of the 1930s, these meanings were negotiated and transformed. For example, the two characters 階 and 級 from classical Chinese were joined together by Qu to make a new contemporary term 階級, which means 'class' in a Marxian sense.[38] The original meaning of 階, namely a 'rank in officialdom', and that of 級, namely a 'step in a flight of stair', would not disturb the contemporary Marxian sense of 'class'. As 階級 is rendered in Latinisation, the visual connection of 階 and 級 to the historical etymology of these two characters drops out of sight. Through Latinisation, Qu transported some useful terms from classical Chinese such as 階 and 級 to the contemporary situation. They are represented in the Latinised orthography side by side with the expressions that have a closer

---

36 Qu, 'Xin zhongguo wen cao'an' [Draft of new Chinese writing], 455.
37 Ou, 'Xin zhongguo wen cao'an' [Draft of new Chinese writing], 439.
38 Qu, 'Xin Zhongguo de wenzi geming' 新中國的文字革命 [Writing revolution for a new China], in *Qu Qiubai wenji: wenxue bian* 瞿秋白文學編 [Qu Qiubai's literary works], vol. 3 (Beijing: Renmin daxue chubanshe, 1998), 313.

11 Linguistic Nationalism and Its Discontents: Chinese Latinisation

relationship to the daily life of common people, such as *cinjy, damen* and *siaohaez* analysed above.

The pedagogic dimension of Latinisation was foregrounded when Qu sought to teach core social theories and distinctions to illiterate people, such as *sennjy giazze* (剩餘價值 / surplus value), *zecaen-gaegi* (資產階級 / bourgeoisie), *siao-zecaengaegi* (小資產階級 / petty bourgeoisie), *baen-zemindi* (半殖民地 / semi-colony), *sin-Zongowen* (新中國文 / new Chinese writing) and *faengemin* (反革命 / counter-revolutionary).[39] A stable orthography would make this new knowledge a constant part of both spoken and written Chinese. One has to write in Latinisation often enough to develop an intuitive and habitual sense of how the hyphen is used to make these polysyllabic words more easily recognised.

The English word 'wage' is another foreign term Qu singled out for discussion. In Qu's time, this term helped define the labour activities of many working people, who had a stake in a proper alphabetised word for 'wage' with which they would become aware of their social positions. Classical scholar and translator Yan Fu first translated 'wage' as a monosyllabic term 庸, which was an expression found in classical Chinese but not in the living speech of his time. Then, there was the translation 賃銀 found in Japanese, which was very much steeped in the socio-cultural milieu of China in the past. Yet another translation, 工資, was provided by the *Kangxi Dictionary*, the most authoritative dictionary dating back to imperial China. Being bi-syllabic, these two translations were perhaps better and closer to the speaking habits of ordinary folk. According to Qu, none of these translations was as good as 工錢, a term circulating among toilers in factories in 1930s Shanghai.[40] As Qu suggested, the character-root *gon* (工/labour) could be combined with another character-root *cien* (錢 / money) to make an accurate and specific translation of 'wage' in an alphabetised form, *goncien* (工錢).[41]

---

39 Qu, 'Xin zhongguo wen cao'an' [Draft of new Chinese writing], 439.
40 Qu, 'Xin Zhongguo de wenzi geming' [Writing revolution for a new China], 301.
41 Qu, 'Xin Zhongguo de wenzi geming' [Writing revolution for a new China], 313.

This method of alphabetisation enables Qu to translate meanings between the past and the present, China and elsewhere. As Tani Barlow points out, Qu was aware that 'written signifiers are by nature unstable. Chinese graphemes or *hanzi* do not flow unscathed through time'.⁴² Translating across Russian and Chinese made Qu develop the habit of annotating, appraising and catechising new words taking shape in contemporary Chinese language. The historical etymology of Chinese characters made Qu aware of how concepts arise out of material history and of how culture moves and transforms. Written language does not remain unchanged. Sometimes, it would seem that an old term from the past could be used to express new content, such as 階 and 級. However, this term might also have an impact on the content. In other words, the content of language changed, but it is hard to determine how this change is related to linguistic or extra-linguistic changes. The process of creating new alphabetised words is a process of translation in language and in history. For Qu, the English word 'wage' is not so much identical with 庸, 賃銀, 工資, 工錢 or *goncien* as it is embedded in a milieu different from the Chinese. Even so, 'wage' is able to create non-repetitive changes in the context of Chinese through a dynamic interaction with the locally specific life of the commoners.

V. N. Vološinov has written about the breaking down of the socio-symbolic order during times of revolutionary change. His observation helps us understand the condition of linguistic volatility that the Latinisation movement addressed by means of writing. In the midst of social crisis, a given ideological sign is shaken from its ground, and thus 'any current truth must inevitably sound to many people as the greatest lie'; in the ordinary conditions of life, on the other hand, the dominant ideology keeps the ideological sign from entering the open semiotic process, trying to accentuate 'yesterday's truth as to make it appear today's'.⁴³ In other words, a sign is not just used to designate things. An assemblage of connotations, resonances and contested meanings hovers around the linguistic structure. It is

---

42 Barlow, 'History's coffin can never be closed: Qu Qiubai translates Social Science', 263.
43 Vološinov, *Marxism and the Philosophy of Language*, 23–24.

this 'more' that makes a sign ideological and open to dispute and appropriation for a wide range of meanings in revolutionary periods.

Lu Xun's 'Diary of a Madman' and Its Latinised Translation

As the Latinisation movement tried to redistribute literacy as well as cultural capital across the class divide, New Writing was used experimentally as a literary language that could be accessible to the masses. *Igo fungz di rhgi* (1936) is a Latinised translation of Lu Xun's short story 'Diary of a Madman' (1918). Translated and edited by Wang Xian and Chenmei, *Igo fungz di rhgi* (A crazy man's diary) indicates the ambition of the Latinisation movement to make New Writing a sophisticated literary language.

Inspired by Nikolai Gogol's story of the same title, Lu Xun's 'Diary of a Madman' tells the story of how a traditional man of letters, or a scholar-gentleman, resorts to diary writing to resist the oppression imposed on him by his family, clansmen and residual feudalism at the turn of the twentieth century. On the one hand, the madman writes, in vernacular Chinese, thirteen diary entries to work through his suspicion of how people around him practise cannibalism and gang up to eat him; on the other hand, the preface-narrator, who claims to be the family friend of the mad diarist, tells us, in classical Chinese, that the madman suffers from a form of persecution complex and that the madman's diary entries are collated and edited by him. Lu Xun's 'Diary of a Madman' dramatised the tension between classical Chinese and vernacular Chinese, at a time when the national language was coming into being. It is a foundational work of modern Chinese literature.

The madman makes a shocking claim in this story:

> [M]y history has no chronology and scrawled all over each page are the words: 'Confucian Virtue and Morality.' Since I could not sleep anyway, I read intently half the night until I began to see words between the lines. The whole book was filled with the two words -- 'Eat people'.[44]

He cites historical instances of leaders in Chinese history who were literally eating human body parts and yet whose authority remained unchallenged. The shocking coexistence of people-eating and ritual propriety in Chinese history and in the madman's perception made this story an odd text for an educated audience, not to say the unschooled commoners, in Lu Xun's time. The strangeness of this story is further intensified in its Latinised translation. As Michael Gibbs Hill suggests, even if all the texts in New Writing were direct translations or transcriptions of Chinese characters, these translated texts are not secondary forms of aesthetic work; rather they are aesthetic texts deserving our close reading. He suggests that *Igo fungz di rhgi* delivers to readers the 'defamiliar' experience of writing and reading in Chinese.[45]

Much of the uneasiness in this reception of the 'Diary of a Madman' resides in the extent to which cannibalism functions as metaphor of cultural power in the text, and/or its historical rootedness in very real material political cannibalism. *Igo fungz di rhgi* leaves behind this binary conception of metaphor and history, revealing how cannibalism brings to the fore the pressure of linguistic and literary expectations set by the intellectuals, as well as the contestation of these expectations by the masses.

Translating Lu Xun's title 'Diary of a Madman' (狂人日記) into *Igo fungz di rhgi*, or 'A Crazy Man's Diary' (一個瘋子的日記), Wang Xian and Chenmei obscure the profound distinction implied in Lu Xun's story between two Chinese characters 狂 and 瘋. Lu Xun's 'madman' (狂人) becomes a 'crazy man' (瘋子) in the Latinised version, rendered as *fungz*. As Tang Xiaobing points out, 狂, translated as 'madness' in English, has a longer history and a richer texture of meaning, referring to a wildly defiant person; whereas 瘋, translated as 'craziness' in English, is of more recent origin, referring to craziness in a pathological

---

44 Lu Xun 魯迅, 'Kuangren riji' 狂人日記 [Diary of a madman], in *Nahan* 吶喊 [Call to arms], trans. Yang Xianyi 楊憲益 and Gladys Yang (Beijing: Foreign Languages Press, 2000), 29.
45 Michael Gibbs Hill, 'New Script and a New "Madman's Diary"', *Modern Chinese Literature and Culture* 27:1 (Spring 2015), 80.

11 Linguistic Nationalism and Its Discontents: Chinese Latinisation

sense, or someone suffering from a migraine attacking like a roaring wind.⁴⁶

In the tenth diary entry, Lu Xun's madman says:

> Then I realized part of their cunning. They would never be willing to change their stand, and their plans were all laid: they had labelled (名目 *mingmu*) me a crazy man (瘋子 *fengzi*). In future when I was eaten, not only would there be no trouble, but people would probably be grateful to them.⁴⁷

The Latinised version goes like this:

> Zhe shxou, wo iu dungde tamndi izhung fazliao. Tamn budan bu keng gai, rcie zaoji ybeixaola, *wo sh igo fungz!* Zianglai gei tamn chidiaoliao, budan xen taiping, kungpa xuan iou rhen iao siesie tamn-ni. Langzcun dagia shuo sh chidiaola igo orhen, ziu sh zhe igo fangfa. Zhe sh tamndi lao faz!⁴⁸
> [Then I realized part of their cunning. They would never be willing to change their stand, and their plans were all laid: *I am a crazy man!* (瘋子 *fengzi*). In future when I was eaten, not only would there be no trouble, but people would probably be grateful to them. When our tenant spoke of the villagers eating a bad character, it was exactly the same device. This is their old trick.]

In Lu Xun's version, the mad diarist says that 'crazy man' is a 'label' imposed on him by the villagers. This label contrasts with the title

---

46 Xiaobing Tang, 'Lu Xun's "Diary of a Madman" and a Chinese Modernism', *PMLA* 107:5 (October 1992), 1226.
47 Lu Xun, 'Kuangren riji' [Diary of a madman], 47. I have made a small but significant adjustment to this English translation, replacing 'madman' with 'crazy man' in this quotation, so as to better represent Lu Xun's choice of word 瘋子 in the quotation and its contrast with 狂人 in the Chinese title.
48 Lu Xun, *Igo fungz di rhgi* 一個瘋子的日記 [A crazy man's diary], ed. Wang Xian, trans. Chenmei (Shanghai: Xinwenzi shudian, 1936), 20. Italics are my emphasis.

'madman' with which the diarist identifies. As Tang Xiaobing indicates, 狂 registers an inner experience of spiritual transgression and eruption, 'an alterity of reason', whereas 瘋 registers an external classification of pathological abnormality. Lu Xun's madman challenges the discursive order and existing value system, bravely defying the Confucian literary culture and seeking to liberate himself from the grip of the cannibalistic crowd. However, in the Latinised version of the same scene, the crazy man speaks to himself and nervously reiterates the 'label' the cannibalistic crowd has imposed on him: 'I am a crazy man!' As in Lu Xun's version, the preface of *Igo fungz di rhgi* reveals how the title of the diary is chosen; however, Wang Xian and Chenmei did not translate 狂人 in Lu Xun's title into a Latinised equivalent but replaced it with a more mundane, less loaded *fungz* (瘋子) in New Writing. This makes a significant difference to the interpretation of the story: The crazy man titles his journal 'A Crazy Man's Diary' after he has recovered from his sickness. As a result, the crazy man does not have the critical edge of Lu Xun's diarist, who titles his bizarre journal 'Diary of a Madman', in defiance of the classification by the cannibalistic crowd.

Translating 'Diary of a Madman' (狂人日記) into *Igo fungz di rhgi* (一個瘋子的日記) would potentially make Lu Xun's story easier for the masses to read. Wang Xian and Chenmei also modified the title with a numeral classifier *igo* (一個) and a possessive particle *di* (的) so as to make the title a grammatically sound short phrase. Since the Latinised orthography cannot represent classical Chinese transparently, Wang Xian and Chenmei also had to turn the preface in Lu Xun's version from classical Chinese into vernacular Chinese and then render it into New Writing. As a result, the preface-narrator and the mad diarist lose their distinctiveness in the use of language. In comparison to the preface-narrator in Lu Xun's version, have not Wang Xian and Chenmei more thoroughly subdued the language of the madman, more violently brought the madman under control by naming him a crazy man and by simplifying and clarifying his language, even if such simplification and clarification is done in the service of the masses, in the name of equality?

The Latinised version ironically tried to make the disconcerting language of the madman 'transparent' to the average readership,

11 Linguistic Nationalism and Its Discontents: Chinese Latinisation

although many users of Latinisation at that time were still learning to decipher Latinised words and thus they might not find those texts 'transparent'. In the tenth diary entry, Lu Xun's madman recites historical instances of cannibalism in Chinese history. Instead of following the chronology of history, the madman tears apart those historical instances into fragments and juxtaposes them in a strange world of Chinese cannibalism, where Yi Ya, Jie and Zhou from ancient time, contemporary revolutionary Xu Xilin and the madman's fellow clansmen from Wolf Cub Village become contemporaries.[49] This indicates the heroic efforts of the madman to reconstitute history on an open-ended horizon. Despite the importance of this part in underscoring such Herculean efforts of the madman, Wang Xian and Chenmei deleted it from the Latinised version. Yi Ya, Jie, Zhou and Xu Xilin belonged to different historical moments, and the masses would likely be confused by the madman's obsession with the literal truth of Chinese cannibalism. Even if Wang Xian and Chenmei had included this part in the Latinised version, they would have needed to annotate it with a footnote, similar to the way they added a footnote to the word *baoxuang* (to report the failure of the crops).[50]

In editing and translating Lu Xun's 'Diary of a Madman' into New Writing, Wang Xian and Chenmei sought to make even the rugged texture of Lu Xun's original version. Without smoothing the textual unevenness in Lu Xun's version, the Latinised version would not be intelligible. In doing so, Wang Xian and Chenmei discipline the language of the madman and diminish his bizarreness, perhaps more violently than the preface-narrator in Lu Xun's version. While the madman in Lu Xun's version seeks to transform the cannibalistic crowd, the crazy man in the Latinised version is preemptively brought under control, inasmuch as he is put into text, transformed into the signifier of the orthographic rules of Latinisation.

In his close reading of *Igo fungz di rhgi*, Michael Gibbs Hill points out a significant contradiction in the third diary entry discussed earlier. Wang Xian and Chenmei retain four Chinese characters 仁義道德 and use them to represent 'Confucian virtue and morality',

---

49   Lu Xun, 'Kuangren riji' [Diary of a madman], 44–45.
50   Lu Xun, *Igo fungz di rhgi* [A crazy man's diary], 5.

whereas they use the Latin alphabet *chrhen* to render 'eat people'. The crazy man tells us that 仁義道德 and *chrhen* are both scrawled into the history book he is reading.⁵¹ According to Hill, while Chinese characters are used here to embody Confucian culture, it is also a calculated rhetorical move of Wang Xian and Chenmei to reveal the anxiety of the Latinisation movement: New Writing cannot totally disentangle itself from the moral values that Chinese characters supposedly represent.⁵² For Hill, the crazy man tears apart the ideology covered over by Chinese characters and discovers the truth – the cannibalistic nature of Chinese tradition – through the medium of the Latin alphabet. In other words, New Writing is ridden with the graphic burden or the literary heritage of Chinese characters; the crazy man can see beyond the 'lingering poison' of Chinese characters and expose the cannibalism beneath them.⁵³

I suggest that beyond the 'lingering poison' of Chinese characters, the juxtaposition of 仁義道德 and *chrhen* in the above passage reveals a profound relation between cannibalism, writing and power. Advocates of the Latinisation movement such as Qu Qiubai, Wang Xian and Chenmei recognised the force of writing in exercising the power of enlightenment. They sought to communise the productive and distributive apparatus of knowledge and culture by instituting a new grammar and a new literature on the basis of the Latin alphabet. As Lydia H. Liu points out, both the Chinese script and Japanese kanji render the word 'civilisation' as 文明, which means 'enlightening through writing and text'.⁵⁴ In the East Asian world, intellectual enlightenment was mediated by a system of script, calligraphy, texts, canons and rituals, which could liberate human beings from the primitive condition and help them establish an understanding of the world, even though such enlightenment might impart an eternal character to a version of truth that buttressed the power holders. In his critique of Western logocentric tradition, as discussed earlier, Jacques

---

51   Lu Xun, *Igo fungz di rhgi* [A crazy man's diary], 7.
52   Hill, 'New Script and a New "Madman's Diary"', 95.
53   Hill, 'New Script and a New "Madman's Diary"', 96.
54   Lydia H. Liu, 'Scripts in Motion: Writing as Imperial Technology, Past and Present', *PMLA* 130:2 (2015), 375–76.

11 Linguistic Nationalism and Its Discontents: Chinese Latinisation

Rancière argues that writing is potentially democratic in that it can be made equally available to the so-called legitimate and illegitimate participants in a community of speaking subjects.

No matter whether it is about maintaining a hierarchy of power or about overthrowing the unfair status quo, whether it is a matter of preserving tradition or creating new values, writing is the necessary medium. In *Igo fungz di rhgi,* the juxtaposition of 仁義道德 and *chrhen* reveals that the crazy man, who is a scholar-gentleman standing at the crossroads of history, becomes a pawn in the power struggle between two forces of writing – the conservative vis-à-vis the progressive. This explains his anxiety and paranoia. The crazy man says: 'I read intently half the night until I began to see words between the lines. The whole book was filled with the two words – : "*chrhen*" (eat people)'.[55] Here the crazy man reveals that 'eat people' or cannibalism is not a metaphor; it is a literal truth, in the sense that the crazy man has become the surface on which traditional values, such as 仁義道德 (Confucian virtue and morality), are inscribed. Scripts and texts shape one's body and life, and conversely, one's body and life give life to scripts and texts. That the crazy man is socially intelligible as a diseased and abnormal person means that he is eaten into by the reason of the society in which he exists.

On the one hand, the crazy man sees through the ideology 仁義道德 shaping him as a diseased person; on the other, he discovers the ideological operation by reading works written in the Latin alphabet. It is *chrhen* (eat people) in the book that reveals to the crazy man how he himself has become the surface for writing or inscription to occur. In other words, he is put into text, eaten away by the emerging language of the masses. As a reader and writer of New Writing, the crazy man is aware of his complicity with and opposition to the masses: '4000 nian ilai, changchang chrhendi difang, gintian cai mingbai, wo ie zai limian xunla xydo nian [It has only just dawned on me that all these years I have been fooling around in a place where for four thousand years human flesh has been eaten]'.[56] Being literate in both the Chinese

---

55 Lu Xun, *Igo fungz di rhgi* [A crazy man's diary], 7.
56 Lu Xun, *Igo fungz di rhgi* [A crazy man's diary], 23.

script and the Latin alphabet, how can the crazy man guarantee that he himself would not end up 'eating people' when exercising his power in and through writing?

Coda: Linguistic Nationalism and its Discontents

As much as Qu tried to extricate the written Chinese language from the graphic burden of the Chinese script, he spent his final days in prison writing poems in the classical style and carving stone seals, seemingly revoking his vision of revolutionary renovation. In its short span as an experimental form of writing, from the 1930s through to the 1940s, New Writing did not eradicate Chinese characters from the horizon of reading and writing. The Latinised texts were mostly read by the intellectually sophisticated, like Qu and his fellow Latinists such as Wang Xian and Chenmei, who worked back and forth between Chinese characters and the Latinised words.[57]

On the surface, it seems that Qu approached speech as an abstract and metaphysical thing to be represented in Latinised orthography, overlooking the material existence of writing (including script and written language) as a medium of social intercourse. This essay contests this phonocentric and logocentric interpretation. It suggests that Qu submerged speech, writing, and even his consciousness in historical contingency. Just as they used to be dreaming in a fabric lined with the most lustrous of silks, intellectuals such as Qu and his fellow Latinists were waking from this dream and seeking to emancipate themselves from what they considered to be the backward thoughts saturating the Chinese script and its ornate literary culture. As history entered their consciousness, these intellectuals could not but recognise the fluidity, not the identity, of the script they used and could learn to use.

---

57 New Writing was studied by urban refugees who took Latinisation's crash courses in makeshift schools, by the averagely educated, adult learners in Beijing, Shanghai, Guangzhou and Hong Kong (where the movement flourished momentarily), as well as by the peasants who took part briefly in Latinisation's winter schools in communist-controlled border areas. In the 1950s, the state-builders of the People's Republic of China retained the character-based script and indefinitely postponed the Latinising goal.

11 Linguistic Nationalism and Its Discontents: Chinese Latinisation

The crazy man in *Igo fungz di rhgi* is a perplexed figure at such historical crossroads. He tries to remake himself into a modern intellectual who learns to read and write in New Writing. Reciprocally, the crowd tries to turn their previously unrecognised 'noises' into articulate 'speech', through a mastery of New Writing. However, this coming together of the crazy man and the crowd in a shifting national community also occurs in conflict. Inasmuch as the crazy man gives life to the living grammar of Latinisation, he might as well eat into the flesh of others, as he attempts to flatten out, in the name of equality, all the depth that Chinese characters embody. Even though Latinisation did not replace Chinese characters, it importantly articulates social differentiation and conflict in the Chinese language. Couldn't Qu continue to ponder the fluidity and materiality of the Chinese script in his final days at the prison?

The Chinese nation was coming together at the same time as the national language in the early twentieth century. In Qu's diagnosis, China needed a strong active national unity, a unity that was to be implicated in daily intercourse among people having different social interests. Rather than suggest that Qu and Latinisation should go into the dustbin of history, this essay argues that they indicate a possibility for us to expand equality as a constituent factor of national citizenship in the modern world. In their critiques of linguistic nationalism, Seton-Watson, Hobsbawm and Anderson examine the roles played by elite-intellectuals, state authority and print capitalism in orchestrating the historical processes through which national language emerges. These critiques focus on the reproduction of national language as a top-down diffusion of cultural influence, or in the case of Anderson, as an imagination of a unitary community. However, they do not show us the possibility of an alternative in the fraught moment of revolutionary change.

Nation-states mystify the productive relations of classes and perpetuate social inequality by proclaiming equality in terms of national interest, regardless of the distinctions of birth, social rank, education and occupation. Equality is then emptied of its material content under the guise of the national interest guaranteed by the state. As against this, Qu and Latinisation importantly expand equality in the actual and material existence of language. Equality is then the democratic participation of people in linguistic activities (such as reading and writing) that affect their material lives. In the historical moment of revolutionary change, the linguistic behaviour of the power holders brought their normative significance to the fore, highlighting the pressure of incontestable linguistic norms. Qu's diagnosis was that the unschooled people of his time held the potential to contest such linguistic norms, despite their late arrival in the world of knowledge, and to reconstitute China and its national language on a solid and strong basis.

Acknowledgements

I thank Michael Gibbs Hill, who gave me assistance in obtaining *Igo fungz di rhgi*. My thanks are due to William Christie and Q. S. Tong, who invited me to speak in the 'China and Global Modernity, 1784–1919' symposium at Sun Yat-sen University in Guangzhou. Special thanks go to Tani Barlow, for her critical comments on a draft of this essay. I have benefited from her analysis of Qu Qiubai from a different angle. I also thank Jacek Fabiszak for organising a guest lecture on this essay at Adam Mickiewicz University, and Arleta Adamska-Sałaciak for her questions at this lecture. All shortcomings in this essay are my own.

About the Contributors

Elizabeth Hope Chang is Associate Professor of English at the University of Missouri, the author of *Britain's Chinese Eye: Literature, Empire, and Aesthetics in Nineteenth-Century Britain* (2010) and the forthcoming monograph *Novel Cultivations: Plants in British Literature of the Global Nineteenth Century*. She is also the editor of *British Travel Writing from China, 1798–1901* (2009), and has published a range of journal articles and book chapters on aesthetic, environmental and textual exchange between China and Britain. Chang is currently at work on a project entitled 'Mobile China', which explicates sensations of sovereignty in British writing from China in the Victorian era.

Kang-Yen Chiu is assistant professor at National Yang-Ming University, Taipei, Taiwan. He received his PhD in English Literature from the University of Glasgow and specialises in the writings of Sir Walter Scott, hospitality and postcolonial theories. He has published in journals such as *The Wenshan Review*, *The BARS Review* and *Scottish Literary Review*. He is working on a monograph, *Sir Walter Scott and China*.

William Christie is Professor and Head of the Humanities Research Centre at the Australian National University, Director of the Australasian Consortium of Humanities Research Centres, and a Fellow of the Australian Academy of the Humanities. He was the founding President of the Romantic Studies Association of Australasia and is widely published in the area of Romantic literature and culture. His publications include *Samuel Taylor Coleridge: A Literary Life* (2006) – awarded the NSW Premier's Biennial Prize for Literary Scholarship in 2008 – *The Edinburgh Review in the Literary Culture of Romantic Britain* (2009), *Dylan Thomas: A Literary Life* (2014), and *The Two Romanticisms, and Other Essays* (2016).

Yinghe Jiang is a Professor of History at Sun Yat-sen University, Guangzhou, China. Her research focuses on Canton Trade, especially the export art in the Qing dynasty. She has published the book *Western Paintings and Canton Port during the Qing Period* (2007), and translated and published several English books on Canton Trade into Chinese. She is now working on a research project on the images of Canton Port from the sixteenth to the nineteenth centuries.

Kendall A. Johnson is a Professor of Literature at the University of Hong Kong. He is the author of *The New Middle Kingdom: China and the Early American Romance of Free Trade* (2017) and *Henry James and the Visual* (2007), the contributing editor of *Narratives of Free Trade: The Commercial Cultures of Early US-China Relations* (2012), and a contributing co-editor of *Oceanic Archives, Indigenous Epistemologies, and Transpacific American Studies* (2019). His articles have appeared in *American Literary History*, *American Literature*, *American Quarterly*, *Literature Compass*, *Modern Fiction Studies*, and elsewhere.

Peter Kitson is Professor of Romantic Literature and Culture in the School of Literature, Drama and Creative Writing at UEA where he teaches and researches British Romantic period writing. He has published widely on the subject including monographs on *Literature, Science and Exploration in the Romantic Period* (Cambridge UP, 2004), *Romantic Literature, Race and Colonial Encounter, 1760–1840* (Palgrave Macmillan, 2007), and *Forging Romantic China: Sino-British Cultural Encounters, 1760–1840* (Cambridge UP, 2013). He has edited three multi-volume editions of writings about slavery and travel writing in the Romantic period for Pickering and Chatto, as well as several collections of essays, including (with Tim Fulford), *Romanticism* *and Colonialism* (Cambridge UP, 1998). His most recent co-edited collection of essays (with Robert Markley) *Writing China: Essays on the Amherst Embassy (1816) and Sino-British Cultural Relations* was published in 2016. He is currently completing his next monograph on *Opium and the Global Romantic Imagination: Travel, Trade and Commerce 1800–1842*.

Robert Markley is W. D. and Sara E. Trowbridge Professor of English at the University of Illinois and editor of *The Eighteenth Century: Theory and Interpretation*. The author of more than eighty articles in eighteenth-century studies, science studies, and digital media, his books include *Two-Edg'd Weapons: Style and Ideology in the Comedies of Etherege, Wycherley, and Congreve* (Oxford UP, 1988); *Fallen Languages: Crises of Representation in Newtonian England* (Cornell UP, 1993); *Dying Planet: Mars in Science and the Imagination* (Duke UP, 2005); *The Far East and the English Imagination, 1600–1730* (Cambridge UP, 2006), and a volume in the Modern Masters of Science Fiction series, *Kim Stanley Robinson* (U of Illinois P, 2019). He has co-edited with Peter Kitson *Writing China: Essays on the Amherst Embassy (1816) and Sino-British Cultural Relations* (Boydell and Brewer, 2016). His current book project examines the emergence of understandings of global climate between 1500 and 1850.

Q. S. Tong is an independent scholar and critic. He is formerly University Professor of English at Sun Yat-sen University, China. He has published extensively, in both English and Chinese, on issues of critical significance in literary and cultural studies, criticism and theory, with special attention to the historical interactions between China and the West. His most recent publication is a book in Chinese entitled *The Meaning of the Chinese Language: Philology, World Literature and the Western Idea of Chinese* (Beijing, 2019). He has served as advisory editor for several international journals including *boundary 2*.

Dongqing Wang is Associate Professor of English at Guangdong University of Foreign Studies (Guangzhou, China). He is visiting scholar at Department of English, University of Illinois at Urbana-Champaign (2018–2019). He received his PhD from the English Department at the

University of Hong Kong. His research interests include the Sino–British cultural interactions during the long nineteenth century. His current research project examines the paradoxical role of British Orientalism in shaping China's revolutionary modernity.

James Watt is Senior Lecturer in the Department of English and Related Literature at the University of York. He is the author of *Contesting the Gothic: Fiction, Genre, and Cultural Conflict* (Cambridge UP, 1999) and *British Orientalisms, 1759–1835* (Cambridge UP, 2019), and he is currently working on a project about popular Orientalism in the Romantic period titled *The Comedy of Difference*.

Lorraine Wong is Lecturer in Chinese Studies at the Department of Languages and Cultures at the University of Otago, New Zealand. Her research focuses on modern and contemporary Chinese literature in the global context, the history of China's script reforms, and the interface of language and history in various forms of linguistic and cultural theory. She has published in both English and Chinese. Her work appears in *Literature Compass*, *City on the Edge: Hong Kong, China, Boundaries and Borderland*, and *Journal of Hangzhou Normal University*. Her latest article, 'Threshold Nationhood: Huang Guliu's *The Story of Shrimp-ball*, Chinese Latinization, and Topolect Literature', is published in *Modern Chinese Literature and Culture*. She is working on a book manuscript tentatively entitled *Script and Revolution in China's Long Twentieth Century*.

Index

Adas, Michael 223
Addison, Joseph 68
Africa 117, 247
agriculture *see* farming
Alcock, Rutherford 268
Alexander, William 11
American Civil War 109, 112
American Revolutionary War 109
Americans in China 72–74, 109–144, 166
Amherst embassy 42, 154, 184, 186, 207, 219
Amherst, William Pitt 75, 150
Amoy 193
Anderson, Aeneas 10
Anderson, Benedict 274
Anderson, John 247, 249
animals 158
Anson, George 15, 25, 42, 64
Arabian Nights, The 156, 221
architecture 174
art 168; *see also* export painting
Asiatic Journal 69
Astor, John Jacob 110

astronomy 6
Atwill, David 253
Austen, Francis William 207
Austen, Jane 71, 207

Baber, Edward Colborne 258, 265, 266, 269
balance of trade 7, 14, 114
Ballaster, Ros 4, 53
Banks, Joseph 65, 71
Baptist missionaries 13, 218
Barber, Peter 172
Barlow, Tani 281, 292
Barrow, John 11, 13, 64, 223, 229
Batavia 114
Baudrillard, Jean 215
Beckford, William 215
Beevers, David 212
Beijing 8, 74, 150, 233
Belknap, Jeremy 113, 115–120
Bell, John 74, 76
Bengal *see* India
Bhamô 267
Bickers, Robert 14

biographies 109–144
Bird, Isabella 266
Blackwood's Edinburgh Magazine 149
Blake, William 66
Blussé, Leonard 181
Bocca Tigris 174, 177
Bogle, George 266
Bonaparte, Napoleon 273
books 216–223
Booth, Martin 201
borders 244–246
Boston 112
botany 71
Braam Houckgeest, Andreas Everadus van 172
Bridges, J. H. 267
British East India Company 6, 7, 13, 14, 25, 82, 171
British Empire 80
British Library 172
Browne, Horace 249, 251, 257
Bruce, James 147
Burma 243, 249, 252, 253, 267
Burton, Richard 75
Byron, Lord 66

Cai Hongsheng 172
cannibalism 293, 294, 297
Canton 6, 8, 40–50, 72, 82, 165–182
Canton Register 192
Canton System 7, 45, 59–68, 80, 110, 114, 165, 166
capitalism 275
Carey, William 218
Carlyle, Thomas 225, 232
Cary, Thomas G. 112
Centurion (ship) 43, 45
Ceres (ship) 208
Chang, Elizabeth Hope 10
Changzhou Mountain 177

Cheape, Hugh 209
Chefoo agreement 260, 265, 266
Chefoo *see* Yantai
Chenmei 293, 294–298
Chi-ming Yang 2
China Inland Mission society 267
Chinese Communist Party 275, 277; *see also* communism
Chinese language 12, 20, 67, 74, 161, 184, 218, 278; *see also* interpreters, linguistic nationalism, translation
chinoiserie 209, 212
chopsticks 57, 58, 69, 73, 210
Christianity
  Chinese attitudes to 6
  influence on European sinology 13, 33, 267
Church Missionary Society 228
cities 29
civil service 236–241
class 38, 46, 67, 72, 149, 180, 230, 274, 290
  and language 274, 276, 286, 291
classical education 229–233, 235
climate 38
Clive, Robert 206
Clunas, Craig 169
Cockney School 149
Coe, Andrew 64
cohong 7, 62, 110, 167
Cole, Lucinda 40
Coleridge, Samuel Taylor 147, 148
collections 215
Collins, Logan 10
Colquhoun, Archibald 266
Columbus, Christopher 113, 115
comic writing 148, 160–163
communism 275, 276, 277; *see also* Chinese Communist Party
concubinage 13, 64

Index

Confucian education 20, 226, 230, 233
Confucianism 298
  European admiration of 3, 225, 227
  translation of Confucian texts 3, 12, 218
consumer culture 35, 166–169
Cornhill Magazine 252
corruption 206
Cotterell, Arthur 10
cotton 7
Cranmer-Byng, John 66
crime and punishment 8, 13, 82–107; see also extraterritoriality
Crossley, Pamela 245
Crossman, Carl 178
customs duties 44, 45, 202, 260
cutlery 56, 69, 73

Dalai Lama 75
Daniel, William 178
Davis, John Francis 12, 14, 18, 74, 153, 183–204, 220, 236
Davis, Samuel 183
De Quincey, Horace 208
De Quincey, Thomas 81, 145, 147, 148, 152, 163
  Confessions of an English Opium-Eater 145, 156, 200
  The Opium Question in China in 1840 208
democracy 225, 230
Deng Tingzhen 193
Dickens, Charles 156, 228
  Nicholas Nickleby 228
diet 41
Dorr, Sullivan 177
dress 56, 67, 74, 77, 154, 171
Dunbar, James 24, 38, 40

East India Company, British 38, 45, 110, 114, 146, 149, 152, 157, 160, 188
  monopoly 202
East India Company, Dutch 114
economic theorists 23–52, 31–40
Edict of Toleration 6
Edinburgh Review 113, 223
education 226–241, 274, 282, 285
Educational Association of China 234
Elliot, Charles 193
Ellis, Henry 219
empire *see* imperialism
Empress of China (ship) 110, 114, 166
Enlightenment thought 25, 55, 285
entertainments 56, 63, 69, 74
Entwisle, E. A. 212
ethnicity 245, 252, 265, 269
examination system 19; *see also* civil service
exceptionalism 8, 15, 24, 24, 157
exploration narratives 262
export painting 18, 165–182
extraterritoriality 8, 14, 17, 80–107, 254

Faa Dei 166
Faber, Ernst 234
Fairbank, John 55, 67
Fang, Karen 148, 157
farming 27, 32, 37, 39
Farrar, F. W. 230
fashion *see* dress
Fichte, Johann Gottlieb 273
food 57, 156, 158
foot binding 64, 146, 150, 161, 171
foreign communities in China 15, 166
foreign embassies in China 9, 76, 110, 207
foreign factories 166, 174, 187
Foreign Language Academy 232, 235

Foreign Management System 166
Fortnightly (magazine) 267
Fourth Anglo-Dutch War 114
Franey, Laura 247
free trade 17, 32, 109, 112, 198, 204
French revolution 10
friendship 16
furniture 70, 212
Fuzhou 177, 193

Galaxy (magazine) 261
Gallagher, Catherine 43
Galland, Antoine 155
Gandhi, Leela 16, 55
Garnier, Francis 263
Gedye, E. F. 240
George III of England 172
Germany 273
Ghosh, Amitav 73
Gifford, William 222
gift-giving 63
Gill, William 264, 266
ginseng 110
Girard, Stephen 110
globalisation 55, 80, 112, 159, 169, 179, 231
Globe Magazine 239
Goethe, Johann Wolfgang von 220
Gogol, Nikolai 293
Gottlieb, Evan 55
grammar 276, 278, 282, 287–292, 289
Great Britain
  increasing assertiveness 7, 14, 157
Great Wall of China 159
Grosvenor, T. G. 258
Guangzhou *see* Canton
guild paintings *see* export painting
guilds 169

Hager, Joseph 75

du Halde, Jean-Baptiste 2, 12, 15, 26, 41, 161
Hall, Basil 219
Haoqiu zhuan (The Pleasing History) 11
Hay, David Ramsay 211
Heshen 10
Hevia, James 8, 248, 261
Hickey, William 16, 56, 64, 166
Higgins, David 151, 158
Hill, Michael Gibbs 294, 297
Hinduism 147
Hobsbawm, Eric J. 274
Hoi Tong Monastery 166
Holland 114, 285
Holmes, Samuel 11
homosexuality 13, 64
Honan Island 166
Hong Kong 110, 177, 185, 186, 193, 197
Hood, Thomas 162
Hoppo 7, 63, 83
hospitality 64, 70, 76
Hsin-pao Chang 192
Huang Shijian 168
humanism 232
Hunt, Freeman 109, 112
Hunt, Leigh 149
Hunter, William 166
Huxley, T. H. 231

imperialism 54, 80, 112, 153, 157, 173, 185, 215, 222, 273, 276, 280
India 7, 37–40, 110, 114, 148, 152, 160, 189, 190
  passage to, from China 249, 253
individualism 113, 268, 270, 282
industrialisation 34, 230
infanticide 13, 64
Ingres, Jean-Auguste Dominique 178
interior decoration 211–216

Index

international law 79
interpreters 12, 184, 220, 249; *see also* translation
Irving, Washington 115
Islam 250, 251
Ismailov, Leoff 76
isolationism 64

Jacotot, Joseph 285
Jakarta *see* Batavia
James, Felicity 158
Japan 276, 291, 298
Jardine, William 188, 192
Jeffrey, Francis 54, 64, 223
Jenkins, Eugenia Zuroski 215
Jesuits
  attitudes to Chinese culture 4
  missionary reports 2, 12, 23, 26, 206
  relations with the Qing dynasty 6, 27
Jones, William 11, 145, 149, 152, 156

Kangxi Dictionary 291
Kangxi Emperor 6
Kant, Immanuel 285
Keats, John 149, 213
Kipling, Rudyard 74
Kitson, Peter 4, 13, 76, 145, 153, 217, 217
Korea 219
kowtow 9, 82, 154

labour 28, 34, 149
Lady Hughes affair 8, 16, 62, 79–107
laissez-faire economics 23, 32, 35, 197, 204
Lamb, Charles 17, 74, 146–163
  'A Dissertation Upon Roast Pig' 154–158, 162
  'Old China' 216
Lamb, Mary 150

Lamqua (painter) 178
Langdon, William 168
Latinisation movement 20, 274–301
Lawrence, Thomas 179
Layard, Austen Henry 249
Leask, Nigel 214
legal texts 12, 13
Levy, Lindsay 220
Leyden, John 218
Lhasa 75
Li Chen 7, 14, 64, 67
Li Yu 220
liberalism 81, 227–242
Lin Zexu 193, 200, 203
linguistic nationalism 20, 273–302
Linton 202
literacy 275, 276, 277, 282, 286, 291, 299
Little, Archibald 257
Liu Haisu 179
Liu, Lydia 10, 248, 298
livestock 43
Lockhart, John Gibson 221, 222
London Magazine 147
London Missionary Society 13
Lu Wan'gai 227
Lu Xun 278, 293–300

Macao 5, 43, 45, 72, 174, 177, 192
Macartney Mission 8–12, 42, 54, 67, 82, 145, 172, 207, 223, 229
  published accounts of 11
madness 294–296
Makdisi, Saree 66, 72
Malacca 15, 114
Malthus, Thomas 32
Mandalay *see* Burma
Mandarin (language) 12
manifest destiny 110

Manning, Thomas 12, 17, 74, 150–157, 266
  'Chinese Jests' 161–163
manufacturing 30, 35, 165, 166
Manwyne 243
maps 258, 267
Margary, Augustus Raymond 20, 243–271
maritime trade ban 5
Marouby, Christian 33
Marshman, Joshua 12, 218
Martin, Robert Montgomery 198
Martin, William A. P. 226, 228–230, 232
Marxism 282
mathematics 6, 75
Matheson, James 188, 192
McCarthy, John 267
medicine 162
memoirs 4
memory 227, 234
mercantile biographies 109–144
merchant guild *see* cohong
meritocracy 4, 19, 236
missionaries 2, 4, 6, 13, 206, 266; *see also* Jesuits
modernity 148, 159, 179, 204, 227, 231
Morrison, Robert 12, 75, 184, 186
Moule, Arthur Evans 227
Murray, John 217, 219, 222
Myanmar *see* Burma

Napier, Lord William 185, 192
national sovereignty 80
nationalism 273–302
Native American peoples 112
nature, attitudes to 33
Navarette, Domingo Fernandez 15, 27–31, 34
Netherlands, the *see* Holland

New Monthly Magazine 161
New Writing 21, 275–301, 275, 278, 283, 286, 293, 298; *see also* Latinisation movement, linguistic nationalism
New York 110
Ningpo 193
Nish, Ian 7

opium 110, 112, 114, 146, 188–204
  effect on trade relations 14, 158, 193
Opium Wars 14
  First Opium War 80, 110, 163, 186, 207, 225
  Second Opium War 160, 197, 200, 203
Oriental Translation Committee 184
Orientalism 15, 52, 66, 72, 76, 156, 214, 241
orthography 289, 296; *see also* Latinisation movement

Packham, Catharine 34
Page, Edward 16, 26, 44–49
Palmerston, Viscount 189
Pankeequa (merchant) 56, 62–68, 67
Pankeequa II (merchant) 69
Pankeequa III 72
pantomime 57
Parker, A. P. 234
Peabody Essex Museum 168, 171, 178
Peacock, Thomas Love 149
Pearl River 110, 171, 172
pedagogy 19, 233, 291
Penang 114, 178
Percy, Thomas 3, 11, 64, 217
Perdue, Peter 261
periodicals 222, 252, 261, 267; *see also* print media
Perkins, Thomas H. 112

Index

Peter the Great of Russia 76
philology 238
physiocrats 32
Pigou, W. H. 83
Pittock, Murray 205
Plato 284
Polo, Marco 33, 258, 264
Pomeranz, Kenneth 31
Pope, John 167
population growth 31
porcelain 4, 6, 11, 147, 149, 157, 210, 216
port cities 8, 114, 174, 177, 179, 193, 202; *see also* Canton
Porter, David 3, 12, 148
Portugal 5, 114
postcolonialism 66, 247
Pottinger, Henry 196
Pottinger, Sir Henry 186
de Premare, Joseph Henri 3
print media 2, 10, 13, 112, 222, 274
progress, notions of 25
Protestantism 13, 230

Qian Zhongshu 54
Qianlong Emperor 6, 10, 165, 172
Qiying (governor-general) 187, 194, 196
Qu Qiubai 21, 275–302
Quarterly Review 222
Quesnay, François 3
Quincy, Josiah 110–112

Rancière, Jacques 284, 285, 298
Reeves, John 71
Reform Act (1867) 230
Reid, Gilbert 239
Revell family 171
revolutionary politics 277–278, 290–293

Ricci, Matteo 2, 5, 227, 229
rice 38, 41
Rigney, Ann 213
Robertson, William 153
Robins, Benjamin 25
Robinson, George Best 192
Romanticism 13, 19, 55, 66, 274
rote learning 229, 234
Royal Asiatic Society 184, 185, 186, 206–224
Royal Corps of Engineers 265
Royal Geographical Society 223, 267
Royal Humane Society 249
Royal Society 184, 223
Russia 8, 15, 76, 274

Said, Edward 76
Saint-Domingue (Haiti) 112
Sang Bing 182
Sanya 177
Saturday Review 254, 266
Schoenfield, Mark 222
schooling *see* education
Scott, Hugh 208, 211
Scott, Walter 19, 205–224
semiotics 292
Serampore 218
Seton-Watson, Hugh 274
Shanghai 177, 179, 193, 254
Shaw, Samuel 17, 82, 109–113, 166
Shin, Leo K. 254
shops 166–167
Siam 253
silk 6
silver 7, 114
Singapore 114, 157, 178, 226
sinology 13, 150, 217
Sladen, Edward Bosc 249, 251
slavery 112, 114
Smentek, Kristel 5

Smith, Adam
  The Wealth of Nations 15, 23–52
  Theory of Moral Sentiments 36
Smith, Charlotte 217
Smith, Sydney 113
smuggling 202
social Darwinism 232
sociology 281
South Africa 177
Spain 42
Spectator 68, 268
Stanley, Lord Edward 194, 198
Staunton, George Leonard 11, 12, 172
Staunton, George Thomas 12, 14, 74, 184, 186
Steeds, David 7
Straits Settlements 114
sublime 146, 157
supercargoes 45
Suqua 46
Swift, Jonathan 54

Taiwan 249
Tang Xiaobing 294
tariffs *see* customs duties
taste 71
Taylor, Hudson 267
tea 4, 6, 11, 110, 114
Terry, Daniel 211
Thelwall, John 147
Tianjin 15
Tibet 75, 150, 151, 153, 265
Tiffany, Osmond 167, 179
Tilden, Bryan Parrot 72
Tongwen Hang (firm) 62
tourism 69
trade 14, 112, 179
translation 11, 13, 21, 75, 184, 290–292;
  see also interpreters
  of Chinese legal texts 12, 13
  of Chinese literature 11, 13, 186, 220, 293–300
  of Chinese medical texts 13
  of Confucius 218
  of the Bible 218
travel writing 69–72, 244, 247–248, 270
Treaty of Nanjing 8, 14, 80, 110, 186, 187, 203
Treaty of Wangxia 110
tributary missions 9, 253

United States of America 15, 17, 109–144
USSR 278; *see also* Russia

Vološinov, V. N. 292
de Vattel, Emerich 79
de Vries, Jan 34

Wade, Thomas 244, 260
wages 25, 31
Waley, Arthur 72
Waley-Cohen, Joanna 246
wallpaper 210–216
Walpole, Horace 215
Walter, Richard 25
Wang Gungwu 55, 67
Wang, S. T. 259
Wang Xian 293, 294–298
Washington, George 110
Wathen, James 69–72
Wedgwood, Thomas 148
Whampoa 110, 174, 176, 177, 202
Wilkinson, James 11
Williams, S. Wells 168
Wills, John 66
women 13, 179, 212
wool 7
Woolf, Virginia 55, 77
Wordsworth, Dorothy 159

Index

Wordsworth, John 207
Wordsworth, William 149, 159
writing systems 276–302; *see also* Latinisation movement, linguistic nationalism
Wu Han Chin 220
Wu Yake 8

Xiamen 177
Xu Xilin 297

Yan Fu 291

Yangtze River 243, 262
Yantai 249
Ye Zhanyan 174
Yi Ya 297
Yongzheng Emperor 6
Yule, Henry 265
Yunnan 250, 252, 259

Zhang Longxi 74
Zhang Zeduan 172
Zhao Yi 172

www.ingramcontent.com/pod-product-compliance
Lightning Source LLC
Chambersburg PA
CBHW050202240426
43671CB00013B/2226